Studies in Natural Language Processing

Semantic processing for finite domains

Studies in Natural Language Processing

This series publishes monographs, texts, and edited volumes within the interdisciplinary field of computational linguistics. It represents the range of topics of concern to the scholars working in this increasingly important field, whether their background is in formal linguistics, psycholinguistics, cognitive psychology or artificial intelligence.

Also in this series:

Memory and context for language interpretation by Hiyan Alshawi
Planning English sentences by Douglas E. Appelt
Computational linguistics by Ralph Grishman
Language and spatial cognition by Annette Herskovits
Semantic interpretation and the resolution of ambiguity by Graeme Hirst
Text generation by Kathleen R. McKeown
Machine translation edited by Sergei Nirenburg
Systemic text generation as problem solving by Terry Patten
Machine translation systems edited by Jonathan Slocum
Relational models of the lexicon edited by Martha Walton Evens
Reference and computation by Amichai Kronfeld

Semantic processing for finite domains

MARTHA STONE PALMER

National University of Singapore
formerly Paoli Research Center, Unisys Corporation

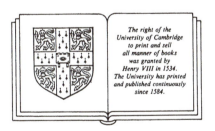

The right of the
University of Cambridge
to print and sell
all manner of books
was granted by
Henry VIII in 1534.
The University has printed
and published continuously
since 1584.

CAMBRIDGE UNIVERSITY PRESS

CAMBRIDGE

NEW YORK   PORT CHESTER

MELBOURNE   SYDNEY

CAMBRIDGE UNIVERSITY PRESS
Cambridge, New York, Melbourne, Madrid, Cape Town, Singapore, São Paulo

Cambridge University Press
The Edinburgh Building, Cambridge CB2 2RU, UK

Published in the United States of America by Cambridge University Press, New York

www.cambridge.org
Information on this title: www.cambridge.org/9780521362269

First published 1990
This digitally printed first paperback version 2006

A catalogue record for this publication is available from the British Library

Library of Congress Cataloguing in Publication data
Palmer, Martha Stone.
Semantic processing for finite domains / Martha Stone Palmer.
p.   cm. – (Studies in natural language processing)
Includes bibliographical references.
ISBN 0–521–36226–1
1. Semantics – Data processing.   2. Computational linguistics.
I. Title   II. Series.
P325.5.D38P35   1990
401′.43′0285–dc20   89–77384 CIP

ISBN-13 978-0-521-36226-9 hardback
ISBN-10 0-521-36226-1 hardback

ISBN-13 978-0-521-02403-7 paperback
ISBN-10 0-521-02403-X paperback

Contents

vi   *Contents*

Figures

Acknowledgements

I have had so much help from so many people, that I could not begin to name them all. I do, however, want to thank many of my readers, especially David Warren, Fernando Pereira, Jerry Hobbs, Ellen Bard, Nigel Shadbolt, Graeme Ritchie, Lincoln Wallen, Leon Sterling, Mary Angela Papalaskaris, Luis Jenkins, and Julia Hirschberg. In particular I would like to thank Lew and Judie Norton and Carl Weir for their painstaking efforts in helping me turn the dissertation manuscript into something suitable for publication. In addition, I owe a special debt of gratitude to:

Bob Simmons, for introducing me to the mysteries and challenges of natural language understanding.

Rod Burstall, who saw so clearly what I was trying to do, and had such good ideas about how to do it.

Bob Kowalski, for his unquenchable enthusiasm and delight in, what else, "logic for problem solving."

Allen Biermann and the CS Department at Duke, for encouraging me and believing in me, and always making me laugh.

Bonnie Webber, who pushed me when I needed pushing, and supported me when I needed supporting – and to all our friends at Penn for the many interesting discussions at La Terasse.

Beth Levin and Mitch Marcus, for their patient reading, their ideas, and their understanding.

Barbara Grosz, who performed the impossible task of getting me up, taking me to work, and sitting me in front of a terminal every day for six weeks – and to the Natural Language Group at SRI, for their suggestions, their disagreements, and their help.

Jim Weiner, for his many valuable contributions, for his constructive criticisms, and for always being there.

My examiners, Henry Thompson and Stephen Isard, for their careful reading and their high standards, and my supervisor, Alan Bundy, the Department of Artificial Intelligence, and the Faculty of Science at the University of Edinburgh, for their patience and tolerance during my somewhat checkered history as a post-graduate student.

This work was supported by SRC grants B/SR/2293 and B/RG/94493 at the University of Edinburgh.

1 Problems in the semantic analysis of text

1.1 Introduction

A primary problem in the area of natural language processing is the problem of semantic analysis. This involves both formalizing the general and domain-dependent semantic information relevant to the task involved, and developing a uniform method for access to that information. Natural language interfaces are generally also required to have access to the syntactic analysis of a sentence as well as knowledge of the prior discourse to produce a detailed semantic representation adequate for the task.

Previous approaches to semantic analysis, specifically those which can be described as using *templates*, use several levels of representation to go from the syntactic parse level to the desired semantic representation. The different levels are largely motivated by the need to preserve context-sensitive constraints on the mappings of syntactic constituents to verb arguments. An alternative to the template approach, *inference-driven mapping*, is presented here, which goes directly from the syntactic parse to a detailed semantic representation without requiring the same intermediate levels of representation. This is accomplished by defining a grammar for the set of mappings represented by the templates. The grammar rules can be applied to generate, for a given syntactic parse, just that set of mappings that corresponds to the template for the parse. This avoids the necessity of having to represent all possible templates explicitly. The context-sensitive constraints on mappings to verb arguments that templates preserved are now preserved by filters on the application of the grammar rules. This allows a more concise and extendable representation of the verb semantics for a given domain since advantage can be taken of linguistic generalizations about certain syntactic mappings.

Two other important characteristics of inference-driven mapping will also be presented here. The use of one level of representation allows the interleaving of several different semantic and pragmatic subtasks. The decompositional *semantic predicate* level of representation will also be described in detail, as well as the way that it makes explicit the verb-independent effect that certain semantic roles, such as INSTRUMENTS, can have on the final representation of a sentence.

Inference-driven mapping is specifically designed for finite, well-defined, i.e., *limited*, domains about a particular topic. The coverage of this type of domain is clearly delineated, and the processes required for the application are straightforward enough to be formalizable, making them especially appropriate for the use of the closed-world assumption [Pereira and Shieber, 1987]. Under the closed-world assumption, a specific application domain is formalized with axioms that allow the truth of a predicate to be proven. If a predicate cannot be proven to be true, it is assumed to be false; i.e., negation as failure [Clark, 1978]. Information that is not relevant to the domain does not need to be formalized, thus allowing the implementer to sidestep the insurmountable task of representing large amounts of general world knowledge.

An example of such a domain is a set of physics word problems for college students involving pulley systems, the *pulley domain*. Each problem is stated in English sentences that completely describe a miniature world of physical entities and relationships between those entities. The goal of the natural language processor is to produce a semantic representation of each problem that is sufficiently detailed to enable a computer program to produce the correct solution of the problem [Bundy, 1979]. This final semantic representation consists of a set of partially instantiated logical terms known as *semantic predicates*.

The formalization of the domain is essential for solving the following basic tasks which are associated with the semantic processing of text:

1. establishing referents for the noun phrases;
2. finding appropriate mappings from the syntactic constituents of the parse onto the underlying semantic representation of the verb;
3. using pragmatic information to assign fillers to semantic roles that do not have an explicit syntactic realization (the term "pragmatic" is used to refer to both discourse knowledge and general and domain-dependent information);
4. expanding the representation of the verb into a more detailed representation that fulfills the requirements of the processing task;
5. constraining allowable inferences so that this semantic representation does not become unmanageably large;
6. appropriately integrating the final representation of the clause with the representations of prior clauses.

These tasks will all be described in more detail, but first certain elementary terms must be defined.

1.2   The semantic representation of sentences

Deriving an appropriate semantic representation for a single sentence in a given context is a difficult problem in natural language processing. It is a non-trivial task, even in a limited domain where one is restricted to discussing inanimate entities and can assume the simplest case of meaning, i.e., where it is assumed that a statement about inanimate entities has a strict meaning and the speaker intends it to be interpreted literally. Given a syntactic parse and a consensus on what the semantic representation should be, there is still the problem of assigning the correct semantic role to each syntactic constituent of the parse, and producing the indicated semantic representation. This requires:

1. formalization of domain-specific information;
2. knowledge of the different syntactic cues that can be used to indicate semantic roles;
3. pragmatic information about the entities mentioned.

This section explores the difficulties associated with each of these requirements, illustrated with specific examples from the pulley domain. Before discussing these factors in detail, examples of the use of **syntactic constituent** and **semantic role** are given.

1.2.1   *Examples using syntactic constituent and semantic role*

The following discussion summarizes one of the more popular linguistic analyses of the use of "subject." It covers three recognized uses of subject: grammatical (G), logical (L), and thematic (T). They can be distinguished by the following examples:

1. John took the largest dog.
   John is assigned G, L, T

2. The largest dog was taken by John.
   dog is assigned G and T
   John is assigned L

3. The largest dog, John gave away.
   dog is assigned T
   John is assigned G and L

The grammatical subject usually immediately precedes the main verb, agrees with it in number, and is not marked by a preposition. The logical subject typically corresponds to the first argument of the logical predicate chosen to represent the verb. The thematic subject indicates the "theme" of the sentence, and can be said to correspond to the topic or focus. It is usually present as the first noun phrase. Generally, "subject" is used here to mean the grammatical subject, unless indicated otherwise. The syntactic category "subject" along with the referent of the noun phrase that the category is associated with, such as John, are indicated by subj(john), where subj is a function symbol with one argument, and john is the instantiation of that argument.

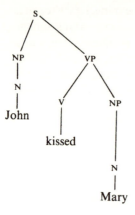

Fig. 1.1.   Syntactic parse

The syntactic structure of "John kissed Mary" is given in figure 1.1.

Generating the parse tree from the string "John kissed Mary" is known as syntactic processing or syntactic parsing, and the noun phrases designated as subject and object are syntactic constituents. In a normal, active, declarative sentence in English, given an unambiguously transitive verb such as *kiss*, the semantic role AGENT can be assigned to "John" and the semantic role PATIENT to "Mary." This is intended to capture the notion that "John" is doing the "kissing" and "Mary" is the one being "kissed." A general semantic representation of *kiss* could be *kiss*(agent,patient). The correspondence between the general representation and the representation of the particular parse can be captured with the following rules:

> Replace agent with john if subj(john)
> Replace patient with mary if obj(mary)

This results in the following semantic representation for the sentence:

> *kiss*(john,mary).

"John kissed Mary" is clearly quite different from "Mary kissed John." The ordering of the words reflects a particular syntactic structure that strongly affects what is being communicated. In "Mary kissed John," the semantic roles assigned to the syntactic constituents would be

> Replace agent with mary if subj(mary)
> Replace patient with john if obj(john)

resulting in the following semantic representation:

> *kiss*(mary,john).

1.2.2   The inherent difficulties in defining semantic representations

The following sections describe two different types of constraints on the formation of logical predicates for producing semantic representations: (1) the demands of the task to be performed for which the representation is required, and (2) the requirements of the process that does reference evaluation and fills semantic roles. For a semantic processor these constraints are actually of great benefit, since the consensus on the nature of semantic representation referred to so lightly above is not so readily obtainable. The next two sections introduce two of the major problems associated with defining semantic representations: (1) the inherent indivisibility of words and (2) verb ambiguities.

Defining primitives

There are essentially two different linguistic approaches to providing semantic representations: semantic markers and decomposition [Jackendoff, 1970]. Both these methods are based on the recognition of fundamental similarities between the ways in which many words can be used. A classic example of the use of semantic markers is the definition of "bachelor" by the markers UNMARRIED and MALE. The standard example for decomposition is the decomposition of "kill" into CAUSE to DIE. The motivation for both of these approaches is to define complex terms as collections of simpler terms, which may themselves be decomposed. Eventually a set of primitive terms will be reached, but this does not end the process. It is not clear that the primitive terms, whatever they may be, can or should be defined [Fodor, 1980]. The difficulty, indeed impossibility, of providing a semantic analysis of language is a well-worn philosophical enigma.

The "vagueness' of semantic notions can easily be demonstrated using the example of "John likes Mary." Given that a "like" relationship exists between "John" and "Mary," i.e. *like*(john,mary), what inferences should then be drawn? Defining the relationship more precisely is very difficult, especially for a computer that has no common fund of human emotional experience to draw upon. Using dictionary definitions such as "fondness," "being pleased with" "having a preference for" merely defers the issue.

The question still remains: Is it possible to derive appropriate semantic representations for verbs, nouns and prepositions that can be composed to form appropriate semantic representations for sentences? The key to answering the question is to sidestep the issue of the compositionality of all of English, and limit the problem to providing a computer with tools that are adequate for a given task. The issue then becomes not "What is the meaning of X?", but rather "What do we need to know about X's meaning in order to do Y?" What is assumed about X should be a proper part of X's "meaning," but should not in any way be expected to give predictions about all of X's meaning.

This is the approach to providing semantic representations that was first exemplified in the pathbreaking implementations of Winograd [1972] and Woods [1973], as described in chapter 2. It has been the cornerstone for much of the research in knowledge representation that has followed [Halpern, 1986; Brachman and Levesque, 1985].

Limited domains

Establishing a useful subpart of X's meaning is a complicated problem in itself. It is somewhat simplified by strictly limiting the context in which X is to be used, so that multiple meanings can be avoided, as well as metaphorical uses. The idealized pulley world described in section 1.3 is an example of a simple, finite, concrete domain. Entities and the relationships between them are clearly defined. In such a domain, a *limited domain*, axiomatizing the information about X that is needed in order to perform Y is a more tractable task.

Verb ambiguities

Another major problem in determining appropriate semantic representations is caused by verb ambiguities; the same verb having more than one definition. The semantic features of the subject or the object of the verb can usually determine how the verb is being used, as in the examples given below. Every new object for **throw** results in a different interpretation. To complicate matters further, "throw a boxing match" could conceivably have two interpretations, "organize a boxing match," and "purposely lose a boxing match"; an ambiguity that would have to be resolved by context. Clearly, the predicates chosen to represent **throw** or **take** would have to change radically depending on the nature of the object. This phenomenon is not restricted to objects. Three different senses of **run** are unambiguously indicated by the subject in the last three examples.

        throw a baseball
        throw support behind a candidate
        throw a boxing match
        throw a party
        throw a fit

        take a book from the shelf
        take a bus to New York
        take a nap
        take an aspirin for a cold
        take a letter in shorthand

        the clock runs
        John runs
        my nose runs

If the semantic features associated with expected semantic roles are used to choose between alternative verb definitions, then the selection process does not necessarily precede the mapping process, but may have to proceed in parallel with it.

In the pulley domain, human emotions and intentionality are ignored and ambiguous verbs such as *throw* and *take* can be avoided. Yet, the task is by no means trivialized. The problem of verb ambiguities is restricted to determining whether similar uses of the same verb represent separate definitions or the same definition. For example, do the uses of *hang* and *suspend* in the following clauses constitute several different definitions of the verbs or are they all really the same?

> a pulley is suspended from a pulley
> at one end of a string a weight is suspended
> a string hangs over a pulley
> weights hang freely on the ends of a string

In changing from the causative form of *hang*, which includes the optional AGENT role, to the stative form which does not, is there a different definition of the verb involved?

> John hung a mass from a pulley.
> A mass hangs from a pulley.

Chapter 5 discusses in detail how the system presented here handles each of these verb usages, and suggests that while for inference-driven mapping they each involve the same definition of the verb, the semantic representation changes radically from phrase to phrase because of the effect of the fillers of the semantic roles.

1.2.3   *Mapping between syntactic constituents and semantic roles*

A major task of semantic analysis is to provide an appropriate mapping between the syntactic constituents of a parsed clause and the semantic roles associated with the verb. Three factors complicate the mapping:

1. the ability of the syntactic constituents to indicate several different types of semantic roles given appropriate contexts;
2. the large number of choices available for syntactic expression of any particular semantic role;
3. preposition ambiguities.

The factors preclude the possibility of a one-to-one mapping between the syntactic constituents and the semantic roles. The pulley domain contains examples of many of these complications but not all of them. It is important to present them in their entirety here, however, since they provided important motivation for the design of previous semantic processors, and since inference-driven mapping is designed to handle them. Problems that are not illustrated fully by the pulley domain, such as semantic-role interdependencies, are discussed in terms of the examples given here, and the techniques by which inference-driven mapping deals with them are described in chapter 3.

Optional and obligatory semantic roles

The first step in the mapping process is the selection of the relevant verb definition. These definitions consist mainly of the appropriate semantic predicate and its associated semantic roles. All of the semantic roles may not be filled in a particular usage of a verb, but this does not necessarily imply a new verb definition. Several verbs such as *open* and *break* have **optional** semantic roles, which means that the roles may or may not appear in the surface structure of a clause containing the verb. Given {AGENT, INSTRUMENT, and PATIENT} as the set of expected roles for *open*, the phrases listed below illustrate the **optional** occurrence of the AGENT and the INSTRUMENT roles:

Optional semantic roles

John opened the door with a key.
The door was opened by John.
The door was opened with a key.
A key opened the door.
The door opened.
John gave Mary the book.
John gave the book to Mary.

The same sets of roles can be expressed using different constituents, as in the last two examples using *give*. The semantic roles seem to be playing musical chairs with the available syntactic constituents, with one or more roles often being omitted. For *open*, the only **obligatory** role is the PATIENT role that is filled by the door. For *give*, all three roles are usually obligatory. *In summary, more than one syntactic constituent may indicate a particular role, and conversely more than one role may be indicated by a particular constituent.*

The associations between semantic roles and syntactic constituents, although complex, are not arbitrary. There is general agreement that for English many verbs use at least three semantic roles, AGENT, PATIENT and INSTRUMENT, and there are indications of rules of etiquette to be followed in their possible mappings to syntactic constituents. These rules are exemplified by the *precedence relations* expounded by Fillmore [1977] in his theory of case. In an active sentence, if the AGENT is present it is the subject, or else the INSTRUMENT (if present) is the subject, or else the PATIENT is the subject. This evidence of some regularity in semantic role assignment is of paramount importance to anyone attempting to understand the nature of the relationship between syntax and semantics. It is essential information for a processor that performs mappings from semantic roles to syntactic constituents.

Some of the examples of alternative syntactic realizations of verbs in the pulley domain are given below. The semantic processor accepts all the possible expressions and produces appropriate representations for them.

Alternative syntactic realizations

A particle is connected to another particle by a string.
A string connects two particles.
A particle is attached at the end of string.
A particle is attached to the end of a string.
A string with particles attached . . . .

Preposition ambiguities

Having seen the subject observe a certain degree of decorum with respect to role assignment, it is tempting to look for other useful regularities in the performance of prepositional phrases. It is true that an INSTRUMENT can be expected to be indicated by either the subject of a BY or a WITH prepositional phrase. But WITH and BY are by no means restricted to introducing instruments. BY can also indicate an AGENT, and WITH is often used as a **comitative**, indicating someone that goes along with someone else, or as a **locative**, indicating a location. This is the case even for verbs that expect INSTRUMENTS. A verb's possible semantic roles do not restrict the use of prepositions in association with that verb. Illustrations of the variety of uses of WITH that can appear with *open* and other INSTRUMENT-taking verbs are given below.

Prepositions performing independently of verb expectations

comitative:
John opened the door with Mary and Jim.

instrumental:
The door was opened with a key.

manner:
The door opened with a solid click.

instrumental:
The door opened with a solid whack.

manner:
John hit the door with a solid whack.

manner:
John kicked the door with a solid whack.

However, the way a preposition can be used is not entirely independent of the verb. It might seem plausible that semantic features on the object of the preposition could exclusively determine its use, but this is clearly not the case. The dividing lines between comitative uses, locative uses, and instrumental uses are hard to draw, but wherever they are, they are strongly affected by the verb semantics. The sentences below give examples of WITH prepositional phrases that can have the same type of object and yet still have a variety of uses depending on the verb they appear with.

Preposition use being determined independently of semantic features on the object

comitative:
Mary started the introductions with John.

instrumental:
The townspeople filled the gap in the firebucket line with the town drunk.

instrumental (?):
Mary flirted with John to get even with Bill.

locative:
Mary put the books with the papers.

instrumental:
Mary stuffed the hole in the window with old newspapers.

comitative:
A kite with paper streamers floated into view.

Semantic role interdependencies

A legacy of the precedence relations mentioned earlier with respect to semantic roles is the constraints they place on prepositions. In spite of the ability of both BY and WITH to introduce the INSTRUMENT role, they cannot typically be substituted for one another. This is illustrated by the following examples.

John opened the door {with/*by} a key.
The door was opened {by/*with} John.

There is a partial explanation for this in the subtle ways in which semantic roles defer to other semantic roles in the assignment of syntactic constituents. The AGENT takes precedence over the INSTRUMENT where the subject is concerned. It is also true that if the AGENT is the subject, the INSTRUMENT cannot usually be indicated by a BY but rather by a WITH. Neither can the INSTRUMENT always be indicated by a WITH if the PATIENT is the subject, as illustrated by the following examples.

> John broke the window with a bat.
> *The window broke with a bat.

In assigning semantic roles there are proprieties that must be observed with respect to other assignments being made. *Semantic roles that have already been associated with syntactic constituents place restrictions on which syntactic constituents can be associated with the other semantic roles.* These restrictions constitute interdependencies between semantic roles that must not be violated.

1.2.4   *The necessity of pragmatic information*

The preceding section concentrated on the way syntactic constituents are used to indicate the semantic roles of a verb. The section preceding that suggested that semantic roles act as arguments to the semantic predicates that indicate lexical entries for verbs. The demands of the particular task for which a natural language interface is designed will provide important constraints on the selection of those semantic predicates. But the requirements of the semantic roles must also be satisfied. These requirements are not restricted to the processing of a single sentence, but extend to the use of information from preceding sentences, i.e., **discourse knowledge**, and to using **knowledge of the domain** to make explicit information that is expressed implicitly in the sentence being represented. As mentioned before, these types of knowledge are referred to as **pragmatic information**. Pragmatic information is also essential for resolving issues in ambiguities, quantification and scoping. However, none of these areas were necessary for this implementation and they are not discussed here.

In describing a complex scene containing entities with relationships between the entities, no one sentence gives more than a partial description. To achieve an appropriate representation for a sentence, the part of the scene being described must be represented accurately, and this representation must be integrated correctly with the current model of the scene derived from preceding sentences.

Semantic roles play an important part in the necessary integration since pragmatic information can sometimes use entities that have already been described to fill roles that are not mentioned explicitly in the sentence. Another important component of successful integration is **reference evaluation**. Previously described entities can be referred to directly in order to provide new information about them. Correct evaluation of such references is crucial to distinguishing between the information in the sentence that is "given" and the information that is "new." The semantic processor described here does not do reference evaluation, but assumes an input in which referents for noun phrases are already fully determined (see section 1.3). The rest of this section concentrates on the requirements placed on the selection of semantic predicates by the process of filling semantic roles.

Filling roles by retrieving fillers

Section 1.2.3 mentioned that many semantic roles, such as AGENTS and INSTRUMENTS, are optional, and do not always appear in the surface structure of a clause. Just because these roles are not mentioned does not guarantee that they do not need to be filled. In "The door was opened with a key," the passivization and the presence of the INSTRUMENT "key" indicate clearly that an AGENT exists, although never mentioned. It is sometimes possible to deduce the AGENT from pragmatic information about the discourse, as in:

> How did the burglar get inside?
> The door was opened with a key.

For a semantic processor to perform this type of deduction it must have access to specific information about the domain represented as implications. To associate the "burglar" with the AGENT of *open*, it is necessary to know that the burglar was inside a house, that houses have doors which are usually locked, and so on. One of the major difficulties involved with implications of this type is deciding when it is appropriate to apply them. Knowledge representation systems generally contain very detailed representations of pertinent entities, with information about their shapes, parts, common properties, etc. Every time a house is mentioned, should inferences be added that list every specific instance of every property associated with that house? Assuming that a system has been told that a burglar is inside a house, should it draw all the possible inferences with regard to actions that the burglar *could have* performed, such as approaching the house, entering the house, searching the house, etc.? This can then result in major "erasing" problems, if it is later discovered that the burglar was the houseowner's spouse, or possibly the dog! These difficulties cannot be ignored, since a complete semantic representation of a sentence in context clearly requires access to global information.

Filling roles by hypothesizing fillers

Not only does the processor need a formalization of the domain that provides a sufficiently rich representation for the recognition of semantic role fillers supplied by discourse, but it may also have to hypothesize the existence of possible fillers. Sometimes there are standard defaults associated with roles that can be overridden. The INSTRUMENT associated with *hit* in the following examples has the default value of being the AGENT's hand if it is not explicitly made something else.

> John hit the wall with all his strength.

John lifted the weighty mallet.
He hit the wall with all his strength.

John hit the wall with his baseball bat.

Even when default values are not given, it is still sometimes the case that unfilled semantic roles need to be filled. In the following sentence there is a clear assumption of an AGENT doing the "crushing," although he is never mentioned explicitly, and one would not normally associate a particular default with **crush**.

The stone wall had been crushed by nothing more than a mallet.

The same pragmatic information that assists in retrieving semantic roles from the discourse is required for hypothesizing roles, but now it must be accessed in a more general fashion to provide a description of a possible filler for the role. This puts an added constraint on the formation of the implications that provide the information, since it would be desirable for the rules to be flexible enough to be used in both tasks.

Filling roles in the pulley domain
Pragmatic information has been introduced as necessary for filling in gaps in semantic role assignment. Semantic role fillers that are not made explicit in the syntactic realization of a verb can sometimes be retrieved from the discourse or hypothesized from general knowledge about the domain. There are clear examples of these implicit semantic role fillers in the pulley domain. In "the pulley is suspended from a pulley," it is clear from pragmatic information about suspension that a STRING, or some type of flexible line segment, is doing the "suspending," but it is never mentioned explicitly. This clause is followed by "and offset by a particle," which cannot be analyzed at all without the STRING having first been recognized as a default value for one of the semantic roles of **suspend**. The processing of this example is described in detail at the end of chapter 4.

The relationships *between* semantic roles are not always made explicit either. Deduction is often required to specify these relationships. In "a string with masses A and B attached at its ends," it is left to the reader to place one "mass" at each "end." In "a string with masses attached," even more deduction is involved since appropriate location points on the "string," presumably the "ends," must be selected for the "masses" to be "attached" to. Fortunately, in the pulley world there are standard configurations of entities that make up part of the common-sense knowledge for that domain.

1.3   The pulley domain

The actual implementation of the approach to semantic analysis described here received as input a syntactic parse of each sentence with all the referents fully determined. This input was based on the output of Chris Mellish's incremental evaluation system [Mellish, 1981]. The term *referent* as used here indicates a unique identifier for a noun phrase to which any attributes associated with that noun phrase can be assigned. Technically, the referent of "pulley" could be T00431, but for the sake of clarity, the referents correspond closely to the head noun of the noun phrases, e.g., pulley1. Determining the referent of a pronoun thus amounts to finding the unique identifier associated with the noun phrase to which the pronoun refers, which is effectively the same as what is known in linguistics as determining a referent.

For instance, for a phrase such as

"A string with a particle attached at its right end . . ."

each noun phrase is given a unique identifier. "A string" becomes **string1**, "a particle" becomes **particle1**, and "its right end," becomes **right1**. In the processing of "its right end," incremental evaluation recognizes that the "it" refers to **string1**, and therefore part of the given information about the referent for the end, **right1**, is that it is a part of **string1**. The type of entity that each of these unique identifiers refers to is captured by a list of **hasname** predicates, where **hasname(string,string1)** indicates that **string1** is a unique identifier for a string. If specific attributes have been associated with any of the entities, such as "a fine string," instead of just "a string," then this is also processed, and is included with the output as **mass**(string1,zero,duration), meaning that the mass of **string1** is **zero** for the **duration** of the problem.

In determining the referent of a noun phrase, prepositional phrases that modify the head noun will also be processed, so they will not be handed over to semantic analysis as part of the parse that requires analysis. For example, given

"A particle of 3 lb attached at its right end"

the **of** prepositional phrase modifies "particle." The information it supplies is part of the information associated with **particle1**.

A plural noun group, such as "two particles" in

"Two particles resting on the table . . ."

is represented by listing each member of the group separately as a member of a plural constituent of the appropriate type. Thus, given referents **particle2** and **particle3** for the particles, "two particles" becomes

pl(subj(particle2))
pl(subj(particle3))

All the plural noun groups involve, implicitly or explicitly, a small finite number of entities, so there is no difficulty in representing them as lists of plural constituents.

1.3.1 Input assumptions

The syntactic parse information is presented in list form rather than tree form, with each syntactic constituent being listed separately. The type of syntactic constituent is indicated by a function symbol, as in subj(particle1). The relative clause in "A string with a particle attached at its right end . . .", i.e., the object of the WITH, "a particle attached at its right end," is represented as:

parse(clause1,attach,[subj(particle1),pp(at,right1)])

The ordering of the noun phrases in the lists corresponds to the order in which they occur in the sentence. This is useful to the processor, as explained in chapter 4.

For greater clarity, the following representation will be used throughout the text:

Verb: **attach**

Constituent list

subj(particle1),
pp(at,right1)

In addition to the syntactic parse, the semantic representations of the referents are also supplied as input.

hasname(particle,particle1)
hasname(string,string1)
hasname(right,right1)
haspart(string1,right1)

1.3.2 Constraints on the desired output

The first of the pulley problems from appendix A is:

Two pulleys of weights 12 lb and 8 lb are connected by a fine string hanging over a smooth fixed pulley. Over the former is hung a fine string with weights 3 lb and 6 lb at its ends, and over the latter a string with weights 4 lb and x lb. Find x so that the string over the fixed pulley remains stationary, and find the tension in it. (Humphrey p. 84, no. 2)

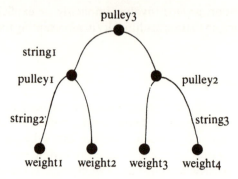

The problem-solver needed the semantic representation for this problem to specify, for the referents of the noun phrases, all of the **contact** and **support** relationships suggested by the verbs. The task to be given the problem-solver also had to be clearly defined. The semantic predicates representing the required level of detail for the first sentence in the preceding problem are explained below. Pulley1 and pulley2 are the referents of the first noun phrase, and they are both instances of "pulleys," as is pulley3. String1 is the referent of the noun phrase that is the object of the BY, and is a string, e.g., **hasname**(string,string1). The following **hasname** predicates, along with the other predicates from section 1.3.1, are given as input.

        hasname(pulley,pulley1)
        hasname(pulley,pulley2)
        hasname(string,string1)
        hasname(pulley,pulley3)

The relationships that must be specified as output include the contact relationships between each of the first two pulleys and the ends of the string. There are two sets of predicates for this, one for each pulley. Each set makes explicit the point on the entity that is at the **sameplace** as a point on the other object. The right end and the left end of string1 are chosen as contact points for pulley1 and pulley2 respectively.

        contact(pulley1,string1)
        locpt(pulley1,pulley1)
        locpt(right1,string1)
        sameplace(right1,pulley1)

        contact(pulley2,string2)
        locpt(pulley2,pulley2)
        locpt(left1,string1)
        sameplace(left1,pulley2)

The string itself is supported by the third pulley somewhere in the middle, a point which is designated as "midpoint" not because it is exactly equidistant from the ends, but simply to differentiate it from an endpoint. The **support** involved here can only occur if there is a direct **contact** between the entities involved, so there also needs to be a set of predicates specifying the **contact** relationship.

support(pulley3,string1)

contact(pulley3,string1)
locpt(pulley3,pulley3)
locpt(midpt1,string1)
sameplace(midpt1,pulley3)

This level of detail is continued for the rest of the problem so that by the end, "X" is clearly defined, and the problem-solver can be instructed to "seek" the measure of "X" and the measure of "tension1," the tension in the string.

sought(X)
sought(tension1)

1.4   Overview

This chapter has introduced several general problems associated with providing a semantic representation of sentences in context, and given specific examples of some of these problems from the pulley domain. It has also defined the input and output conditions for the pulley domain implementation. This section gives an overview of the next four chapters. The overview includes a description of inference-driven mapping, illustrated by an example, and uses the same example to compare it to the template approach. The main difference between the template approach and inference-driven mapping is that the latter bypasses the intermediate levels of representation used by templates, and maps the syntactic constituents directly onto the predicate-arguments of the "deep" semantic representation. This has significant advantages, in that one level of representation allows more efficient and integrated processing, and it provides a clear distinction between the verb definition used to produce the semantic representations, and the semantic representations themselves.

One of the main goals of any semantic processor is to provide an appropriate mapping between the syntactic constituents of a parsed clause and the semantic roles associated with the verb. As demonstrated in section 1.3.2, three factors complicate the mapping: (1) the large number of choices available for syntactic realization of any particular semantic role, (2) the ability of the syntactic constituents to indicate several different types of semantic roles given appropriate contexts, and (3) semantic role interdependencies.

Chapter 2 discusses two traditional approaches to semantic processing which are referred to here as the *linguistic* approach and the *template* approach. The *linguistic* approach attempts to adhere closely to a prevalent linguistic theory of semantic analysis, usually either a variation on Fillmore's case grammar [Simmons, 1967], or generative semantics. The most radical implementations are Schank's and Wilks's, which claim to skip over syntactic parsing entirely and achieve a semantic representation directly from a string of English words [Schank, 1975; Wilks, 1976]. However, clear similarities can be seen between their implementations and the more traditional case implementations, which will be discussed in detail. The generative semantics school is exemplified primarily by Norman and Rumelhart's [1975] implementation based on Lakoff's cognitive grammar. The goal of generative semantics is to include the decomposition of the verb in the process of parsing the sentence, so that the semantic deep structure is produced as the end result of the parse.

One of the main problems with all of these implementations is that the linguistic theories they are based on were not developed as theories for computational processors, but rather as descriptions of different levels of representation. As a result, there are no obvious correlations to standard processing techniques. The code that produces the required level of description tends to be extremely opaque and special purpose. Another major problem is that the descriptions that are generated are basically similar to what is known as a case-frame description, which has certain serious inadequacies. It consists of a flat-predicate argument structure that is not flexible enough to capture the representation of complex events. This is discussed in more detail in chapter 2. The result is that the implementations then apply pragmatic rules to augment the case-frames, and derive more complex semantic representations similar to the decompositions favored by generative semantics. There is no generally accepted formalism for creating these types of pragmatic rules, and there is general concern over how many of them there should be, and when they should and should not be applied. This is referred to as the problem of constraining pragmatic inferences.

The *template* approach places the emphasis on transparent processing rather than any one linguistic theory, and since it is thus more transportable it is quite popular. It maps a sentence through several successive levels of description in order to derive the semantic information from the syntactic parse. Since this is the most widely used current approach that makes explicit use of a syntactic parse, it is the most important approach to compare with inference-driven mapping. The main difference is that the *template* approach maps syntactic constituents onto semantic roles and <u>then</u> derives deeper semantic representations by drawing domain-specific inferences. *Inference-driven mapping* expands the verb into its deeper representation, and performs the mappings <u>during</u> the expansion while establishing the appropriateness of the representation. Inference-driven mapping and templates produce equivalent sets of mappings since the inference-driven mapping rules are effectively grammar rules that generate the same sets of mappings as the ones captured by the templates themselves.

This is illustrated in the next section which briefly describes the template approach using a specific example, and then shows how inference-driven mapping handles the same example. Both these examples are given in terms of the six tasks originally outlined in the introduction, and restated here:

1. establishing referents for the noun phrases;
2. finding appropriate mappings from the syntactic constituents of the parse onto the underlying semantic representation of the verb;
3. using pragmatic information to assign fillers to semantic roles that do not have an explicit syntactic realization;
4. expanding the representation of the verb into a more detailed representation that fulfills the requirements of the processing task;
5. constraining allowable inferences so that this semantic representation does not become unmanageably large;
6. appropriately integrating the final representation of the clause with the representations of prior clauses.

1.4.1 *The template approach*

In general, the template approach can be described as using basically three levels of semantic representation which are illustrated below. The first level, referred to here as the *template level*, corresponds to a set of patterns that represent the possible syntactic realizations of sentential units for an individual verb. Each ⟨slot⟩ in the template represents the position of a syntactic constituent in a particular realization. The slots usually have semantic markers associated with them, referring to the semantic role the syntactic constituent is expected to play with respect to the verb. (The semantic markers in the example below refer to physical objects, PH-OBJ, and location points on those entities, LOC-PT.) Specific syntactic parses can be matched directly with these templates. Matching parses onto templates achieves the mapping of the syntactic constituents onto the underlying semantic representation. In the following examples subject is indicated by subj(X), and prepositional phrases are indicated by pp(Prep, Y), where Prep can be given the value of a particular preposition such as BY or WITH. The variables X, Y and Z can be given the value of the referents of the noun phrases corresponding to the syntactic constituents being indicated.

The second step is to match the templates with an intermediate level, the *canonical level*, which is sometimes termed the "case-frame level." The canonical level consists basically of the verb or the predicate chosen to represent the verb, and a union of all of the semantic roles the syntactic constituents can be associated with. Inferences can then be drawn from this intermediate level to first fill unfilled semantic roles, task 3, and then expand the representation of the verb, task 4, to produce the final and third level, the *predicate level*. Care must be taken to constrain these inferences, task 5, and then task 6, the integration of the representation with the prior discourse, must be achieved.

Sentence:

A particle is attached to the end of a string.

Template:

⟨PH-OBJ1⟩ **attach** to ⟨LOC-PT2⟩ of ⟨PH-OBJ2⟩

Canonical form:

attach(⟨PH-OBJ1⟩,⟨PH-OBJ2⟩, ⟨LOC-PT1⟩,⟨LOC-PT2⟩)

Predicates:

contact(⟨PH-OBJ1⟩,⟨PH-OBJ2⟩)
locpt(⟨LOC-PT1⟩,⟨PH-OBJ1⟩)
locpt(⟨LOC-PT2⟩,⟨PH-OBJ2⟩)
sameplace(⟨LOC-PT1⟩,⟨LOC-PT2⟩)

From the parse level to the template level

Applying this approach to the following alternative syntactic configurations from the pulley domain results in the set of templates immediately below.

"A particle is attached	at the end of a	string."
⟨PH-OBJ1⟩	⟨LOC-PT2⟩	⟨PH-OBJ2⟩
subj(X)	**attach** at pp(at,Y)	of pp(of,Z)

"A particle is attached	to the end of a	string."
⟨PH-OBJ1⟩	⟨LOC-PT2⟩	⟨PH-OBJ2⟩
subj(X)	**attach** to pp(to,Y)	of pp(of,Z)

Matching the first sentence onto its corresponding template achieves the following set of mappings:

PH-OBJ1 is particle if subj(particle)
PH-OBJ2 is string if pp(of,string)
LOC-PT2 is end if pp(at,end)

The template to the canonical level

The same canonical form can be associated with both templates, and can be described as a **case-frame** for ***attach***:

Case-frame:

attach(⟨PH-OBJ1⟩,⟨PH-OBJ2⟩, ⟨LOC-PT1⟩,⟨LOC-PT2⟩)

In going from the template level to the canonical level the problem of unfilled canonical arguments has to be addressed. In the set of mappings just given, there is no mapping for ⟨LOC-PT1⟩. One approach is to examine the canonical arguments after matching them with the template arguments. With these examples, the match is straightforward, since the semantic markers give the arguments unique names. The match consists of filling a canonical argument with the referent of the template argument that has the same name. Any arguments that were not filled by the template can then be filled by pragmatic information, if the argument has been marked as requiring a filler. For example, ⟨LOC-PT1⟩ can be marked, and the following type of implication can be used to derive an appropriate filler. This implication states that if the referent of ⟨PH-OBJ1⟩ has the shape of a point, then it can be its own location point.

if shape(⟨PH-OBJ1⟩,point)
then ⟨LOC-PT1⟩ = ⟨PH-OBJ1⟩

The canonical level to the predicate level

Having filled the missing arguments, a rewrite rule such as the one below can be applied to the canonical form to expand it into a "deeper" representation; the predicate level.

contact(⟨PH-OBJ1⟩,⟨PH-OBJ2⟩) →
locpt(⟨LOC-PT1⟩,⟨PH-OBJ1⟩)
locpt(⟨LOC-PT2⟩,⟨PH-OBJ2⟩)
sameplace(⟨LOC-PT1⟩,⟨LOC-PT2⟩)

A general problem with deriving the predicate level is deciding exactly how detailed the representation should be. There is no accepted method for choosing which inference rules to apply, and final representations could be much more detailed than this one. This can result in having to store a great deal of unnecessary information, as well as a heavy computational overhead in deriving the information.

1.4.2 *Inference-driven mapping*

The main difference between templates and inference-driven mapping centers on the levels of description being used. Inference-driven mapping begins by decomposing the verb into its "deep" semantic representation which in the template approach is known as the predicate level. All the tasks of semantic analysis can be performed using the same level of description, allowing significant gains in efficiency and in integration of similar tasks such as filling the predicate-arguments, either by syntactic constituents or by pragmatic deduction.

This is possible because inference-driven mapping has a very different goal from the template approach. Templates select an appropriate representation of the verb, and then expand that representation by drawing inferences. It is possible that the inferences being drawn could be inconsistent with previous information, so constant consistency checking must be done, as well as constraining the inference drawing so that it does not become unmanageable. Inference-driven mapping, on the other hand, does not commit itself to a representation of the verb until its definition has been fully expanded. A full expansion is defined as a decomposition including all those predicates whose arguments can act as semantic roles for the verb. It is by making the assignments to the semantic roles in the decomposition while it is being built, and testing the consistency of these assignments, that the appropriateness of the representation is established. The goal is selecting a verb definition. The predicates that constitute the expansion of the verb are set up as subgoals. When the subgoals have been established, the definition has been selected. The representation corresponds to a collection of the instantiated subgoals.

In order to integrate the mapping process with the expansion process, domain-specific information must be divided into three categories:

1. lexical entries – the logical implications that are directly associated with the semantic relationships suggested by verbs;
2. mapping constraints – the linguistic information relating to associating syntactic constituents with the arguments to the semantic relationships;
3. pragmatic information – the more pragmatic implications required by the specific task to be performed in the domain.

This division is exemplified by the formalization of the pulley domain presented in chapter 3.

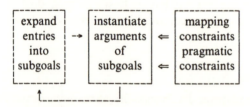

Fig. 1.2 Basic structure of inference-driven mapping

Traditional semantic roles are defined as **types** of arguments of the semantic predicates that appear in the lexical entries. The predicate-arguments are instantiated during the processing of the entries. A possible instantiation of an argument is the referent of a syntactic constituent of the appropriate syntactic and semantic **type**. The syntactic constituent instantiations correspond to the desired mapping of syntactic constituents onto semantic roles. Other instantiations can be made using pragmatic information to deduce appropriate fillers from knowledge derived from previous sentences or from domain knowledge. This process is illustrated in figure 1.2.

This approach therefore considers the mapping problem to be a member of the set of problems involved in finding instantiations for the arguments to the semantic predicates. The mappings are derived by providing a set of syntactic and semantic constraints on the instantiation of each **type** of predicate argument, depending on the particular **predicate environment** it is in. The predicate environment as explained below contains information about the predicate and the other arguments. The constraints make use of intuitions about syntactic cues for indicating semantic roles embodied in the notion of *case* [Fillmore, 1977] and use the **predicate environment** to preserve semantic role interdependencies.

If there is no syntactic constituent for a particular semantic role it may be filled by deductions based on pragmatic information. The use of pragmatic deductions depends on whether the semantic role is considered to be **optional**, **obligatory**, or **essential**. **Optional** roles are merely marked "absent," **essential** roles are filled by deduction, and an unfilled **obligatory** role causes a failure resulting in the derivation of a new set of mappings. The ability to instantiate arguments by syntactic constituents or by pragmatic deduction is essential for the correct integration of the sentence representation within the current model of the scene being described, as illustrated by the examples in section 4.3. The following sections describe this process in more detail.

Expanding the verb representation

In inference-driven mapping, producing a semantic representation of a particular sentential unit can be seen as "proving" that the verb involved has been used appropriately for the domain. Prolog is an obvious language for such an approach and the rules are expressed as Prolog clauses. (In conventional Prolog notation Q ← P corresponds to P → Q; strings starting with upper-case letters correspond to variables; and predicates, function symbols, and constants are all lower-case.) For example, R1, the lexical entry for *attach*, can be read as, "A contact between an entity, OBJECT1, and another entity, OBJECT2, can be expressed using the verb *attach*." In order to "prove" that *attach* has been used appropriately, **contact** can be set up as a subgoal. Chapter 3 defines the lexical entries used for the pulley domain.

R1

attach ←
    contact(Object1, Object2)

R2 defines **contact** in terms of three subgoals, **locpt**, **locpt** and **sameplace**. The following entry, R2, can be read as "If a location point on an entity, LOCPT1, and a location point on another entity, LOCPT2, are at the sameplace, then the entities are in contact with each other."

R2

    contact(Object1,Object2) ←
        locpt(Locpt1,Object1)
        locpt(Locpt2,Object2)
        sameplace(Locpt1,Locpt2)

The next section describes how the mappings from the syntactic constituents to the semantic roles are made during the process of establishing the subgoals. Then R1 and R2 can be used to produce the same semantic representation produced by the templates for a sentence S1, by simply listing the instantiated subgoals that are established during the process of proving the appropriateness of the verb usage.

S1

"A particle is attached to a string at its right end."

Note that the semantic roles are represented as logical variables. This allows the instantiation of a general verb rule to correspond to a particular syntactic realization of a verb. And it allows for the same semantic role to occur in more than one predicate, and be assigned the same logical variable without having to know the instantiation of that variable. Then, when it is finally instantiated, both instances of the role will automatically share the same referent. It also allows for a model–theoretic interpretation of the verb representation. Given a domain model that includes a representation of things (i.e., entities and situations) and relations between things, the general verb rules can be seen as representing types of relationships between entities and things (i.e., between entities and entities, or between entities and situations). The denotation of an instantiated representation is the general relationship corresponding to that verb as represented in the domain model.

At the moment, a model–theoretic interpretation of the verb representations does not provide any further utility. Later on, when this work has been extended to include verb modifiers and quantification, the logical status of the verb representations will be essential.

Filling semantic roles

Chapter 3 introduces the mapping constraints that are used in conjunction with the lexical entries to guide the instantiation of predicate arguments with the referents of surface syntactic constituents. The mapping constraints make use of intuitions about syntactic cues for indicating semantic roles first embodied in the notion of case [Fillmore, 1980]. For the application of these rules to be useful, it is essential they preserve the same semantic role interdependencies handled by templates. This is accomplished by making the application of the mapping constraints "situation-specific" by the use of a predicate environment.

An example of a general mapping constraint involves the OBJECT1 from R1. OBJECT1s are similar to PATIENTS and, like PATIENTS, can usually be indicated by the subject. For a general constraint, the predicate environment is simply a variable, Y, given after the "/," as in M1. (M1 is an informal example of the mapping constraints that are defined more precisely in chapter 4.)

M1: Object1 is X if subj(X)/Y

Given [subj(particle1),pp(to,string1),pp(at,right1)] as the constituent list of S1, application of this constraint results in OBJECT1 being instantiated with "particle1."

The mapping rule for the OBJECT2 from the "attach" example is not as general, and gives an example of how mapping constraints can be restricted. An OBJECT2 of a **contact** relationship can be indicated by a pp(to,X), but an OBJECT2 of a **support** relationship cannot. In order to make the application of the constraints situation-specific, the predicate environment can be partially instantiated. It contains information about the "context" of the semantic role, exemplified here by the predicate name and the other arguments. The predicate environment for the term OBJECT2 on the right-hand side of R1 is **contact**(Object1,Object2). By associating a **contact** predicate environment with the **pp(to,X)** mapping constraint, as in the following example, the constraint can be restricted to OBJECT2's which are arguments to **contact** predicates. This allows the term OBJECT2 to be instantiated with **string1**.

M2: Object2 is X if pp(to,X)/contact(Y,Object2)

The associated predicate environments act as filters on the possible mappings for the arguments, so that the final set of mappings arrived at is within the limitations of the domain [Palmer, 1983]. This is described in detail in chapter 3.

The only terms remaining to be instantiated in the decomposition of ***attach*** are the LOCPT1 and LOCPT2 terms; M3 is a general constraint for instantiating LOCPT1 or LOCPT2 with the referent of the object of a pp(at,X), regardless of the predicate environment.

M3: Locpt is L if pp(at,L)/Y

This takes care of the location point on the string, LOCPT2, which becomes instantiated with the referent of the right end, **right1**. However, it does not supply a location point for the particle. Location points are classified as *essential* roles, so that if they are not filled by syntactic constituents they have to be deduced. Pragmatics allows entities with the shape of a point to be their own location point, so LOCPT1 is instantiated with **particle1**.

To summarize the mapping of syntactic constituents to semantic roles that has been performed during the expansion of *attach*, the subj(X) and the pp(to,Y) are assigned during the first decomposition of *attach* into **contact**:

contact(particle1,string)

Then R2 further expands the set of subgoals, and the pp(at,X) is assigned to LOCPT2. The instantiation of LOCPT1 is found by the application of pragmatic information.

locpt(particle1,particle1)
locpt(right1,string1)
sameplace(particle1,right1)

Integrated semantic analysis

The ability to instantiate arguments by syntactic constituents or by pragmatic deduction has allowed any gaps in the assignment of syntactic constituents to semantic roles to be filled during the expansion of the verb, so clearly the tasks of expanding the verb, task 4, performing the mappings, task 2, and filling unfilled roles with pragmatics, task 3, have all been completed simultaneously. Perhaps not so obviously, the remaining tasks, constraining the inferences, task 5, and integrating the representation appropriately, task 6, have also been performed. The inferences are constrained automatically, since the decompositions of the verbs are restricted to predicates whose arguments are semantic roles, in other words whose arguments can be filled by syntactic constituents. Allowing unfilled roles to be filled by pragmatic deduction is essential for the correct integration of the sentence representation within the current model of the scene being described, since pragmatics can often supply fillers from discourse information about previous sentences. Detailed examples of the use of pragmatics to fill unfilled roles are given in chapter 4.

The key to the simultaneous solution of all of these semantic tasks is filling the semantic roles, either by syntactic constituents or pragmatic deduction, *during* the expansion of the verb representation. The filler of a semantic role can have a profound effect on exactly how the verb representation is to be expanded. It is this close tie between the desired representation of a verb and the referents that act as arguments to it that provides the basis for inference-driven mapping.

Comparing inference-driven mapping to templates

The general mapping constraints are very similar to the syntactic cues traditionally associated with cases. However, the addition of the predicate environments restricts the mapping constraints so that semantic role interdependencies are still preserved, allowing much more generality. The restricted mapping constraints together with the lexical entries can be seen as a grammar for generating the same sets of mappings captured by templates, or possibly a superset of the templates. This is explained in more detail in chapter 3. As such, they are capable of producing the same set of mappings between syntactic constituents and semantic roles that is produced by the templates, with important advantages. The various tasks associated with semantic analysis are performed simultaneously rather than in several stages, resulting in a more efficient analysis with fewer redundancies in the levels of representation required. Analysis by synthesis is used to perform all of the semantic analysis tasks in a process that has only a few more steps in it than the single stage of template matching, and is thus extremely efficient.

Using semantic predicates as a central level of representation provides another important benefit in that their effect on the path of the semantic analysis can be clearly demonstrated. This has previously been obscured by the separate stages of the template method. Because of the inadequacy of case-frames most systems are forced to derive "deeper" representations which are often decompositional in nature, such as the LNR representations. The implementations that derive the deeper representations unfortunately do not give clear rules for their derivations, as is pointed out in chapter 2. Decompositions represent complex events more appropriately than case-frames by capturing complex interactions of relationships between roles. In complex verbs such as *shoot*, an AGENT uses an INSTRUMENT to put a projectile into motion, and that projectile eventually strikes an entity. Several different semantic predicates need to be defined to capture even a portion of the meaning of *shoot*. A more detailed discussion of complex events along with a possible definition of *shoot* is given in chapter 2.

It is impossible to capture this complexity in a flat predicate-argument structure like a traditional case-frame, which is designed to handle a single event. By simply listing the semantic roles involved, without specifying how the presence of one of them affects relationships between the other, the complexity is lost. A major criticism of the case-frame approach is that the semantic roles are nothing more than argument positions [Charniak, 1976]. With inference-driven mapping, however, the inclusion or non-inclusion of certain **optional** roles such as AGENT or INSTRUMENT has a major impact on the decomposition of the verb itself. This impact takes the form of choosing or not choosing to include the semantic predicate to which the role is an argument. Including a new semantic predicate in the decomposition occasions the application of an additional lexical entry during the expansion of the verb so that the correct decomposition is achieved. The semantic predicates uniquely associated with these semantic roles are termed *case predicates* and their lexical entries, introduced in chapter 3, give an unequivocal statement of the desired *case meaning* for the relevant semantic role as it is defined in chapter 2. For one class of roles, the INSTRUMENT class, the case meaning is independent of the verb in which the semantic role appears, and there are indications that this same lexical entry will prove transportable to other domains, as mentioned in chapter 5.

The general influence of certain semantic roles on the decomposition of the verb is captured concretely in the form of lexical entries, providing a transparency of processing not available in the template approach. It also allows a distinction to be made between the verb definition, i.e., the lexical entry, used to produce a semantic representation, and the semantic representation that is produced. The same lexical entry can be seen to produce widely different semantic representations due to the influence of certain semantic roles. These final semantic representations differ in their structure as well as in which roles have been filled. This could provide an interesting tool for linguists investigating the difference between similar usages of a verb, such as intransitive and transitive usages of *hang*.

1.4.3   *Implementation*

The processor that is presented in chapter 4 performs inference-driven mapping by imposing a procedural interpretation on the lexical entries very similarly to the way that Prolog imposes a procedural interpretation on Horn clauses. Horn clauses are logical implications with only one consequent. The lexical entries are in fact Horn clauses, and the semantic roles that are arguments to the predicates are terms consisting of function symbols with one argument. The procedural interpretation drives the expansion of the lexical entries, and allows the function symbols to be "evaluated" as a means of instantiating the arguments. The predicate environments associated with the constraints on instantiation correspond to possible snapshots of the procedural interpretation of the entries. This allows the same argument to be constrained differently depending on the instantiations of the other arguments or on the particular predicate. Therefore one lexical entry can correspond to several different syntactic expressions of the verb without losing necessary interdependencies. Procedural interpretation also allows different entries to apply given different instantiations of predicate arguments. The representation of a single lexical entry for *break* can be constrained so that INSTRUMENTS can only be filled by WITH prepositional phrases if the AGENT is instantiated. The subgoals that are established correspond to the set of predicates that make up the semantic representation of the clause.

Chapter 3 explains how the lexical entries can actually be thought of as grammar rules. A particular lexical entry and the other entries that can expand it can be combined with the general mapping constraints to produce all the possible syntactic expressions of that verb. In this way, the lexical entries and the mapping constraints can be seen as grammar rules that generate the sets of mappings corresponding to the sentences of a language. The predicate environments act as filters to ensure that the sets of mappings being generated are within the limitations of the domain. Theoretically, the processor could be used to generate all the possible syntactic realizations of a single verb and then match one of them to the clause waiting to be analyzed, in much the same way that the templates described in chapter 2 are used. It is much more efficient to compare each possible mapping as it is being generated with the constituent list of the clause so that the processor can immediately discard those mappings that involve constituents not on the constituent list.

Thus, the only complete sets of mappings produced are always sets that will match the constituent list. These sets are achieved with surprising directness by using the order of the arguments of the semantic predicates to control the order in which possible mappings are considered. The ordering of the mapping rules and the arguments follows the natural ordering of syntactic constituents as defined by the precedence relations mentioned in section 1.2.3. So the lexical entries encompass the same syntactic realizations as a set of templates, but allow the semantic processor to go directly from the syntactic parse level to the "deep" semantic representation without requiring the intermediate level of representation exemplified by a case-frame.

In summary, inference-driven mapping performs analysis by synthesis efficiently and directly using a procedural interpretation of the Horn clauses that correspond to the lexical entries of each verb. One lexical entry can produce alternative semantic representations given different sets of syntactic constituents. These representations provide the level of detail necessary for the problem-solver, but also retain certain useful pieces of information regarding the surface structure of the clauses and represent complex events more adequately than case-frames. The greater flexibility of representation is a major factor in the ability of inference-driven mapping to perform the tasks associated with semantic analysis simultaneously, without requiring the separate levels of description and corresponding separate stages of processing used by templates.

2 Previous computational approaches to semantic analysis

The preceding chapter presented the basic difficulties associated with producing semantic representations of sentences in context. This chapter surveys several well-known natural language processors, concentrating on their efforts at overcoming these particular difficulties. The processors use different *styles* of semantic representation as well as different *methods* for producing the chosen semantic representation from the syntactic parse. Ideally, clearly defined methods of producing semantic representations should be based on a linguistic theory of semantic analysis; a theory about the relationships between the given syntactic and semantic representations, and not just on the particular style of semantic representation. Computational linguistics has a unique contribution to make to the study of linguistics, in that it offers the opportunity of realizing the processes that must underlie the theories. Unfortunately, it seems to be the case that those systems that adhere most closely to a particular linguistic theory have the least clearly defined processing methods, and vice versa.

Another important aspect to examine is whether or not any of the methods make significant use of procedural representations. An important contribution hoped for from computational linguistics is an understanding of procedural semantics as "a paradigm or a framework for developing and expressing theories of meaning" [Woods, 1981, p. 302]. It is argued that adding procedures to a framework should greatly enrich its expressive power [Wilks, 1982]. In spite of the intuitive appeal of this argument, much work remains to be done before the benefits can be convincingly demonstrated. The only two systems that have attempted to make significant use of procedural verb representations, SHRDLU and LNR, have some of the least clearly defined theories of semantic analysis; perhaps simply because procedural verb representations are still so new.

Whether procedural or not, an essential component of a natural language processor is the type of verb representation used. Some implementations make explicit use of a representation associated with a particular linguistic theory. Other implementations modify a single theory, or combine two or more theories to produce an entirely new representation. Still other implementations eschew any direct ties to linguistic theories, and use representations developed primarily to aid the processing techniques employed. Comparing and contrasting implementations is complicated, since a processing method is generally inextricably linked to the type of representation that has been chosen. There are several possible points of comparison, including:

1. the linguistic theories themselves;
2. the adherence or non-adherence to those theories;
3. any variation in the processing of similar theories;
4. how well a theory lends itself to processing;
5. the transparency of the processing techniques;
6. overall advantages and disadvantages of an individual implementation.

The task would be difficult enough if the domains chosen were the same or even similar, but they are invariably quite different. A discussion of computational linguistics is not the place to argue competitive merits of linguistic theories, but most of the other points are addressed in this chapter, giving rise to the following conclusions.

In general, implementations fall into two categories: those that are concentrating on the adequacy of the representation produced by the theory being used, and those that are concentrating on the transparency of the processing techniques. These approaches appear to be more or less mutually exclusive since rich, complicated representations tend to result in unusually complex processing techniques. The first section discusses the systems that can best be compared in terms of their processing techniques, including Woods' [1973, 1977, 1981] and Novak's [1976]. Although they do not claim to be adhering to standard case theory, all of these systems use an intermediate level of representation of the verb that is very similar to a case-frame. This is the only representation that spans both categories. It consists of a simple flat predicate-argument structure that contains the semantic roles generally associated with a verb. This use of case with respect to semantic roles represents a deviation from the standard linguistic use of "case markings" to indicate syntactic cases, as explained in section 2.2. While a case-frame cannot adequately represent complex events, it does give more semantic information than a syntactic parse, and provides a general representation for a verb from which inferences can be drawn. It also seems to be an appropriate level for indicating syntactic cues for expressing the semantic roles or cases, although it has been somewhat disappointing in this respect, as discussed in section 2.2. Systems that are mainly concerned with the representational advantages or disadvantages of case are discussed in this section, and these include Simmons [1967, 1973], Schank [1975], Norman and Rumelhart [1975], and Wilks [1975a, 1975b, 1976, 1982]. This section ends by presenting multiple embedded predicates as an alternative to case as a deep structure representation. These are complex predicate-argument structures that can more appropriately represent verb semantics and are somewhat similar to the structures from generative semantics. The lexical entries for inference-driven mapping that are introduced in chapter

1 and explored in more depth in chapter 3 are based on these embedded predicates.

In spite of the popularity of case-frames as tools for deep structure representation, there are several fundamental problems with them. Case-frames were originally suggested as the deep structure to be produced by a syntactic parse using a case grammar, a type of transformational grammar [Fillmore, 1977, 1980]. As such, the ties between the syntactic constituents and the cases were built into the grammar rules. Since case was supposed to greatly simplify these ties by capturing linguistic generalizations, making the ties an intrinsic part of the grammar was not considered a problem. However, a comprehensive investigation of case grammar [Stockwell, Schacter and Partee, 1973] brings to light positional idiosyncrasies that can only be handled by allowing certain verbs to have more than one case-frame or by changing fundamental aspects of the grammar itself. Computational implementations sidestep this issue by using only the case-frame representation and not the case grammar itself. Perhaps a more serious problem with case revolves around the difficulty linguists have in agreeing on a single set of cases for English. Since case is basically a method of decomposing verbs into more primitive concepts, it falls heir to all the fundamental problems associated with decomposition. Implementations reflect this disagreement, since each presents a slightly different set of possible cases, or arguments to the verb predicates. The final serious problem with case-frames is that they fall so short of being useful semantic representations. Every implementation that uses case-frames as a level of representation has to augment the case-frame by a more complex representation that spells out the relationships between the cases, usually multiple embedded predicates. In trying to cope with these difficulties, implementers continue to modify their use of case, until, as claimed by Charniak, they are not using case for anything more than a notational device, and there are no resulting case benefits [Charniak, 1975]. This criticism and Wilks' reply [Wilks, 1976] are explored in section 2.2.4.

Generative semantics represents a serious effort by linguists to ameliorate some of these problems, most particularly the representation problem [Fodor, 1977]. The deep structure used by generative semanticists is itself a multiple embedded predicate structure, and the grammar rules are designed to parse the sentence into that structure. The motivation was to allow semantics to play a more important role in a syntactic parse. Unfortunately, the transformational paradigm being used did not lend itself to flexible use of semantic information, resulting in rather opaque and unnatural grammar rules. Implementers such as Norman and Rumelhart, whose LNR system was largely inspired by this approach, did not make use of the generative semantics grammar rules, but developed their own technique of producing a generative semantics deep structure from the parse. They make explicit use of a case-frame as an intermediate level of representation, and in practice LNR turns out to be quite similar to the systems that were supposedly based on case grammar, but also had major departures from the actual theory. The end of section 2.2 discusses the multiple embedded structure in isolation from the transformational framework, and compares it to case-frames simply on the basis of its richer expressive power. The main disadvantage of multiple embedded predicates when compared to case-frames is that there is no defined method for associating syntactic cues with the predicate-arguments. The lexical entries for inference-driven mapping make use of a *predicate environment* to capture the syntactic cues for the predicate-arguments, as explained in chapter 3.

2.1 Performing mappings before drawing inferences

This section surveys two different natural language processing systems: **pattern–action** rules [Woods, 1973, 1977, 1981], and sentence schemas [Novak, 1976]. Both systems are representative of a common approach to semantic processing that occurs in at least two stages: the mapping of syntactic constituents onto the semantic roles associated with the verb, and the drawing of inferences implied by that verb. Sometimes the mapping is done after a syntactic parse has been found, and sometimes it is done in conjunction with the syntactic parsing. Whether or not parsing and mapping occur as one stage or two separate stages does not affect the mapping technique that has been chosen, or when the inferences are drawn. These systems all use variations of the template approach for performing mappings, in that alternative syntactic expressions for a particular verb are each given individual predicate-argument representations. Such multiple predicate-argument representations are not dissimilar to multiple case-frames, although unlike case-frames they can be restricted to only those arguments that can be indicated by major syntactic constituents. Woods' **pattern–action** rules and Novak's sentence schemas are more similar to multiple case-frames since they also include arguments that can only be indicated by prepositional phrases. Another important aspect of the template approach, or variations on it, is that the lexical entries of the verbs always consist of static data structures. It has often been suggested that the most useful contribution of a computational approach to semantic analysis should be procedural word representations [Woods, 1981]. None of the processors surveyed in this section attempt to make such a contribution.

2.1.1 *Templates vs. procedures*

There are two basic techniques for finding semantic role assignments that are used by the processors discussed here: the *template* approach and the *disjunctive* approach.

One of the most popular current approaches (used in ISAAC, CHAT, LADDER) is to create templates for every possible syntactic realization of a verb and its semantic roles. This has the advantage of preserving dependencies, but is somewhat redundant, since verbs that take similar assignments cannot be expressed with general templates, but must each have their own set of templates, no matter how similar. This makes it cumbersome for very large domains. Although there is no claim made that the template approach represents a theory of semantic analysis, or is derived from a theory of semantic analysis, it is actually fairly comparable to using multiple case-frames. These have been suggested as a method of dealing with the problems of accounting for positional variations of cases (see section 2.2.2).

Templates are constructed by listing, for a particular domain, all the possible syntactic configurations in which a single verb is expected to appear. Generally, an appropriate semantic feature will be associated with each syntactic constituent. The object of the processor is to match the syntactic parse of a sentence with one of the templates involving the main verb of the parse.

Having matched a template, the sentence is locked into the system so that it can proceed towards full semantic expression. There are general inference rules associated with each verb around which a set of templates has been grouped. Rather than creating inference rules that deal with each template individually, it is often considered more efficient to associate a more general, i.e., *canonical*, level with a specific group of templates. This intermediate level of representation usually consists of the verb itself (or perhaps a more primitive semantic predicate chosen to represent the verb) and a list of possible roles, i.e., arguments to the predicate. These roles correspond loosely to a union of the various semantic types indicated in the templates. Multiple case-frames such as the ones suggested by Levin [1977, 1979] would correspond to the templates, and they could be mapped onto a canonical case-frame before applying inference rules. One set of inference rules then applies indirectly to a group of templates, by being applied to the instantiated canonical form that represents that group. If this method is chosen, there must also be rules for mapping each of the individual templates onto the canonical template.

The templates required for the *open* examples, from chapter 1, assuming an active–passive transformation or some sort of redundancy rule, are as follows:

⟨AGENT⟩ open ⟨PATIENT⟩ with ⟨INSTRUMENT⟩
⟨INSTRUMENT⟩ open ⟨PATIENT⟩
⟨PATIENT⟩ open

The portion of each semantic role implies the associated syntactic constituent, e.g., ⟨AGENT⟩ is in the SUBJECT position.

An alternative to templates would be to associate a procedure with each semantic role that would be responsible for finding the syntactic constituent assignment. Each procedure would be defined as a *disjunction* of the possible syntactic role assignments for that semantic role. The approach taken by the natural language interfaces at BBN uses combinations of templates and disjunctions [Woods, 1977]. An example of this approach, using the *open* verb examples again, is:

Verb: ***open***

AGENT   (SUBJECT)
INSTRUMENT   (OR (SUBJECT)(WITH PP)(BY PP))
PATIENT   (OR (SUBJECT)(OBJECT))

This approach is more general, and one can conceive of different verbs sharing the same procedures for the same semantic roles. However, the assignments as stated operate entirely independently of any other role assignments that are being made. There is no way to take into account dependencies between semantic roles and possible constituent assignments. For example, there is no way of checking if SUBJECT had been assigned to the AGENT or the PATIENT before assigning a BY PP to the INSTRUMENT. Neither could a test be made to see if the AGENT had been given any kind of assignment before assigning the INSTRUMENT to a WITH PP. As long as the sentences to be analyzed could be assumed to be grammatical and locally unambiguous this would not technically be a drawback. However, it is clearly not an approach that could be extended later to synthesizing sentences as well. The inability of procedures based on disjunctions to account for semantic role interdependencies leaves little alternative to the template approach.

Combining templates with procedures

Much of the most impressive work in natural language processing has been directed by Bill Woods at BBN. The examples in this section come from his dissertation, which contains a clear account of the techniques for semantic analysis that were later implemented [Woods, 1973, 1977, 1981]. The particular component focused on in this section is the method for mapping semantic roles onto syntactic constituents. The thesis also includes interesting techniques for quantification, handling anaphoric expressions and question-answering, but they are not particularly relevant to the issues being discussed here.

After first achieving a syntactic parse, semantic representations are derived from the parse by repeated applications of semantic interpretation rules, called S-rules. In some of the BBN implementations, the rules are applied during the parse, and in others after the parse. This does not affect the manner in which dependencies between semantic role assignments are dealt with. The interpretation rules take the form of **pattern–action** rules, where, if the left-hand **pattern** matches, the right-hand **action** is executed. There are several different patterns for a single verb. In this sense patterns correspond to templates. They do, however, allow alternative syntactic constituents or even alternative verbs in the same pattern, which adds flexibility to the standard template approach. In this way patterns combine the disjunction method with the template method.

Patterns are broken up into subcomponents, each one roughly equivalent to a semantic role. The pattern includes information about what kind of syntactic constituent, or possibly kinds of syntactic constituents, can indicate this semantic role in constructing this particular pattern. Each component also has associated with it tests to make on the possible filler of the semantic role in the form of semantic predicates or structural information about where the syntactic constituent under consideration fits in the parse tree. In the following example of an S-rule involving *fly*, as in "AA-57 flies from Boston to Chicago," the action part of the rule indicates the semantic predicate chosen to represent the information in the sentence. For this rule that predicate is CONNECT.

> 1-(G1: FLIGHT((1)) and (2) = fly) and
> 2-(G3: (1) = from and PLACE((2))) and
> 3-(G3: (1) = to and PLACE((2))))
> ⇒ CONNECT(1-1,2-2,3-2)

In this example, G1 and the two G3s correspond to subtrees that will match subtrees of particular parse trees. G1 matches the first noun phrase of a clause and the verb that immediately follows, and the G3s match prepositional phrases. The preposition for the first G3 has to be *from*, while the noun phrase should satisfy the semantic constraints of being a PLACE. The preposition for the second G3 must be *to*, and the noun phrase must also be a PLACE. The noun phrase from G1 must be a FLIGHT, and the verb must be *fly*. There is no required ordering on the G3s, so this rule would match "AA-57 flies to Chicago from Boston" just as easily. The right-hand side of the arrow, CONNECT(1-1,2-2,3-2), represents the three subcomponents for CONNECT, CONNECT(FLIGHT,PLACE,PLACE), as indicated by the subscripts, and is essentially the same as a domain-specific case-frame for CONNECT.

Three more S-rules for the sentence "AA-57 flies from Boston to Chicago" are:

> S1   1-(G1: FLIGHT((1)) and ((2) = fly
>   or (2) = depart
>   or (2) = go) and
>   2-(G3: (1) = from and PLACE((2)))) and
>   3-(G3: (1) = to and PLACE((2))))
>   ⇒ CONNECT(1-1,2-2,3-2)

> S4   1-(G1: FLIGHT((1)) and ((2) = fly
>   or (2) = leave
>   or (2) = go) and
>   2-(G3: (1) = from and PLACE((2))))
>   ⇒ DEPART(1-1,2-2)

S6   1-(G1: FLIGHT((1))) and ((2) = fly
                    or (2) = go) and
        2-(G3: (1) = from and PLACE((2))) and
        ⇒ ARRIVE(1-1,2-2)

S1 is an expanded version of the example S-rule above. Notice that this rule can apply whether the verb involved is *fly*, **depart** or **go**, as indicated by the disjunction, ((2) = fly or (2) = depart or (2) = go). S1 would match the example sentence, as well as the following sentences:

AA-57 departs from Boston to Chicago.
AA-57 departs to Chicago from Boston.

AA-57 goes from Boston to Chicago.
AA-57 goes to Chicago from Boston.

The other two rules in figure 2.1 would also match the first sentence, only they would produce a different **action**. S1 would result in CONNECT(AA-57, Boston, Chicago), because the FLIGHT, AA-57, has the first slot in the first subcomponent, 1-1, Boston is the PLACE in the second subcomponent, 2-2, and Chicago is the PLACE in the third subcomponent, 3-2. S4 would result in DEPART(AA-57,Boston), and S6 would result in ARRIVE(AA-57,Chicago). It seems a bit strange that S4 and S6 would match, since they do not match the entire tree, but only part of it.

S-rules can take advantage of certain generalities by giving alternative verbs for a particular rule. But there is no way for these alternatives to test what is going on in the other subcomponents, so alternative prepositions usually result in additional rules. The following rule matches "AA-57 leaves from Boston for Chicago."

S2   1-(G1: FLIGHT((1))) and ((2) = leave
                    or (2) = depart and
        2-(G3: (1) = from and PLACE((2))) and
        3-(G3: (1) = for and PLACE((2)))
        ⇒ CONNECT(1-1,2-2,3-2)

The **action** portion of an S-rule is similar to an instantiated case-frame. It is a flat predicate-argument structure that takes particular semantic types of arguments. The relationships between the arguments, however, still have to be spelled out. Executing an action corresponds to applying a new set of inference rules at this stage to spell out those relationships, and produce whatever kind of semantic representation is required.

By using disjunctions, the S-rules can take advantage of generalizations among verbs more effectively than multiple case-frames, which treat each verb separately. However, verb dependencies in semantic role assignments still have to be captured explicitly in separate templates. S-rules are similar to multiple case-frames, although Woods does not claim to be implementing case theory.

Sentence schemas

ISAAC [Novak, 1976, p. 1] is a program that can "read, understand, solve, and draw pictures of physics problems stated in English." The ISAAC techniques most relevant to this discussion are those concerning the natural language processing rather than the problem-solving that ISAAC also performs. ISAAC makes explicit use of the template approach, although Novak uses the term *schema* instead. In a domain of equilibrium problems such as ISAAC's, the sentence "A rope supports one end of a scaffold" could match a schema like "⟨physobj⟩ SUPPORT ⟨locpart⟩." The word ordering here implies that the first ⟨physobj⟩ is the logical subject (SUBJ) and the ⟨locpart⟩ is the logical object (OBJ).[1] Other likely schemas for sentences involving *support* are listed here:

  1. ⟨physobj⟩ SUPPORT ⟨physobj⟩
  2. ⟨physobj⟩ SUPPORT WHAT ⟨force⟩
  3. ⟨physobj⟩ SUPPORT ⟨force⟩
  4. ⟨nil⟩ SUPPORT ⟨locpart⟩

The SUBJs and OBJs of a parse are matched with the schema positions, checking that they have the appropriate semantic features. The main advantage of the schemas is that particular verb idiosyncrasies can be accommodated by simply constructing individual schemas that match each syntactic realization. The *support* schemas above are designed to match the following sample sentences:

  1. The lever is supported by a spring.
  2. What load does each pier support?
  3. The scaffold supports 500 lb.
  4. The other end of the scaffold is supported.

In matching a sentence to a schema, the head noun of the syntactic constituent being matched must be of the correct semantic type. "Levers," "springs," and "piers" are all physical objects so they match ⟨physobj⟩. "Load" matches ⟨force⟩, while "the other end of the scaffold" is a location part and matches ⟨locpart⟩.

ISAAC makes no attempt to account for every possible use of *support* in the English language. The schemas only need to cover the expected sentences in a given domain. However, there are schemas, such as the one below, that would be missing not only from ISAAC, but from any set of schemas for an English physics-world domain because they correspond to unacceptable sentences.

---

[1] These examples assume that the object of a BY prepositional phrase of a passive sentence is the logical subject, and that the subject of a passive sentence is the logical object.

* ⟨nil⟩ SUPPORT ⟨force⟩
50 g are supported.
30 lb are supported at the end.

It is not natural to discuss a force being supported without mentioning explicitly the object doing the supporting, as in "The scaffold supports 500 lb." This is a clear example of the interdependencies between semantic roles that affect how they can be expressed in the surface structure of a sentence. For *support*, a "physical object" or a "location part" of a physical object can naturally be expressed as "⟨physobj⟩ is supported," where the object doing the supporting, the AGENT, is inferable. This does not hold true for ⟨force⟩.

Summary

Novak's schemas handle instances of interdependencies by assigning semantic features to template slots, and giving a full set of relations for each sentence complete with positional information. Woods' more general **pattern–action rules** would also require an additional S-rule to account for this type of dependency.

Novak's schemas also include the overall sentence construction, which is important for guiding the application of inference rules. Since, for Novak, the semantic roles of the verb are not separated from the type of sentence in which they appear, he has nothing to gain by mapping his schemas onto verb-specific canonical predicate-argument representations. The inference rules applied to the schemas are concerned just as much with propositional information as with verb semantics, so each schema requires its own set of rules. This makes the system more domain-dependent than Woods' S-rules which are embedded in a natural language processor that handles quantification independently of the verbs.

In summary, Novak and Woods both use variations of a template approach to derive a semantic representation from a syntactic parse. Novak relies on clearly defined schemas that encode the essential semantic role information, as well as important aspects of the overall sentence structure. These schemas ensure that no context-sensitive restrictions on semantic role assignment will be overlooked, and allow Novak to apply inference rules directly based on the construction of the individual sentences. The main drawback to this type of approach is that the schemas are quite redundant, and extending the set of allowable sentences even slightly requires new schemas along with new sets of inference rules. Adding new information would be less tedious if greater use could be made of verb and sentence generalizations. The system is very domain-dependent.

Woods' system is designed to be more domain-independent and uses a more general approach for solving the task of semantic role assignment. This approach allows cross-verb generalizations to be made by combining verb disjunctions with standard templates. However, alternative syntactic expressions of individual verbs still have to be treated separately, as well as idiosyncratic interdependencies. The action portion of his pattern–action rules corresponds to an intermediate level of representation to which inference rules can be applied. As such it is similar to an instantiated case-frame, although the predicate involved is not a specific verb, but, rather, a more general semantic predicate appropriate for the application of inference rules.

System designers such as Woods and Novak who are not committed to using case are still forced by semantic role interdependencies into using verb representations that are not dissimilar to multiple case-frames. These representations can be described as templates which constitute patterns with empty slots that can be matched to actual syntactic parses. There must be a template for each alternative syntactic realization of a verb. The instantiated templates correspond to the same kind of intermediate level of representation as that represented by instantiated case-frames. This intermediate level contains the assignment of semantic roles to syntactic constituents, and inference rules must next be applied to make explicit the semantic relationships between the semantic roles that are indicated by the verb.

2.2   The use of case in semantic analysis

Fillmore's theory about universal cases for verbs has had a pervasive influence on linguists and computer scientists interested in semantic analysis [Fillmore, 1980]. The set of cases has been revised, the rules have been amended, yet the basic thrust still remains. The intuition that syntactic choices are largely a reflection of underlying semantic relationships is very appealing although difficult to define precisely or to implement satisfactorily. Implementations such as Simmons' that attempt to adhere closely to a linguistic analysis of case get bogged down in trying to model the necessary semantic representations, and in accounting for all the "exceptions" to the generalizations. These "exceptions" seem to form a larger set than the verbs that conform, with the result that most verbs seem to require individual sets of prepositions for indicating cases. Other implementations have much clearer processing methods, but reduce the use of case to a mere notational device. They use case-frames as predicates with arguments, but the arguments could just as easily be indicated by ARG1 and ARG2 as by AGENT and INSTRUMENT.

2.2.1   Introducing case

The term *semantic role* was used in chapter 1 to refer loosely to the semantic relationships betwen the noun phrases in a clause and the verb of that clause, including AGENT, PATIENT, LOCATIVE, and INSTRUMENT. These same relationships have also been labelled as *cases*, and there has been a great deal of

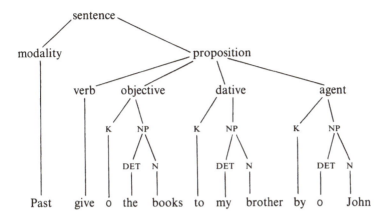

Fig. 2.1. "John gave the books to my brother"

controversy over exactly what level of representation cases correspond to, and over which semantic roles should be considered to be cases. The traditional linguistic use of case is a purely syntactic one, while for Fillmore cases define interrelations between syntax and semantics [Fillmore, 1977]. It seems intuitively plausible that there are syntactic methods, *case forms*, for indicating important semantic relationships, *case functions*, and that these relationships should be reflected in the underlying semantic representation. However, this has been surprisingly difficult to achieve.

Fillmore's original claim was that case functions were expressed in the deep structure of a generative transformational grammar. This claim was motivated in part by the evidence presented in chapter 1 concerning the various semantic roles that can be indicated by the same syntactic constituent. Fillmore rejected SUBJECT and OBJECT as the underlying universal syntactic–semantic relations and proposed a more abstract representation containing case functions, i.e., cases. This representation separates out a **modality** component from the **propositional** component of the sentence. **Modality** includes information about negation, tense, aspect, and so on, that operates over the entire sentence, while the **propositional** component is the verb with its associated cases. Transformations operate on this deep structure to produce all the alternative syntactic realizations of the verb. While this approach is basically a generative approach, it could in principle be equally applicable to analysis. In fact, the computational linguists who have made use of it in one form or another have all been concerned with analysis rather than generation.

Fillmore's original "deep structure" for "John gave the books to my brother" is given in figure 2.1. The cases used here are objective, dative, and agent, and represent a subset of the original set of cases he defined.[2] The cases with the verb constitute a *case-frame* for the semantic representation. K (for *kasus*), is used to indicate the appropriate case-form, while NP stands for noun phrase, DET stands for determiner, and N for noun.

These cases were supposed to be universal to all languages and to provide a common terminology for representing the deep structures of all verbs. Fillmore postulated a set of general rules for the syntactic realization of his list of cases in English:

If there is an Agentive, it becomes the SUBJECT; otherwise, if there is an Instrumental, it becomes the SUBJECT; otherwise, the SUBJECT is the Objective.

The Agentive preposition is BY; the Instrumental preposition is BY if there is no Agentive, otherwise it is WITH; the Objective and Factive prepositions are typically ZERO; the Benefactive preposition is FOR; the Dative preposition is typically TO; the Locative and Time prepositions are either semantically nonempty (in which case they are introduced as optional choices from the lexicon), or they are selected by the particular associated noun [*on the street, at the corner* (= intersection of two streets), *in the corner* (of a room); *on Monday at noon, in the afternoon*]. Specific verbs may have associated with them certain requirements for preposition choice that are exceptions to the above generalization. [Fillmore, 1977, p. 32]

Fillmore proposed other useful restrictions as well, such as:

No case can appear twice in the same clause.

Only noun phrases of the same case can be conjoined.

Each syntactic constituent can fill only one case.

2.2.2   *Case as an intermediate level of representation*

The original motivation for case was the need for a bridge between syntax and semantics for both analysis and generation. Cases were intended to define universal interrelations between syntactic constituents and the underlying semantic representation of a sentence. However, one of the greatest difficulties involved in using case is the lack of consensus on what constitutes such an underlying representation. This lack has led to a proliferation of alternative sets of cases, each set designed to emphasize a particular aspect of semantics that the designer sees as central. One of the main criticisms of case is that the names of the cases reflect a multitude of assumptions about semantic representations that are never made explicit. Case enthusiasts are trying to use cases to refer to meaningful relationships without committing themselves to any theories of meaning. The problem of semantic representation is so complex that

---

[2] Since this set was subsequently redefined, and since there are competing sets of cases from other linguists, the names of the cases are not really of interest here. The important contribution offered is the idea of universal interrelations between syntax and semantics.

most researchers want to avoid it, and the hope is that case will provide the necessary vehicle for skipping over the problem. To a certain extent, that is exactly what case does. However, there are clear limitations. Case is inadequate for completely expressing possible syntactic configurations of verbs, and it is also inadequate for providing a semantic explanation for certain linguistic phenomena. The following discussion of implementations illustrates these inadequacies, and they are discussed more fully in section 2.3.2.

Implementations of case grammars

The UCLA grammar [Stockwell, Schacter and Partee, 1973] makes explicit use of case grammar in a transformational approach to English, as Fillmore originally intended. There are minor variations in the names of the cases, and an extension of case grammar to analyze noun phrases such as "the destruction of the environment," as well as verbs. Each verb has associated with it the prepositions that are likely to introduce particular cases. Verbs whose prepositions conform to Fillmore's generalizations have **unmarked**, or natural, prepositional cues. Exceptional verbs, such as "ask" in "He asked a question of Mary," where Mary as the dative case is indicated by OF rather than the expected TO, are said to use **marked** prepositions. The MIND grammar implementation [Kay, 1973] treats cases and the associated prepositions similarly.

A major drawback to the transformational approach is that, though it does allow marked prepositions to indicate cases for idiosyncratic verbs, the transformations that produce the various subsets of the cases that can appear in the surface structure do not handle positional idiosyncrasies [Levin, 1977, 1979]. For all except a few verbs the neutral case always comes either before or after the dative case or the locative case. However, it is generally accepted that *swarm, familiar* and *spread* can be expressed in both ways, as in the following examples:

> Bees are swarming in the garden.
> neutral bees, locative garden
>
> The garden is swarming with bees.
> locative garden, neutral bees
>
> The book is familiar to me.
> neutral book, dative me
>
> I am familiar with the book.
> dative I, neutral book
>
> He spread butter on the bread.
> neutral butter, locative bread

He spread the bread with butter.
locative bread, neutral butter

Levin proposed various alternatives for extending the case-grammar approach to handle positional alternatives:

1. allow verbs to have more than one case-frame;
2. have two underlying case orders;
3. formulate rules that allow the case-frame to be reordered, and which would have to depend on grammatical relations or on the cases involved.

The UCLA grammar uses the third method of reordering rules to overcome potential inadequacies. They define new transformations dependent on particular cases that can override the ordering constraints of the more general transformations, but there are still problems. The first alternative, allowing verbs to have multiple case-frames, is the safest, and effectively comparable to the template approach defined in section 2.1. However, the proliferation of case-frames is cumbersome and seems at odds with the semantic generalizations hoped for from cases. Levin preferred a set of rules that could be applied to two different orders of cases, the second order allowing a *shifted* neutral, but her general dissatisfaction with the semantic limitations imposed by the flat predicate-argument structure of case-frames kept her from pursuing this approach. (See section 2.3.)

The inadequacy of the flat predicate-argument structure is perhaps best illustrated by looking at a natural language system modelled by Simmons, who made a serious attempt to capture the semantic representations of certain verbs using cases, with some success. But the resulting processing techniques are quite opaque, due to the large amount of verb-specific information stored with each verb for achieving reasonable semantic interpretations. Simmons was also forced to depart from several of the standard restrictions associated with Fillmore-like cases in an effort to get more semantic mileage out of his case-frames.

Augmenting cases with pragmatic deductions

Computational linguistics is indebted to Simmons for his pioneering use of semantic networks in the representation of complex relational structures [Simmons, 1967]. The arc between two nodes of a semantic network is considered to be logically equivalent to a predicate, with the nodes as its arguments. Semantic networks give a visual display of the amazingly complex interweavings of relations to be found in the representation of even a small section of text.

Simmons, along with several others, uses some of the results from case grammar for analysis rather than generation. He makes explicit use of an intermediate level of semantic representation by going directly from a syntactic parse to an instantiated case-frame. He relies on *deep case structures* for the case-frame to be derived from the syntactic constituents of the sentence. The first noun phrase (the SUBJECT) and the verb are parsed before an attempt is made to begin assigning the cases associated with the lexical entry of the verb to the **nominal arguments**, i.e., syntactic constituents. The cases are chosen from a surprisingly small set; causal actants (CA1 similar to agentive, CA2 similar to instrumental), theme (T), locus (L), source (S) and goal (G). Simmons departs from Fillmore's original restrictions in allowing a sentence to contain more than one argument of each type. For example, in "John (CA1) broke the window (T) with the hammer (CA2)," both the hammer and John are considered causal actants. Another major departure is the filling of cases by deduction rather than solely by syntactic constituents as in the following *run* example. This results in a case-frame representation that is more complete than it would normally be expected to be.

The cases defined above are intended to be unusually flexible. The example given below shows several different uses of the verb *run* that are covered by the following definition – RUN theme (incurs rapid motion), causal actant 1 (animate instigator), causal actant 2 (instrumental cause of motion), goal (condition of cessation of motion). The different interpretations of *run* in the following sentences can all be captured by varying the case assignments of the nominal arguments.

> John ran to school.
> CA1 John, T John, G to school
>
> John ran a machine.
> CA1 John, T machine, CA2 motor, G unknown
>
> The machine ran.
> CA1 unknown, T machine, CA2 motor, G unknown
>
> The brook ran.
> CA1 unknown, T brook, CA2 gravity, G unknown

One drawback is that animate instigators are always assumed "CA1 unknown" even if they are not mentioned. It is not clear that one would want to make this assumption with respect to the brook.

The representation desired by Simmons goes farther than Fillmore-like case-frames by including pragmatic information that could only be deduced using common-sense inference rules, for instance, the acknowledgement of "gravity" as the instrumental cause of the motion of the brook, or the presence of a motor in a machine. Including such detailed semantics with the case-frame represents another important deviation from other uses of case-frames. For

Simmons, case-frames are augmented to include much of the information that is yet to be inferred from case frames in other implementations. They are not, however, the final "deep" semantic representations, which are implicit in the paraphrase rules that relate case-frames for similar verbs.

In the implementation, a function finds the head noun of the nominal argument and, given the cases to be associated with the verb and the irrelevant semantic features, attempts to assign a case to the nominal argument. It is not clear how this function goes about determining the relevant information for the sophisticated case assignments described above. After the verb has been parsed and the first noun phrase assigned, subsequent noun phrases and prepositional phrases are all passed along for case assignment. In later implementations Simmons used a method much closer to the template approach described in section 2.1.

One advantage of Simmons' representation is that much of the surface syntactic information is retained, as illustrated by the following two sentences. This can be an advantage in finding the focus of a sentence for both appropriate question answering and resolution of anaphora.

Wellington defeated Napoleon at the Battle of Waterloo.
DEFEAT;

CA I WELLINGTON, T NAPOLEON,
L BATTLE OF WATERLOO

Bonaparte lost the Battle of Waterloo to the Duke of Wellington.
LOSE;

S BONAPARTE, T BATTLE OF WATERLOO,
G DUKE OF WELLINGTON

In preserving the surface syntactic information the similarity in meaning between the two sentences is obscured, and must be inferred explicitly using paraphrase rules associating LOSE and DEFEAT. The more general representations implicit in the paraphrase rules can be thought of as a final "deep" representation that is derived from the augmented case-frame.

Although case information is meticulously preserved throughout the application of the rules, having to define explicit paraphrase rules to exploit semantic generalities seems to depart from some of the original goals of Fillmore's case. Processing efficiencies should be obtained if one could preserve surface structure information but still retain easy access to semantic generalities. For most implementations there seems to be a trade-off between intermediate levels of representation that are general enough for one set of pragmatic rules to apply but have lost all the surface syntactic information, and intermediate levels that still preserve surface syntactic information but then require several alternative sets of pragmatic rules.

2.2.3   Combining case with generative semantics

One possible solution to the problem of augmenting case-frames is to replace them with more complex predicates. The LNR system discussed in this section – as well as conceptual dependency nets and preference semantics described in the following sections – all seem to make this choice, but with somewhat strange qualifications. An embedded predicate representation is certainly richer and has definite advantages, but many of the relationships between syntactic constituents and cases are no longer directly applicable. This places a heavier burden on the production of the semantic representation from the syntactic parse. Conceptual dependency nets and preference semantics sidestep this issue by claiming they do not use syntactic information at all, although that claim is open to question. Norman and Rumelhart have a more compli-cated solution. They borrow their semantic representations from generative semantics, which is a linguistic theory quite distinct from case grammar, but their implementation still uses case-frames in between the syntactic parse representation and the generative semantics style of deep structure. The final result is not dissimilar to the way Simmons maps a syntactic parse into a case-frame deep structure, and then augments that by pragmatics.

Generative semantics
In generative semantics the deep structure of a sentence is not a case-frame but rather a decomposition of the verb predicate into several embedded predicates. For example, a possible case-frame for *kill* is:

kill(agent,patient)

Generative semantics prefers a more componential representation along the lines of:

cause(⟨agent⟩, *become*(*dead*(⟨patient⟩))))

This representation is actually supposed to be part of the syntactic deep structure of a sentence, as in the parse tree for "We killed dragons" in figure 2.2.

All of the verbs, *cause*, *become* and *dead*, can eventually be collected together by the application of transformations, at which point the lexical entry for *kill* can be substituted. These transformations do not have to apply, however, and two other sentences can also be derived from this deep structure: "We caused dragons to become dead" and "We caused dragons to die." Two of the most important motivations for generative semantics were (1) including the deep semantic representation in the parse tree so that it could directly affect the eventual surface syntactic structure, and (2) defining lexical entries as decompositional deep semantic representations [McCawley, 1968]. Unfortu-nately, the transformations for manipulating the resulting parse trees are fairly

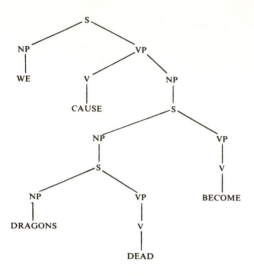

Fig. 2.2.   "We killed dragons"

complicated, and many intermediate structures are generated that have no direct correspondence to possible sentences. These two drawbacks leave some doubt as to the suitability of the transformational paradigm for capturing the original goals of generative semantics.

LNR

At any rate, although Norman and Rumelhart [1975] are in agreement with the goals of generative semantics, especially with the decompositional approach, they do not use similar transformational rules for LNR. Instead they define verbs as predicate representations which are basically case-frames, map the syntactic constituents onto the predicate arguments, and then expand the case-frame into the SOL representation. SOL (Semantic Operating Language) is a language that interprets verb representations procedurally. The SOL representations are very similar to generative semantics deep structures, even if they are not derived in a similar manner.

For example, the predicate representation (case-frame) of *give* is:

X *gives* O to Y (at-time T)

where X, O and Y are AGENT, PATIENT and RECIPIENT respectively, and are all considered obligatory, and T is for time information, and is optional. LNR produces the following mappings from syntactic constituents onto semantic roles for the sentence, "Bert gave a boat to Ernie on his birthday." It is never made very clear exactly how the mappings are produced, or whether or not

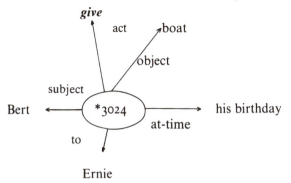

Fig. 2.3.   "Bert gave a boat to Ernie on his birthday"

other definitions of *give* are needed to handle sentences such as "John gave only a book," "A book was given to Mary" and "A book was given by John."

> subject(Bert) → X
> object(boat) → O
> indirect object(Ernie) → Y
> at-pp(his birthday) → T

The SOL structure instantiates the arguments of *give* with the respective mappings. This does not seem very different from the case-frame representation, since there is no embedding in a representation of *give*. A representation of *kill* would show more variation, since it decomposes into an AGENT causing a PATIENT to die, with the appropriate embeddings. The important difference between the SOL structure and the case-frame above is that *give* has been classified as an act which affects the way the structure is interpreted. Acts can be embedded in other acts, and so on, allowing SOL structures to be very complex (figure 2.3).

After the SOL structure has been produced by the interpreter, it is passed to the COMPREHENDER, which applies it in the way that a procedure is applied. The application of this *give* structure actually changes the internal representation dealing with the possession of the boat. It did represent that the boat was possessed by Bert; it now represents that starting from "his birthday" the boat is possessed by Ernie, as well as the information that this involves a change in possession.

SOL offers enormous potential for studying the impact of procedural representations, although at the moment the methods for going from the syntactic parse to the case-frame are unfortunately not well-documented. As with many experimental implementations from this period, the system itself quickly reached a stage where it could not be easily extended because of implementation limitations.

Procedural representation of verbs in SHRDLU

An important difference between LNR and the case-oriented systems is the status of the deep structure representations, which in LNR are supposed to be procedures as well as static data structures. The case systems all use static data structures for the lexical entries of the verbs, whether they are called case-frames, conceptual dependency nets, formulas, S-rules or templates. The only other system that has attempted to make significant use of procedural representations of verbs is Winograd's SHRDLU [Winograd, 1972]. Unfortunately, there is no clear method of semantic processing in either SHRDLU or LNR that reflects a corresponding theory of semantic analysis. However, given the potential for possible impact, it is worthwhile to examine briefly Winograd's use of verbs before continuing the review of other computational approaches to semantic analysis.

Winograd's SHRDLU program includes a graphics simulation of a robot that can manipulate blocks and pyramids. It has a detailed factual representation of its blocks world, including knowledge of various sizes and colors of blocks and information about which blocks are supporting other blocks, which blocks have clear tops, etc. These facts are essential to both the mechanism that finds noun phrase referents and the one that determines the meaning of verbs.

After being recognized as such by the syntactic parser, a noun phrase is processed by two noun group semantic specialists. They first recognize the main noun and then collect modifiers in the form of adjectives or relative clauses. These modifiers are added as properties of the main noun to the data structure that will be used by a procedure to find a referent for the noun phrase. When run by Micro-Planner, a theorem-prover written in Lisp, this procedure locates a specific "block" with the appropriate properties. The data structure for "a big red cube which supports the pyramid" contains the following predicates, where $X1$ is the cube in question and $B5$ refers to the pyramid:

is($X1$,block)
equidimensional($X1$)
color($X1$,red)
support($X1$,$B5$)

The selected referent for $X1$ must result in a "true" value for each of the predicates.

Predicates are also used for representing verbs, with even greater impact. There are really two types of verbs processed by SHRDLU – descriptive verbs and imperative verbs. Descriptive verbs, such as *support*, are simply recognized as providing an additional attribute of the SUBJECT, e.g., that it is supporting some other object. The support relationship is represented by a **support** table with pairs of entries. Information about changes in support relationships is noted by changing the entries in the table. Imperative verbs, on the other hand, indicate complex actions for SHRDLU to perform, giving rise to one of the first procedural interpretations of verb semantics. For SHRDLU, a verb definition is not simply a static, formal description of correct usage, but a process to be executed. One test of "understanding" the verb is the ability to perform the action, or at least deduce preconditions of that action and the effect it would have on the state of the world.

The definition of *grasp* requires SHRDLU to first establish that the object it is trying to grasp can be manipulated, that its hand is empty, and that nothing is on top of the object to be grasped which might fall off. Assuming all of the above, SHRDLU's hand can move to grasp the object. These requirements are represented informally by the following predicates:

> manipulatable(X)
> empty(hand) if grasping(Y) then get-rid-of(Y)
> cleartop(X)
> movehand(topcenter(X))
> → *grasp*(X)

Winograd's project set high standards for discourse with a computer, but it is difficult to see how to extend his approach to other domains. The level of detail required is staggering. Equally discouraging are the inherent difficulties involved in decomposing more abstract verbs. The large problem areas that Winograd touched on lightly, such as "time" and "semantics of discourse," are still unsolved. Neither does SHRDLU come to grips with the semantic role assignment problems defined in the preceding chapter. In the blocks world, verbs such as *support* and *sit* always have the same assignments of "blocks" as SUBJECT and OBJECT, so that the meaning of the verb is rarely changed by the introduction of a different kind of object. Verbs like *grasp* and *pick up* have an active AGENT which is always the robot. The AGENT of *own* is always Winograd himself. By fine tuning the verb definitions to these specific AGENTS and PATIENTS, word sense problems can be avoided giving impressive results. An obvious extension of this is to combine Winograd's procedural verb representations with a coherent method of semantic analysis that allows for flexible role assignment. This is the goal of inference-driven mapping.

2.2.4 *Case as a deep level of semantic representation*

The preceding sections have not shed much light on the controversy over what actually constitutes cases, how many there are, and how they can be used effectively [Bruce, 1975]. Are case-frames a separate stage on the way to finding a deep semantic representation as Fillmore thought, or are they an intrinsic component of a more complicated theory of semantic analysis that preempts case? A basic underlying premise behind the interest in case was the hope that including case would improve semantic processing. Having found the cases, they should simplify all of the other tasks associated with semantic analysis (see chapter 1).

Explicitly including the cases in one's representation of language will provide many simplifications to one's theory (system) of language. We will call the simplifications *case benefits*. [Charniak, 1975, p. 3]

Schank and Wilks took much more radical approaches than Simmons in trying to capture the elusive case benefits [Schank, 1975; Wilks, 1975a,b, 1976, 1982]. In particular, they eschewed the traditional syntactic cues for indicating cases, and concentrated on the generalizations case could provide for deep semantic representations. Charniak argues convincingly that this resulted in the reduction of case to a mere notational device. He claims that to justify labeling the subject of a clause as an AGENT, there must be some independent interpretation of the role of an AGENT that can then be applied. Wilks strongly denies this criticism, asserting that case interpretation is essential to the inferences his system draws. Since many semanticists now agree that cases have no independent existence themselves, but are merely arguments to semantic primitives [Fodor, 1980], it is instructive to examine the AI case controversy in more detail.

Charniak lists four conditions he deems necessary for establishing a legitimate instance of a case benefit:

1.   A case meaning should be independent of the predicate or predicates it is associated with.
2.   A case meaning should apply to more than one predicate.
3.   A case meaning should offer beneficial inferences.
4.   There must not be a better way to accomplish 1 through 3.

In order to fully analyze Charniak's criticisms of Schank and Wilks, a brief review of their systems is necessary.

Conceptual dependency nets

Schank investigated semantic representation for a very general domain, one including "people" with "beliefs" and "desires." His system shares certain similarities with Wilks', namely the lack of formal syntactic parsing and the basing of verb definitions on a small set of **primitives**; linguistic strings that cannot be decomposed into more basic linguistic strings. Schank's lexical entries for verbs appear as **conceptual dependency nets** (CDN). The CDN for the verb *give* is something like the network given below.

There is an obvious similarity between a CDN and a standard case-frame, although Schank sometimes seems more comfortable avoiding case-frame terminology, and calls his semantic arguments *conceptual cases*. Being independent of case allows him to develop his networks without being constrained by the supposed links between syntactic constituents and traditional cases. In fact, CDNs often decompose verbs into concepts that could not appear in the surface structure of a clause using the verb.

Another difference between a CDN and a case-frame is that the "predicate" of a CDN is a member of a small set of primitives which has been chosen to represent the verb being processed. The set of primitives varies somewhat, but is generally considered to include at least INGEST, ATRANS (transfer of abstract object), PTRANS (transfer of physical object), MTRANS (transfer of mental object), PROPEL, MBUILD (mental construction), and so on. Certainly for the examples Schank gives his choice of primitives is adequate. His original claim that they will be equally applicable to all of English has been modified.

CDNs also include four *conceptual cases* as basic building blocks: OBJECTIVE, RECIPIENT, INSTRUMENTAL and DIRECTIVE. They form intrinsic parts of the acts on which they depend. One of the clearest separations between Schank and Fillmore can be seen in Schank's division of the traditional case functions into two separate types of entities. Conceptual cases are semantic relationships that correspond to some of Fillmore's original case functions while some of the other case functions become arguments to the conceptual cases, or in Schank's terminology, slot fillers. In the example below, the RECIPIENT conceptual case has two slot fillers, Mary, the recipient of the book, and John, the donator. In this example, the donator "slot" is presumably automatically filled by the filler of the INSTRUMENTAL conceptual case.

The method used for filling the slots in CDNs is not clearly described, but occurs during the processing of the sentence. It relies heavily on the semantic "expectations" of the CDN being satisfied by properties (semantic markers) of a particular noun phrase. Once the slots are filled, the CDN contains detailed information about the action involved that can be drawn out by applying inference rules. For example, food or liquid **ingested** by an AGENT can be inferred as then being inside the AGENT. When it only includes slots that correspond to cases, Schank's instantiated CDN bears a strong resemblance to Simmons' instantiated case-frame, and can be seen as an intermediate level of representation. The extra slots, however, usually represent information that would normally be inferred from such an intermediate level and thus constitute a CDN that corresponds more to the LNR deep level of representation. This gives an appearance of inconsistency to the various CDNs, since some of them offer much more detailed decompositions of verbs than others do. It is not clear what general principles are being used to choose the limits on the decompositions.

The previous representation of *give* should have used the primitive ATRANS,

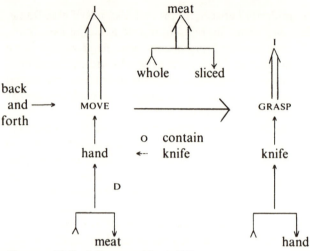

Fig. 2.4.   "I sliced the meat with a knife"

meaning "transfer of possession." "John gave the book to Mary" could be represented by the CDN given below.

```
                    to
I            O    R├──── Mary
John ⇔ Atrans ← book ←  │
                    ├──── John
                   │ from
```

The primitives chosen for the verbs determine what inferences can be drawn regarding the conceptual cases and slot fillers, rather than the type of conceptual case or slot. Although John may be classified as the INSTRUMENTAL in "John gave the book to Mary," it is the primitive ATRANS that cues successive inference rules, rather than anything to do solely with INSTRUMENTALS. John could just as easily be classified as ARGI of ATRANS, and the same rules applied. Simply recognizing John as an INSTRUMENTAL does not in itself constitute a definition of what it is to be an INSTRUMENTAL. Herein lies the main thrust of Charniak's concern about the wholly positional use of case.

Schank's diversion from standard case theory is even more apparent in his representation of "I sliced the meat with a knife," in figure 2.4. The CDN gives a good example of a very detailed decomposition in contrast to the CDN for *give* from above, and is so complex as to be almost unreadable since so much knowledge about slicing is built into it. It says basically that meat goes from being "whole" to being "sliced" by being the object of a "slicing" action which is performed by an AGENT "I" grasping a knife in a hand, and moving the hand containing the knife back and forth (presumably while in contact with the meat, although this is not made explicit).

This may be a very practical deep semantic representation, but clearly contains several arguments that would not be present in a standard case-frame. One of the main advantages to case-frames is the constraints they make on what can and cannot be present in the surface structure of a clause. "Hand," though clearly acting as the OBJECTIVE conceptual case for MOVE, would scarcely be expected to appear in a clause about slicing. It could, however, be considered part of our understanding of the action of slicing, or at least of holding a knife, since "Holding the knife between the second and third fingers of my right hand I managed to slice the cheese," does not seem completely unnatural.

In summary, Schank ignores the syntactic properties of cases, but concentrates instead on possible semantic generalizations. In doing so he departs to a large degree from Fillmore's original use of case. Some of Fillmore's original cases are defined in Schank's framework as conceptual cases which are semantic relationships, and other cases are defined as arguments of the semantic primitives used in the conceptual dependency nets. The conceptual dependency nets also contain other arguments that could not appear in the surface structure of a clause, and there is no distinction made between these arguments and the more case-like arguments. Neither are any clear guidelines given for introducing these new arguments. The arguments themselves do not influence what inferences can be drawn, and the application of inference rules is determined entirely by the semantic primitives. It is not clear that Schank is left with any generally accepted case benefits, and would be justified in claiming to have preempted the use of case by his CDNS.

Preference semantics

With the goal of building an English–French translator to handle fairly general sentences, Wilks also forgoes standard syntactic parsing, and uses a preprocessor that separates the sentences into manageable fragments. The preprocessor does, however, make use of many syntactic cues in doing the fragmenting. The occurrence of a second verb, or an "ing" verb, or a preposition, all indicate places to divide the sentence. Each fragment is then matched to a three-place **template** (not to be confused with templates as defined in section 2.1) of the form AGENT–ACTION–OBJECT, in order to recognize which particular phrase played the role of the AGENT, or ACTION, or OBJECT. The key to a successful match is finding the template whose ACTION matches the main predicate in the verb **formula**. Formulas are similar to case-frames but also involve decomposing the verb into a set of primitive semantic predicates. Traditional cases correspond to arguments of the semantic predicates.[3] Prepositions correspond to **paraplates**, which are very similar to templates, and treated as ACTIONS with dummy AGENTS. Before definitely selecting a word as

---

[3] There seems to be a superficial similarity here to Jackendoff's use of thematic relations – see section 2.3.

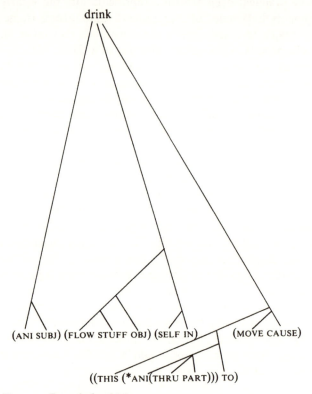

Fig. 2.5.   Formula for *drink*

an AGENT or as an OBJECT of a particular ACTION, semantic markers associated with the words are checked for compatibility with the prospective template slot. These markers, or **preferences**, are stored next to the cases in **formulas** for each verb, as in the formula for *drink*, in figure 2.4. Formulas should be read from right to left, with the first (X Y) on the right representing the main predicate of the formula. Loosely interpreted, the formula indicates that a drinking action is one by which an animate subject causes a liquid (flow stuff) object to move to a thru part of the animate subject with a final location of being inside the animate subject itself.

An agent for the action of drinking should be marked ANI as indicated by the semantic marker on SUBJ. Wilks uses SUBJ for the AGENT case, while OBJ, IN, and TO represent the OBJECT, CONTAINMENT and DIRECTION TOWARDS cases respectively. This use of grammatical relations and prepositions to indicate cases reflects Wilks' basic accordance with the general tenor of case theory.

The semantic markers are seen as semantic preferences that do not necessarily have to be satisfied. A fragment may match more than one template. The set of matches between words and cases that satisfies the most semantic preferences is selected as the correct one from all possible sets of matches. If there are difficult instances of word sense ambiguity or pronoun reference that do not resolve easily, the formulas for actions can be expanded and deeper inferences drawn. The above formula would allow "The wine is in John" to be inferred from "John drinks the wine." The head predicate of each action formula, such as (CAUSE MOVE), must be a member of a set of primitive predicates used for drawing inferences. The set of primitives themselves is larger and more complex than Schank's.

The use of templates and formulas obscures somewhat the process of assigning words to cases, though Wilks claims to find case information essential to his system. He denies Charniak's claim that his *drink* formula includes cases that cannot appear in the surface structure of a clause using *drink*. He offers the sentence "John drank the beer up through his nose with a straw and into his brain" [Wilks, 1976, p. 26] as evidence to the contrary. The very awkwardness of the sentence lends itself more to substantiating Charniak's criticism than to refuting it.

Wilks does not give independent definitions for his cases, stating instead that "no system, Fillmore's included, has given precise definitions of the cases beyond the most general indications . . ." He does claim, however, that his "case specialists" can operate without looking at the predicate involved. His system does infer that INSTRUMENTS are "used" and GOALS are "attained" independently of the predicate involved, which may be the closest anyone has come to actual case benefits.

Summary

One senses a certain ambivalence in Charniak himself as to the reality of case benefits. Doubtful of his conditions ever being met, he suggests four possible positions one could presently take with regard to case [Charniak, 1975, p. 27].

1. Replace very deep semantic representations with much more 'surface' representations, à la Simmons.
2. Drop case entirely and retain the present deep structures.
3. Drop case as a semantic representation, and add it to syntactic parsing.
4. Compromise between the needs of case, and the needs of inferencing by finding a level of representation deep enough to accommodate inferencing without excluding case.

He favors the third position as being the most honest, but sees the last position as one envisioned by Fillmore in later observations on case.

[Fillmore] suggests that 'I hit the ball over the fence' should be converted into something more like 'My hitting the ball caused it to go over the fence.' Clearly, from the viewpoint of simplifying inference, this is a step in the right direction. But it should be clear that if such a representational level exists, finding it will require the most delicate intellectual balancing. For this reason such a position is quite risky, and frankly

I do not see much hope for it given some of the problems caused by deepening the semantic representation. [Charniak 1975, p. 28]

2.2.5   Summary

This section surveyed several well-known natural language systems and discussed connections between these systems and Fillmore's use of case as a means of defining interrelations between syntax and semantics. In spite of extremely creative attempts to take advantage of the potential generalizations offered by case, several problems have arisen. The two most serious difficulties concern (1) the proliferation of alternative sets of cases, all of which represent efforts to capture accurately varying sets of assumptions about underlying semantic representations, but none of which make these assumptions explicit, and (2) the inherent inadequacy for representing the complex events indicated by verbs that is found in the flat predicate-argument structure exemplified by a case-frame. Case adherents are left with the unsatisfying prospect of representing alternative realizations of verbs by multiple case-frames, that do no more than list each alternative separately. Natural language experts who are not committed to case have not found an alternative theory of semantic analysis that can cope with interdependencies between semantic roles, and use variations of a template approach which are more or less similar to the construction of multiple case-frames. All of these approaches rely on static data structures for the representation of verbs, without taking advantage of the potential for procedural representations illustrated by SHRDLU's complex "understanding" of actions like grasping.

There are two divergent approaches to incorporating case into a computational system that have been discussed here. Simmons' deep case structures offer an example of case-frames being used as an intermediate level of representation where an attempt is made to capture both syntactic and semantic properties of cases. The complex requirements of underlying semantic representations forced Simmons to depart from Fillmore's use of case in several ways. Chief among these is the use of pragmatic deduction to assign fillers to cases not mentioned explicitly at the surface level. This occasionally leads to anomalies such as the assumption of an animate instigator in the running event indicated by the sentence, "The brook runs merrily." Simmons also allows sentences to contain more than one instance of the same kind of case, another departure from Fillmore. Having achieved a fully instantiated case-frame, inference rules are then applied to derive a "deeper" representation.

Perhaps the system closest to Simmons in overall approach is the LNR system implemented by Norman and Rumelhart. The LNR system also produces a syntactic parse, maps the parse onto a case-frame, and then expands the case-frame representation into a deeper representation. The main difference is that this deeper representation is written in SOL, a language that allows the representation to be interpreted procedurally to further expand the knowledge base. The deep representation is also consciously modelled after the deep structure representations of generative semantics, with a strong decompositional flavor. Unfortunately, there is no clear description given of the method of mapping the parse onto the case-frame representation, and LNR, while being one of the most semantically rich systems, is also one of the most unwieldy.

Winograd's SHRDLU is another semantically rich system that does not offer clear guidance to a method of semantic analysis. His "meanings" for some of his verbs are literal procedures that are run by the robot, SHRDLU, after being "understood." However, since there is little diversity among the fillers for the semantic roles corresponding to the arguments to the procedures, he does not really address the problem of semantic role assignment that is of major concern here. He does, however, raise interesting philosophical questions about the role of procedures in semantic representations.

Schank and Wilks ignore the syntactic properties of cases and concentrate on using them to capture semantic generalities. They both evolve "deep" semantic representations that are not very similar to the original use of case. Schank represents some of Fillmore's cases as semantic relationships and some of the others as participants in those relationships. His complex networks that constitute verb representations, conceptual dependency nets, also contain slots representing concepts that could not be expected to appear in the surface structure of a clause using the verb, a major departure from case. An even more significant variation involves the application of inference rules for deriving "deeper" representations. These rules are attached to the semantic primitives chosen to model the verbs, and there is no use made of the kind of verb-independent generalization Fillmore originally intended case to capture. Wilks also represents traditional cases as participants in semantic relationships defined by semantic primitives and his verb representations include "cases" that would not be expected to appear in the surface structure of clauses involving the verb. He does, however, claim to infer from the presence of an INSTRUMENT that it is being "used," and that GOALs are "attained." It is not clear what it means for something to be "used" or "attained," but assuming they could be defined these would represent verb-independent case benefits.

2.3   An alternative to case

In spite of Charniak's pessimism, there does seem to be a certain amount of support for a level of representation that still incorporates case. Whether consciously or unconsciously supporting this position, linguists such as Jackendoff, although moving away from a Fillmore-like approach to cases, have not discounted it entirely. Without denying the extremely useful ties between syntactic constituents and semantic cases, Jackendoff questions the ability of case to capture complex semantic relationships [Jackendoff, 1972]. Levin argues a similar point, though with slightly different motivation [Levin, 1977, 1979]. Both of these positions are briefly described in the next two sections. The consensus seems to be that case-frames should indeed be replaced by more complex predicate-argument structures such as the ones used by generative semantics. These are in fact the semantic representations that are used in chapters 3 and 4 in describing the implementation of inference-driven mapping. Choosing similar representations does not, however, require choosing similar methods of semantic analysis, and this is an important point of difference between Jackendoff and the generative semantics school. The method of semantic analysis described in chapter 4 is even more different, and manages to preserve the ties between syntax and semantics that were hoped for from case by associating the syntactic cues with the arguments to the semantic predicates. In order to capture idiosyncrasies and interdependencies, a context for the arguments, called the *predicate environment*, is introduced.

Jackendoff offers a method of semantic interpretation within the framework of generative grammar which has very different goals from generative semantics. The complex predicate-argument structure is not considered to be the deep structure of the syntactic parse, but is to be derived from that deep structure. Just as Fillmore's case grammar separates a modal component from the case-frame, so does Jackendoff's version of generative grammar, and these two components are now termed the functional component and the modal component. Two other components are separated out as well: a coreferential component, and a focus and presupposition component. All of the components except the functional component are associated with levels of the syntactic derivation in between the deep structure and the surface structure. The functional component is obviously the most relevant to this discussion. *Functional* is used by Gruber [1976] and Jackendoff [1972, 1983] to refer to the semantic role that a noun phrase *functions* as. Since there is a confusion between this use of function and the mathematical use of function, this type of representation will generally be referred to as a multiple embedded predicate representation.

2.3.1   Thematic relations

Jackendoff's main objection to standard case theory is that it does not allow a noun phrase to be assigned more than one case [Jackendoff, 1972]. In examples like "Esau traded his birthright (to Jacob) for a mess of pottage," Jackendoff sees two related actions:

The first is the change of hands of the birthright from Esau to Jacob. The direct object is Theme, the subject is Source, and the to-object is Goal. Also there is what I will call the secondary action, the changing of hands of the mess of pottage in the other direction. In this action, the for-phrase is Secondary Theme, the subject is Secondary Goal, and the to-phrase is Secondary Source. [Jackendoff, 1972, p. 35]

This, of course, could not be captured by a Fillmore-like case-frame. Jackendoff concludes that

A theory of case grammar in which each noun phrase has exactly one semantic function in deep structure cannot provide deep structures which satisfy the strong Katz–Postal Hypothesis, that is, which provide all semantic information about the sentence. [Jackendoff, 1972, p. 35]

Jackendoff is not completely discarding case information, but rather suggesting a new level of semantic representation that tries to incorporate some of the advantages of case. Making constructive use of Gruber's system of thematic relationships [Gruber, 1976], Jackendoff offers the following extension:

The thematic relations can now be defined in terms of [these] semantic subfunctions. Agent is the argument of CAUSE that is an individual; Theme is the argument of CHANGE that is an individual; Source and Goal are the initial and final state arguments of CHANGE. Location will be defined in terms of a further semantic function BE that takes an individual (the Theme) and a state (the Location). [Jackendoff, 1972, p. 39]

Another way of expressing the information that is captured by thematic relations is by the following logical predicates.[4] This representation does not correspond directly to Jackendoff's representation for "Esau traded his birthright (to Jacob) for a mess of pottage," although it is fairly similar.

> change-of-poss(agent(Esau),
>   source(Esau),theme(birthright),goal(Jacob))
> change-of-poss(agent(Esau),
>   source(Jacob),theme(mess-of-pottage),goal(Esau))

The similarities to other semantic representations using embedded predicates can be seen more clearly in the representations of *buy* and *sell*. Again, this representation has been put into the general notation used, and is not identical with Jackendoff's. Notice that the same semantic role fills the traditional AGENT position as well as either the SOURCE or GOAL positions.

buy
> cause(agent(buyer),
>   change-of-poss-for-money(agent(buyer),
>   source(seller),theme(T),goal(buyer)))

---

[4] This notation is introduced here and will be used throughout as a general form of semantic representation using logical predicates to indicate the central semantic relationship involved, and function symbols to indicate the type of semantic role a particular argument plays. This notation in fact corresponds directly to the semantic representations used in the next two chapters. This does not constitute a claim that representation of semantic relationships in terms of logical predicates is being introduced here, since of course philosophers and linguists have been using logical predicates for years. However, one of the advantages to inference-driven mapping is the direct procedural interpretation of the semantic representations, and their direct correspondence to a general form of logical representation.

sell
cause(agent(seller),
      change-of-poss-for-money(agent(seller),
          source(buyer),theme(T),goal(seller)))

There are also some similarities here to the systems proposed by Schank, Wilks, and Norman and Rumelhart. It is perhaps closest to LNR, since it does assume a syntactic parse, and a syntactic deep structure that is separate from the semantic representation. However, thematic relations do not use case-frames as an intermediate level of representation. Indeed, Jackendoff's view is one example of a trend away from case noted by Janet Fodor [1980] as

it may be more revealing to regard the noun phrases which are associated in a variety of case relations with the LEXICAL verb as the arguments of the primitive SEMANTIC predicates into which it is analyzed. These semantic predicates typically have very few arguments, perhaps three at the most, but there are a lot of them and hence there will be a lot of distinguishable 'case categories.' (Those which Fillmore has identified appear to be those associated with semantic components that are particularly frequent or prominent, such as CAUSE, USE, BECOME, AT.) [Fodor, 1980, p. 93]

Fodor summarizes with

As a contribution to semantics, therefore, it seems best to regard Fillmore's analyses as merely stepping stones on the way to a more complete specification of the meanings of verbs. [Fodor, 1980, p. 93]

Chapter 3 introduces the formalization of the mechanics domain for inference-driven mapping. All of the verbs from this domain are defined in the logical notation used above in terms of a finite set of semantic predicates that includes several of Fodor's "case categories." These definitions prove to be very flexible and efficient for producing appropriate semantic analyses of sentences from this domain. In order to produce the semantic analysis, it is also necessary to find the ties between this type of semantic representation and the syntactic parse of each sentence. This was the one loose end in the neat summation of case; its relation to syntax. Fodor continues,

Whether there are any SYNTACTIC properties of case categories that Fillmore's theory predicts but which are missed by the semantic approach is another question . . . [Fodor, 1980, p. 93]

Chapter 3 demonstrates how syntactic cues can be associated directly with the arguments of the semantic predicates, preserving the syntactic properties of case without falling heir to the inherent problems of case-frame representations.

2.3.2   Necessary capabilities for an alternative to case

Levin argues for a similar point of view in her criticism of case-frames as flat predicate-argument structures that are not rich enough to capture the complex actions described by verbs in English sentences [Levin, 1977]. Her two major objections are that:

1. case systems adopt arbitrary categorizations because they cannot represent the complexity of events;
2. case names encode semantic concepts without explicitly defining their properties and interactions.

The second objection is reminiscent of Charniak's complaint about case being used as a mere notational device. It is difficult to see what else it could be used for, if cases are no more than names for undefined semantic concepts.

Levin first looks at two particular verbs, **break** and **shoot**, to illustrate the inadequacy of case-frames as verb representations, and then goes on to examine the use of INSTRUMENTS in detail [Levin, 1979]. Having demonstrated that verbs require more complex representations, she proposes a **control** relation for distinguishing between **marked** and **unmarked** INSTRUMENTS. These results are summarized here.

Levin argues that assigning INSTRUMENT to hammer and LOCATIVE to wall in the following sentences using **break** does not say anything about the manipulation of the objects. In the first sentence the hammer is being manipulated, and in the second it is the vase itself.

> John broke the vase with a hammer.
> John broke the vase against the wall.

Fillmore's second analysis of **break** assigns GOAL to the vase and PATIENT to the hammer in the first sentence, but assigns PATIENT to the vase, and GOAL to the wall in the second sentence [Fillmore, 1977]. By assuming that the PATIENT is being manipulated, the similarity between the hammer in the first sentence and the vase in the second can be captured. However, it is no longer clear what is being broken. Levin suggests that there are two events being described by **break**, a state change and the manipulation necessary to achieve the state change, and that both must be included in a representation of **break** for that representation to adequately account for its linguistic usage. Specifically, the representation must account for the difference between "The vase broke," and the previous sentences, which rests on the ability to distinguish between the state-change event alone and the state-change event combined with the manipulation event.

Shoot also offers evidence for complex semantic relationships. The problem lies in finding an appropriate case assignment for the rifle in the following sentences [Levin, 1979]. Is it being used as an INSTRUMENT or a SOURCE or both?

(a) John shot the turkey with a rifle.
(b) John shot the turkey with a bullet.
(c) John shot the turkey with a bullet from a rifle.
(d) *John shot the turkey with his rifle (of?) a bullet.

Again, Levin sees the center of the difficulty as being the *combination* of events being described by *shoot*. The rifle is the INSTRUMENT being used to **launch**, or propel a bullet. As such it is the SOURCE of the motion of the bullet. The bullet is the INSTRUMENT by which John effects a contact with the turkey. The two events are therefore a launch event and a contact event, but they are not independent of each other.

Shoot can be represented more appropriately by using a multiple embedded predicate representation similar to Jackendoff's thematic relations. A propellant verb requires an INSTRUMENT by which the agent applies force to an entity to be put into motion. This INSTRUMENT is the rifle. The bullet is put into motion with the SOURCE of the motion path being the rifle and the GOAL of the motion path being the turkey. The other event suggested by *shoot*, the contact event, can also be described using an INSTRUMENT, where contact is effected between John and the turkey by an INSTRUMENT which is the bullet.

A suggestion for a partial representation of this use of *shoot* is given below. This representation is based on the style of lexical entry used by inference-driven mapping, which uses multiple embedded predicates and is defined more thoroughly in chapter 3. The "contact" between John and the turkey is much more complicated than the simple contact predicate indicated here and there is no mention of intentionality or John's desiring to harm the turkey, etc. The importance of this representation is simply to demonstrate how easily multiple role assignments can be captured by a multiple embedded predicate representation. An effect predicate is used rather than the USE predicate normally associated with INSTRUMENT, since another criticism of Levin's is that the traditional use of INSTRUMENT fails to adequately capture the relationships *between* semantic roles. For example, the rifle *propels* the bullet and the bullet *strikes* the turkey. A slightly fuller representation is given at the end of the section which spells out more completely the relationships between the semantic roles.

"John shot the turkey with a bullet from a rifle"

shoot ←
effect(instrument(bullet),
    contact-event(john,turkey)),
effect(instrument(rifle),
    cause-motion(agent(john),
    move(object1(bullet),object2(Path),time(Per))).

The importance of the INSTRUMENT case in these examples motivated Levin to examine INSTRUMENTAL WITH [Levin, 1979]. Her conclusions are that "An underlying representation must include semantic relations between noun phrases as well as the predicate–argument relations of noun phrases to a verb" [Levin, 1979, p. 1]. Her main criticism of both case and thematic relations with respect to INSTRUMENTS is that they cannot account for locative phrases that have instrumental functions. She defines these locative phrases as **unmarked** INSTRUMENTS, while phrases that would traditionally be assigned the INSTRU-MENT case are ***marked***.[5] She suggests that the presence of a marked INSTRU-MENT introduces a control relation between the INSTRUMENT and the user of the INSTRUMENT that is missing when the INSTRUMENT is unmarked.

An example of an unmarked instrument is the rock in "John cut his foot on a rock." Even though *cut* expects an INSTRUMENT, and the rock is the thing that does the cutting, it does not have the same relationship to John that the rock has in "John cut his foot with a rock." The same inferences should not be drawn. Another example of an unmarked instrument is "At one end of a string a weight is suspended." The string is normally an instrument for suspension, but it is usually indicated by SUBJECT, WITH or BY, rather than AT. The analysis of this example, using the notion of an "unmarked" instrument, is described in detail in chapter 4.

Chapter 3 defines the **effect** predicate which is used to indicate the INSTRU-MENTAL function in the multiple embedded predicate representation used by inference-driven mapping. This predicate can be used to capture Levin's control relation as well as to expand the representation of ***shoot*** from above into the fuller representation given below. This expansion is described in more detail in chapter 5.

> contact-event(john,bullet)
> contact-event(bullet,turkey)
> cause-motion(agent(john),
>   move(object1(rifle),object2(Path),time(Per)))
> cause-motion(agent(rifle),
>   move(object1(bullet),object2(Path),time(Per)))

2.3.3   *Summary*

Jackendoff and Levin present serious objections to the use of case as an intermediate level of representation that can adequately encompass both the syntactic realizations of verbs and the underlying semantic representations. One of Jackendoff's main objections is that in case grammars each noun phrase is associated with a unique case. This restriction makes it impossible to account for the multitude of functions being performed during transfer events. Levin also objects to the inability of case to adequately capture the complex relationships suggested by ***break*** and ***shoot***, and postulates that many verbs indicate the occurrence of more than one event. Case-frames are specifically designed to capture single events.

---

[5] This terminology is unfortunately inconsistent with the previous use of **unmarked** as a normal syntactic indication of a case, and **marked** as an idiosyncratic syntactic indication.

Another objection to the use of case is that the case names suggest underlying semantic relationships that are never made explicit. It is difficult to compare competing sets of cases since they are usually based on very different assumptions about semantic priorities. Jackendoff's use of Gruber's thematic relations as arguments to semantic predicates chosen to represent verb meanings corresponds to an attempt to make these underlying assumptions explicit. Any effort in this direction requires taking a position on an appropriate theory of semantics, at best a rather risky venture. One of the apparent advantages of case was that it seemed to offer an intermediate position that could avoid making explicit the underlying semantic representations. This, however, is exactly where case has proven to be inadequate, and future speculation about interrelations between syntax and semantics will necessitate at least a token attempt to formalize the semantics involved.

Since all of the previous approaches to semantic analysis, even the ones claiming to be implementing case theories, have ended up augmenting their representations through the use of pragmatic deductions, the inadequacy of case is hardly argumentative. These previous approaches offer various versions of more complex representations, from Schank's conceptual dependency nets to the LNR SOL structures, but the one thing they do not offer is a well-defined method of producing such structures. The most important need is not for a more complex representation, since that is available in the form of decompositions, but for a well-motivated method for producing that representation from the syntactic parse.

In working with a limited domain such as the pulley domain, a sublanguage is involved, rather than all of natural language. The finite nature of a sublanguage allows the researcher to take that "risky position" on an appropriate theory of semantics, and commit to a particular semantics for the domain. There may be alternative formalizations for the same domain. Any one of them may not hold for other domains, and certainly may not be appropriate for all of natural language. From the point of view of the computational linguist, there are three motivating factors in choosing such a formalization. It should be adequate to account for the alternative semantic configurations of the domain, and it should have some relevance to linguistic theories about semantics, and it should allow for transparent processing.

For inference-driven mapping, a formalization for the mechanics domain has been chosen that allows for efficient, integrated analysis of paragraphs of text. This formalization is based on the multiple embedded predicates that have been presented here as a rich medium of semantic representation. These predicates are interpreted procedurally to drive the assignment of syntactic constituents to semantic roles, as well as the other semantic analysis tasks. Chapters 3 and 5 demonstrate how the multiple embedded predicate representations used by inference-driven mapping overcome many of the inadequacies associated with case-frame representations that have been discussed here. They clearly distinguish between the lexical entry that can be used to produce representations for several different syntactic realizations of a verb, and the representations themselves. The representations follow Jackendoff in allowing noun phrases to be assigned to more than one semantic role, and also spell out many of the relationships between the semantic roles as desired by Levin. The relationships are in terms of predicates that are associated with a particular domain, and do not constitute a philosophical definition of the meaning of the verb. However, within the limits of the domain they make explicit the underlying semantic notions that are associated with the introduction of the various semantic roles. By associating the mapping rules with the predicates representing these notions, case-like linguistic generalizations can be made, and the mapping process can be performed during the procedural interpretation of the lexical entry.

3   A domain formalization

This chapter presents the formalization of the pulley domain. In this domain, the entities involved tend to be simple solid entities like particles and strings, while the relationships between them include notions of support, contact, or motion of some form. Section 3.2 describes the formalization of the pulley world in terms of the types of entities and their properties. The relationships are used for the decompositions of the verbs which are described in section 3.3 where the lexical entries of the verbs are listed. Each verb is subcategorized in terms of the primary relationship involved in the decomposition. The semantic roles are arguments of these relationships. The lexical entries include the decompositions of these primary relationships. Section 3.5 introduces the mapping constraints for assigning syntactic constituents to semantic roles. Examples demonstrate how the syntactic cues can be used with predicate environments to preserve the same semantic role interdependencies that are preserved by templates. The last section describes the semantic constraints used in conjunction with the mapping constraints to test that the referent of a syntactic constituent is of the correct semantic type. The last category of constraints described, the pragmatic constraints, are used by inference-driven mapping to fill semantic roles that do not have mappings to syntactic constituents. Chapter 4 describes how inference-driven mapping interprets the lexical entries procedurally to drive the semantic analysis of paragraphs of text.

Prolog was chosen for the implementation because it has two powerful features which are characteristic of logic programming languages in general. Firstly, there are two separate readings of each logical statement, the declarative reading and the procedural reading [Pereira and Shieber, 1987]. This allows the verb rules to be understood at both a declarative level and a procedural level. Hence the separation of the declarative discussion in chapter 3 from the procedural discussion in chapter 4. Secondly, the use of logical variables with the associated operation of unification provides an especially suitable mechanism for filling in the verb arguments. Prolog does have limitations which make it difficult to express naturally all the relevant linguistic information, and many linguists and logicians would argue in favor of a non-monotonic logic instead. However, Prolog has one other advantage, which is that it is widely available in well-documented and efficient implementations, and therefore an eminently practical programming language choice. It is hoped that the careful reader will be able to actually implement the procedures described in this text based on the information in the appendices.

3.1 Introduction

Chapter 1 stated that successful semantic analysis depends partly on the formalization of the domain, and mentioned some of the difficulties associated with formalizations. As explained there, by choosing a limited domain, i.e., a clearly delineated domain, many of these difficulties are sidestepped, and it is possible to commit to a formal semantics for the domain. Jerry Hobbs has recently been extending this approach to several different areas that are crucial for common-sense reasoning, such as spatial reasoning, composition of objects, and reasoning about abrasion [Hobbs *et al.*, 1986]. It is important to bear in mind, however, that a limited domain formalization might not extend to natural language as a whole. Many words may be assigned interpretations that, while appropriate for their usage in the domain, seem to contradict their general usage in a broader domain. An interesting question to be asked about such a formalization is: which parts of it can be extended, and which parts cannot? The formalization presented here consists of three distinct components:

1. the lexical entries for both the verbs and the predicates comprising the decompositions of the verbs;
2. the entity hierarchy;
3. the syntactic, semantic and pragmatic constraints that are used to select instantiations for the predicate-arguments of the lexical entries.

These components are used to produce a semantic representation of a syntactic parse of a sentence. The approach taken by inference-driven mapping is to apply the lexical entry associated with a verb to decompose it. The decomposition will consist of one or more semantic predicates which will have decompositions of their own. Before decomposing these semantic predicates, inference-driven mapping first attempts to instantiate the predicate-arguments of the verb's decomposition. These predicate-arguments correspond to semantic roles, and can be filled by referents of syntactic constituents from the syntactic parse. The syntactic and semantic constraints are used to try to find mappings between the semantic roles and the parsed syntactic constituents. If these fail, then the pragmatic constraints can be applied in an attempt to deduce a possible filler for the semantic role. It is not necessary for a filler to be found, and the semantic role can be left as a variable. The verb decomposition is then decomposed in turn, and the process begins again with any new unfilled semantic roles. It is possible for a semantic role to remain unfilled until the final decomposition, when enough information will at last be available to find an appropriate filler.

The approach itself, the alternation of decomposition and semantic role filling, is considered to be general, but lexical entries and associated constraints are not. It does appear, however, that the syntactic cues associated with semantic roles that are most closely aligned to traditional cases, such as OBJECT1 (PATIENT), LOC (LOCATIVE) and LOCPT (LOCATIVE), may be fairly extendible. At any rate, they are similar to the syntactic cues traditionally associated with cases, which are supposed to be general. There are also indications that the decompositions of the basic semantic predicates such as **contact** and **move**, as well as the ones for the *case predicates*, **cause-motion** and **effect**, may be applicable to other domains. This remains to be demonstrated by future research.

The pulley domain is represented by the problems listed in appendix A. There are 79 different syntactic clauses in these problem statements that involve 31 different verbs. Each problem statement averages approximately six clauses, with an occasional WITH prepositional phrase thrown in. Most verbs have two or three alternative syntactic realizations, either individually or in conjunction with synonymous verbs. The verbs which shaped the development of the semantic processor were the **contact**, **support**, **location**, and *move* verbs, 26 out of the 33 verbs. Of these, half are **location** verbs, while the rest are fairly evenly distributed among the other categories. The remaining verbs are **quantity** verbs, which indicate the variables to be solved by the problem-solver. The problem-solver was originally designed to take as input a "reasonable" semantic representation of the information in the problem statements. The decisions about what would be reasonable were made primarily by the author after several discussions with the other group members, and then tested by running the problem-solver on some of the representations. The problem-solver specifically requires the **sought** predicate and the **mass** predicate.

3.2   Entities and their properties in the pulley domain

The standard approach in knowledge representation is to begin with a very general category such as "entity," and define the items in the relevant domain as specializations of this category [Brachman and Levesque, 1985]. This is equivalent to the computational use of typing for structuring data objects for a program [Goguen and Mesequer, 1988; Weiner and Palmer, 1981; Cardelli, 1984]. The tree in figure 3.1 presents most of the simple entity hierarchy that defines the inheritance of *types* in the pulley domain. The subtree underneath the quantity node is given in the next section. *Properties* and *parts* are associated with individual nodes on the tree, i.e., types of entities, and are automatically inherited by all of the *subtypes* of that node.

In the representation of entities in the pulley domain, the emphasis is on achieving a simple, easily managed data base. This emphasis results in semantic anomalies such as the inclusion of "shapes," i.e., points and lines, as types of

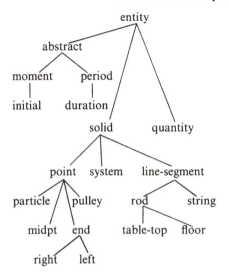

Fig. 3.1.   Entity hierarchy

solid entities as well as the definition of "animate" as a property of a type of point (see section 3.2.2). This allows the entities in the domain to be represented by one simple tree hierarchy, greatly simplifying the rules that express generalities about the tree.

The same semantic analysis approach can be used with a richer and more sophisticated representation of the domain. There are two points of contact with the domain model: the predicates in the verb representations and the tests included in the semantic constraints. The tests here are mostly simple class membership tests, but they could be arbitrary Prolog procedures, and so could take advantage of a more complicated knowledge representation schema. The predicates themselves could be any predicate that has a definition in the knowledge base, so they are also fairly unrestrained. It would only be necessary to avoid circular definitions.

Section 3.2.1 explains the entity hierarchy and the inheritance of types in detail. Section 3.2.2 gives examples of the association of properties with types, and the resulting inheritance of properties. Parts of entities are also described; they can also be inherited in much the same way as properties. This simple formalization of the entities in the pulley domain is fundamental to the semantic analysis of sentences, since semantic properties of the referents of noun phrases are essential to the successful assignment of semantic roles to syntactic constituents. The conventions of upper-case notation for variables and lower-case notation for predicates, function symbols and constants are used throughout.

3.2.1   *The typing of entities*

There are two main supertypes in the pulley domain, solid entities and quantities. Solid entities are more complex than quantities and will be examined here in more detail. The **isa2** predicate in the following assertion expresses the supertype relationship between entity and solid. It should be read as "solid is a subtype of entity."[1]

> isa2(entity,solid)

Solid entities are divided into two subtypes, those with the shape of a line-segment and those with the shape of a point, as illustrated by the next two **isa2** predicates:

> isa2(solid,point)
> isa2(solid,lineseg)

A pulley system can have all the properties of a solid entity, so it is said to be solid, but is not given any dimension since it is not really a point or a line-segment.

> isa2(solid,system)

The three most common entities in the pulley domain are particles, pulleys, and strings. For the purposes of problem-solving, physics textbooks idealize particles and pulleys as dimensionless solid entities, or "points," while strings are "flexible line-segments." Their positions in the type hierarchy are defined by the following three predicates:

> isa2(point,particle)
> isa2(point,pulley)
> isa2(lineseg,string)

These are by no means the only possible entities. A pulley system can be referred to, as well as masses, weights, men, rods, ropes and cords. For the purpose of solving a problem, masses and weights are assumed to be members of the set of particles, which is indicated by the **hasname** predicate. This is used to associate a specific instance of an entity with its type. So, in the following example, a particular mass, mass1, and a particular weight, weight1, are designated as members of the set of particles, so that all the properties of particles can be associated with the mass and the weight.

---

[1] The semantic predicates correspond exactly to the representation of this information in the Prolog program. The **isa2** predicate is used to define the type hierarchy, while the **hasprop** predicate associates attributes with entities.

hasname(particle,mass1)
hasname(particle,weight1)

Ropes and cords are assumed to be members of the set of strings.

hasname(string,rope1)
hasname(string,cord1)

A rod is also a line-segment, but is distinguished from a string because it is inflexible, or rigid. Since in the pulley domain we consider the world to be two-dimensional, table-tops and floors can be idealized as rigid line-segments, or rods.

isa2(lineseg,rod)
isa2(rod,table-top)
isa2(rod,floor)

Line-segments can have endpoints and midpoints. These are similar to particles in being points and, since they are parts of solid entities, being solid as well. There are two kinds of ends, right ends and left ends, and an entity can have more than one midpoint, since a midpoint is not constrained to being halfway between two endpoints.[2]

isa2(point,end)
isa2(point,midpt)

isa2(end,left)
isa2(end,right)

There are two more subtypes, which are not included in the solid entity hierarchy, but which need to be mentioned for the sake of completeness. They can be considered abstract entities, and are used to indicate periods of time. They are *moments* of time and *periods* of time, and can have the subtypes listed below. Initial moments of time indicate the beginning of a period of time, while the duration of the period indicates the entire motion event associated with a pulley word problem.

isa2(moment,initial)
isa2(period,duration)

Several attributes are associated with the various entities. These attributes are inherited by the entity's subtypes. Every attribute of a solid entity is inherited by every subtype of a solid entity. The relationship between a type and its subtypes is captured by the transitivity of the **isatype** predicate, as indicated by the following logical implications. The first implication merely

---

[2] This is an unfortunate departure from the standard mathematical usage, where a midpoint is considered to be exactly midway between two endpoints, and is due to historical reasons.

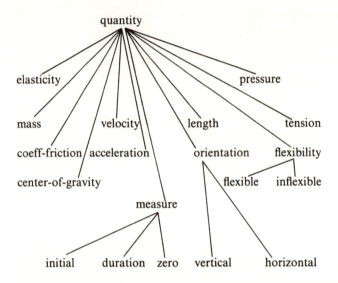

Fig. 3.2.   Quantity hierarchy

states that if Ent1 is a subtype of Ent, then there is also an **isatype** relationship between Ent and Ent1. The second implication states that if Ent1 is a subtype of Ent2, and there is also an **isatype** relationship between Ent2 and a third entity, Ent, then there must also be an **isatype** relationship between Ent and Ent2's subtype, Ent1. In other words, the isatype relationship represents the transitive closure of the isa2 relationship.

> For all Ent and Ent1:
> isa2(Ent,Ent1) →
>   isatype(Ent,Ent1)

> For all Ent, Ent1 and Ent2:
> isa2(Ent2,Ent1)   &   isatype(Ent,Ent2) →
>   isatype(Ent,Ent1)

3.2.2   Properties and parts

In a physics world domain, it is not surprising that most of the properties to be inherited consist of quantities such as mass or acceleration. Many of these properties are common to all solid entities, or to solid entities of a particular shape. The following list of **isa2** predicates encodes some of the information represented in the quantity hierarchy given in figure 3.2.

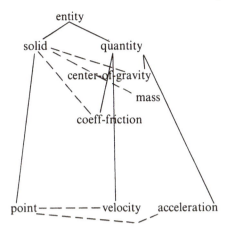

Fig. 3.3.   Illustrating **hasprop** links

isa2(quantity,mass)
isa2(quantity,tension)
isa2(quantity,coeff-friction)
isa2(quantity,acceleration)
isa2(quantity,pressure)
isa2(quantity,velocity)
isa2(quantity,elasticity)
isa2(quantity,measure)
isa2(quantity,orientation)
isa2(quantity,length)

The following list of **hasprop** predicates associates the different types of quantities with the appropriate types of solid entities. Notice that while every solid entity can have a mass, a center-of-gravity, and a coefficient of friction, only points can have velocities or accelerations. As mentioned before, strings are flexible and can have tensions, while rods are rigid, but can have elasticity, a somewhat contradictory combination that does not seem to bother authors of applied physics textbooks. Pulleys can have pressure exerted on them, and every line-segment, whether flexible or inflexible, can have an orientation and a length. If the quantity hierarchy were included on one large sheet of paper with the rest of the entity hierarchy, each **hasprop** relationship would represent a horizontal line connecting a member of the quantity type hierarchy with a member of the solid entity type hierarchy. The entire tree would be quite unreadable, so a small portion of it is given in figure 3.3 to illustrate the use of **hasprop**.

hasprop(solid,center-of-gravity)
hasprop(solid,mass)

hasprop(solid,coeff-friction)
hasprop(solid,shape)

hasprop(point,velocity)
hasprop(point,acceleration)
hasprop(point,animate)

hasprop(lineseg,orientation)
hasprop(lineseg,length)

hasprop(string,tension)
hasprop(flexible)

hasprop(rod,inflexible)
hasprop(rod,elasticity)

hasprop(pulley,pressure)

These properties are often given values in the statement of the problem, and these values are considered to be measured. In figure 3.2, initial and duration refer to values for periods of time, which are included in the entity hierarchy as abstract entities rather than solid ones. Vertical and horizontal refer to line-segment orientations, while zero can be a measure for a mass, a velocity or an acceleration. Often a property of an entity is given a particular measure, such as a "mass of 4 lb," or a "weightless pulley." These measures are expressed as three-argument predicates, where the first argument contains the token by which the measure is referred to, the second argument the numerical component, and the third argument the actual units of measure that have been indicated. Having two predicates to represent this information rather than one corresponds more closely to the linguistic usage, where the quantity information is often indicated by a prepositional phrase such as "of 4 lb." The "mass of 4 lb" and "weightless pulley" would become:

"mass of 4 lb"
mass(mass1,m1)
measure(m1,4,lb)

"weightless pulley"
mass(pulley1,zero)
measure(zero,0,lb)

In the problem set in appendix A, a man is introduced as "pulling himself up a rope." For this usage, the man is idealized as a particle, a dimensionless weight that can have a velocity and acceleration. These are the only attributes that have any bearing on the problem-solving. A man is distinguished from a particle only because he can also have the property of being animate, which a particle does not. The following predicates allow a man to be recognized as an AGENT of an Event for linguistic purposes, and also as a solid entity for problem-solving purposes.

>   hasprop(man,animate)
>   isa2(point,man)

The inheritance of attributes can be modelled by the following logical implications. These implications indicate that if there is a direct **hasprop** link between an entity, Ent, and a property, Prop, then **hasprop1** is true of the Ent and the Prop. The predicate **hasprop1** is also true if there is a direct **hasprop** link between another Ent1 and the Prop, as well as an **isatype** link between the Ent and the Ent1. This is the same **isatype** link that was defined in the preceding section as the transitive closure of the **isa2** relationship. It is being used here to examine all of the possible supertypes of an Ent, to see if any one of them has the Prop in question.

>   For all Ent and Prop:
>   hasprop(Ent,Prop) →
>   hasprop1(Ent,Prop)

>   For all Ent, Prop, and Ent1:
>   isatype(Ent1,Ent) & hasprop(Ent1,Prop) →
>   hasprop1(Ent,Prop)

The **isa2** hierarchy has already indicated that there are endpoints and midpoints. But those points have not been directly associated with line-segments. This is accomplished by the **part** predicate. It also establishes that table-tops have surfaces and edges.

>   part(table-top,surface)
>   part(table-top,edge)
>   part(lineseg,right)
>   part(lineseg,left)
>   part(lineseg,midpt)

Just as attributes can be inherited, so can parts. Anything that is a type of line-segment has a left end, a right end and multiple midpoints. This includes table-tops and floors. The following implications establish the inheritance of parts, and are essentially the same as the **hasprop1** implications.

>   For all Ent, Part:
>   part(Ent,Part) →
>   haspart(Ent,Part)

For all Ent, Part, Ent1:
isatype(Ent1,Ent) & part(Ent1,Part) →
     haspart(Ent,Part)

3.2.3   Summary

The entity hierarchy with its associated attributes plays an essential role in the semantic analysis of any domain. One of the main goals of the analysis is to determine the semantic roles played by the syntactic constituents of a sentence. The next section introduces the lexical entries for the verbs which contain the semantic roles. The following section describes how case-like syntactic cues can be associated with each type of semantic role, to indicate a likely syntactic filler for a semantic role. These cues can be used to generate a set of mappings between the syntactic constituents of the sentence being analyzed and the semantic roles associated with the verb. However, there is often more than one possible set of mappings between the syntactic constituents and the semantic roles. One method of determining which set is appropriate is by testing certain semantic features on each proposed filler of a semantic role. For instance, a filler of an OBJECT1 role in a **contact** relationship should be a solid entity. This can be tested by proving that **isatype**(solid,Object1) is true.

The entity hierarchy and the rules for traversing the hierarchy provide the necessary tools for testing whether or not a syntactic constituent has indicated an instantiation that is semantically appropriate. These tools are also important in deciding whether or not an uninstantiated semantic role should be filled, and what should fill it. The semantic and pragmatic constraints that make use of the entity hierarchy to perform these tasks are described in section 3.6.

3.3   Lexical entries for verbs

The selection and definition of the basic semantic relationships of the domain are constrained by two important factors: (1) the inclusion of all the semantic roles that can be associated with a verb that includes the semantic relationship in its decomposition, and (2) the necessity of including semantic relationships required by the problem-solver.

The lexical entries described in this section decompose the verb into groups of semantic predicates. These predicates correspond loosely to the semantic information that can be expressed by sentences in this domain. The set of all arguments to the semantic predicates is the same as the set of semantic roles for this domain. All except two of the predicates form a subset of the set of predicates required by the problem-solving task. Examples of the additional predicates that are suggested by the requirements of the problem-solving are given in section 3.3.1. The two predicates that are not required by the problem-solving, but are necessary for the semantic analysis, are **cause-motion** and **effect**. These are explained in detail at the end of this section.

There is an intentional one-to-one correspondence between the semantic roles normally associated with a particular verb and the set of predicate-arguments that can be associated with that verb through decomposition. There is no consensus in linguistics as to which semantic roles should be considered universal, so the predicate-arguments in this implementation cannot be considered exactly equivalent to any accepted set of semantic roles. There is no claim here that this set of predicate-arguments constitutes a theory of universal semantic roles. The only claim is that the multiple embedded predicates that make up the decompositions contain all of the information necessary to map the "semantic roles," i.e., the predicate-arguments, onto syntactic constituents accurately and efficiently. In order to achieve this mapping, syntactic information must be associated directly with the predicate-arguments in the form of mapping constraints. In this sense the predicate-arguments correspond to semantic roles, so they will be referred to as such from now on.

The verbs used in the pulley problems can be subcategorized according to the concrete semantic relationships that they are decomposed into, including **contact**, **support**, **quantity** and **motion**. A **contact** relationship can be decomposed into a set of predicates that make explicit additional relationships between the entities that could be involved in the **contact**. These relationships include the existence of suitable location points on each entity at which the **contact** can occur, and the location points being at the same place, e.g., **sameplace**(Locpt1,Locpt2). More than one verb can adequately express a **contact** relationship, so many verbs include **contact** in their decomposition. Other verbs decompose into **support**, **motion**, or **quantity** relationships. These four relationships can be seen as defining four distinct categories of verbs.

The four concrete relationships are not mutually exclusive. In fact, the **contact** relationship acts as a building block in the decomposition of both **support** and **motion** relationships. For example, in this domain, for one entity to **support** another there must be a **contact** between them. Section 3.5.2 discusses how this "sharing" of predicates for decomposition simplifies the problem of semantic role assignment by allowing case-like generalizations to be made about the arguments to the shared predicates. Since several verbs share the same predicate-argument, and the same syntactic cues for that argument, the resulting cross-verb generalizations about the argument and its syntactic cues are "case-like."

The verbs in a particular category are not necessarily synonymous. *Connect* and *attach* are clearly verbs that both express **contact** relationships even though they are not interchangeable. In this domain, "A string connects two particles . . ." unambiguously indicates a string with a particle at each end, whereas "A string attaches two particles" seems somehow incomplete. However, "A particle attached at the end of a string . . ." is a straightforward enough noun phrase, while "A particle connected at the end of a string" is the awkward phrase. The difference between *attach* and *connect* in this domain is captured by including an **effect** predicate in the decomposition of *connect* which the decomposition of *attach* does not have. The **effect** predicate is less tangible than the concrete semantic predicates previously mentioned. It is based on the USE relationship generally associated with INSTRUMENTS, and spells out explicitly how the inclusion of the INSTRUMENT affects the decomposition of verbs in this domain. Another, the **cause-motion** predicate, is introduced for showing the influence of AGENTS on the decomposition of **motion** verbs. Since both the **effect** predicate and the **cause-motion** predicate are aimed solely at delineating the influence certain semantic roles have on the further decomposition of a verb, they are termed *case predicates*.

This section presents the simple verbs which can be decomposed in a straightforward manner into the concrete semantic predicates of the domain. It also presents the case predicates, **cause-motion** and **effect**, and shows how more complicated verbs can be decomposed using these predicates. For example, concrete predicates can be embedded in the **effect** predicate in the same way that Jackendoff's thematic relations are embedded. The decompositions here go farther than Jackendoff's thematic relations or other uses of decomposition in that they clearly define the influence of the case predicate on the verb reresentation as a whole. For instance, the inclusion of a marked INSTRUMENT in a typical **contact** verb (or **location** verb) results in two **contact** relationships, (or two **location** relationships), with the INSTRUMENT filling an argument position for both. This is explained in more detail below. This decomposition of the case predicate, like the decompositions of all the predicates, is independent of the verb itself. Since the arguments to the predicates are semantic roles, the case predicate decompositions correspond to Charniak's independent case definitions as described in chapter 2, and provide evidence for the retention of a modified notion of case in a theory of semantic analysis, at least for limited domains.

3.3.1   Verb categories

In this chapter, the emphasis is on finding the verbs that most appropriately express particular sets of predicates. The lexical entries presented here can be thought of as backwards implications. The collections of predicates on the right-hand side of each rule can imply the use of a particular verb to express those predicates. More than one verb could express the same set of predicates. The basic semantic predicates such as **contact**, **support**, and **motion** can be decomposed in turn, and these decompositions are expressed in lexical entries for these predicates. The verb entries are designated by the left-hand predicate being expressed in ***bold-face italics***, while the left-hand predicate of the semantic predicate entries is merely **bold-face**. The convention of using underbar, "_", to stand for variables which are irrelevant to the current discussion is also used.

The predicates on the right-hand side of each rule generally share arguments with the predicate on the left-hand side, and instantiations of these arguments are preserved in the rewriting. If the variables in the arguments on the right-hand side have been instantiated, the corresponding variables on the left-hand side will receive the same instantiation. The lexical entries are Horn clauses, in that the left-hand side never has more than one predicate.

A simple example of this kind of lexical entry is given below.[3]

> For all X,Y,Z,S, and T:
> **pred1**(X,Y,Z) $\rightarrow$ pred2(S,X,Z), pred3(T,Y,Z)

The following sections all begin by giving examples of verbs that can express a basic semantic notion, as well as sample phrases expressing these verbs. They then present the lexical entry of the basic semantic predicate. Each section also lists the simple verbs that belong in the category represented by this lexical entry. Verbs that are not mentioned explicitly in this chapter can be found in appendix D.

Contact verbs

Attach has already been mentioned as an example of a verb that appropriately expresses a certain kind of **contact**. The "kind" of **contact** relationship is a simple fixed contact between two entities, meaning that it will last for the duration of the motion event suggested in the pulley problem. The lexical entry for *attach* is given below, and can be read as: "For any two entities there exists a time period, duration, during which, if a contact exists between the two entities, the verb *attach* may appropriately be used." OBJECT1 and OBJECT2 are introduced here as the semantic roles corresponding to the entities in question. The processing that can eventually associate the particle 1 from subj(particle1) with OBJECT1 is explained in the latter half of this chapter, and in more detail in chapter 4.

> For all OBJECT1,OBJECT2 there exists a duration such that
> *attach* $\rightarrow$
> contact(Object1,Object2,duration)

Phrases from this domain that illustrate the use of *attach* include:

> "A particle is attached at the end of a string . . ."
> ". . . a string with weights attached at its ends."

In the first phrase, the particle and the string are the entities in contact, and

---

[3] There is a deliberate correspondence between the form of these lexical entries and the form expected of Prolog clauses. For instance, the "&'s" have been replaced by commas. This is to make it easier for the reader to recognize the corresponding Prolog code in the appendices.

the end of the string is the location point at which the contact occurs. In the second phrase, there are two separate **contact** relationships, one between each weight and the string. The location points are again the ends of the string.

In describing a **contact** relationship, reference is often made to a specific location point on one or more of the entities where the **contact** occurs, so location points are semantic roles for **contact** verbs. The lexical entry for **contact** must therefore include predicate-arguments, i.e., semantic roles, that correspond to these location points. These semantic roles are indicated by LOCPT1 and LOCPT2. **Contacts** fall into two categories: (1) fixed **contacts** which can be counted on to hold for the *duration* of the problem-solving, or (2) movable **contacts** which may not continue to hold true after the *initial* moment during which the problem situation is set up. Another predicate-argument must be included to distinguish between fixed contacts and movable contacts; in this case it is the time period. For the general **contact** relationship, this time period is a variable, Time, since the relationship must be applicable to verbs that indicate fixed contact as well as verbs that indicate moveable contacts.

The left-hand side of the **contact** lexical entry is a **contact** predicate with three arguments, the two solid entities and a time period:

contact(Object1,Object2,Time) ←
    locpt(Locpt1,Object1,Time),
    locpt(Locpt2,Object2,Time),
    sameplace(Locpt1,Locpt2,Time)

A **contact** can decompose into three predicates, a **locpt** predicate that indicates a location point on each of the solid entities, and a **sameplace** predicate that indicates that the two location points are in the **sameplace**. Since location points ideally have no dimension, just like particles, it is not impossible for them to share the same space. In a more realistic domain, **contact** might more appropriately decompose into a **next-to** predicate instead of **sameplace**. **Contact** relationships are symmetric.

Support verbs

Another fundamental notion in the pulley domain is the notion of **support**. A **support** relationship is indicated between two solid entities, with one doing the supporting and one being supported. **Support** is not symmetric. As in **contact**, some **support** relationships can be expected to hold for the duration, whereas others may not last past the initial setting up stage. Two simple **support** verbs are *sustain* and *support*. Notice that each of the following phrases includes a pp(at,X) that indicates a location point.

"A string sustains a mass at one end . . ."
". . . a string supporting at one end a weight of mass 4 lb . . ."

The lexical entries for the simple **support** verbs are listed below. The first entity, OBJECT1, is the one doing the supporting, and the second entity, OBJECT2, is the one being supported.

> ***carry*** ←
>> support(Object1,Object2,initial)
>
> ***sustain*** ←
>> support(Object1,Object2,initial)
>
> ***support*** ←
>> support(Object1,Object2,initial)

The **support** predicate on the left-hand side of the following **support** entry has three arguments. The first argument corresponds to the supporter, the second argument corresponds to the supportee, and the third argument indicates the time period for which this **support** relationship can be expected to hold.

>> support(Object1,Object2,Time) ←
>>> force(Up,Object1,Time),
>>> force(Down,Object2,Time),
>>> contact(Object1,Object2,Time)

Support can decompose into two **force** predicates and a **contact** predicate. There must be an upward **force** exerted by the entity doing the **supporting**, an equal downward **force** exerted by the entity being **supported**, and the two entities must be in a **contact** relationship.[4] Of course, **contact** decomposes into location points being at the same place, hence the natural inclusion of pp(at,X)'s in **support** phrases.

Location verbs

Many of the verbs in this domain can express **support** indirectly by indicating that a **location** of an entity is on or above another entity. For a **location** of an entity to be more than momentary in a physics domain that includes gravity, the entity must be **supported**. So verbs that indicate precise **locations** include **support** in their decomposition. The **location** lexical entries given below appear to be quite similar, though they actually represent quite different decompositions. In the first decomposition the entity *doing the supporting* is the location of the entity being supported. In the second decomposition the entity *being*

---

[4] Strictly speaking, this lexical entry stretches the original restriction that the arguments of the predicates should be mentioned in sentences of the domain. None of the pulley problems explicitly mention a **force** directly resulting from a **support** relationship. They do however sometimes refer to the "pressure" on the pulley, an indirect reference to such a **force**. It has also been demonstrated that in a similar domain, Novak's equilibrium problems, **forces** are mentioned at the surface structure. These considerations combined with the requirements of the problem-solver resulted in the decision to include the **force** predicate.

supported is the one indicating a location. These inferences are tied to the manner in which the location relationship is expressed. If the entity being given a location is indicated as being *above* the location entity, the location entity is the one doing the supporting. If the entity being given a location is indicated as being *below* the location entity, the location entity is being supported. In a domain which included magnets, the relationship between **location** and **support** would not be as straightforward.

$$\text{location(Object1,Loc,Time)} \leftarrow$$
$$\text{support(Loc,Object1,Time)}$$

$$\text{location(Object1,Loc,Time)} \leftarrow$$
$$\text{support(Object1,Loc,Time)}$$

Simple examples of **location** verbs in this domain are *pass* and *rest*. Their entries are given below along with the other **location** verb entries.

> *lie* ←
> location(Object1,Loc,initial)
>
> *pass* ←
> location(Object1,Loc,initial)
>
> *place* ←
> location(Object1,Loc,initial)
>
> *rest* ←
> location(Object1,Loc,initial)
>
> *run* ←
> location(Object1,Loc,initial)
>
> *sling* ←
> location(Object1,Loc,initial)

They are used in the following types of phrases:

> ". . . a string passing over a pulley . . ."
> "A mass of 9 lb resting on a smooth horizontal table . . ."
> ". . . a string . . . passes under a movable pulley . . ."

Motion verbs

The most complex notion necessary for the pulley domain is that of **motion**. There are not many examples of the motion verbs in the pulley problems. There are, however, two verbs which clearly describe motion events: *drop* and *descend*. A simple **move** lexical entry accommodates the use of motion in the pulley problems.

Drop and *descend* occurred in the following two phrases:

"... this latter [a weight] has dropped one metre ..."
"... the larger mass descends with acceleration g/7 ..."

The motion event being described here includes directional information. The lexical entries below supply a downward **direction** for the motion that can be expressed by *dropping* or *descending*.

> *drop* ←
> > move(Object1,Path,Time)
> > direction(down,Path,Time)

> *descend* ←
> > move(Object1,Path,Time)
> > direction(down,Path,Time)

The **move** predicate from the motion lexical entry that follows has three arguments; the entity in motion, OBJECT1, the path along which it is moving, Path, and the period of time during which the motion takes place, Time. A motion event can always be decomposed into the **acceleration** and the **velocity** of the entity.

> move(Object1,Path,Time) ←
> > acceleration(Object1,Accel,Time)
> > velocity(Object1,Vel,Time)

The only other explicit description of a motion event in the pulley problems is actually an indication of a "lack" of motion, represented here as a velocity of zero. There were very few examples of these descriptions, so they have been treated more superficially than the other verbs. The problem statements generally describe a system of pulleys with various weights and constraints on the positioning of the strings and then "let the system go from a position of rest." The actual phrase "let go from a position of rest" occurs, along with phrases such as "initially at rest." A phrase such as "remains at zero" indicates that the motion in the current state is the same as the motion in a previous state, namely the velocity is zero. These phrases can all be seen as indicating that the initial velocity of the system is zero. Examples of the lexical entries that capture this are as follows:

> *is-at-rest* ←
> > velocity(Object1,zero,initial)

> *remains-stationary* ←
> > velocity(Object1,zero,duration)

Quantity verbs

The only category of verbs that have not been dealt with are the **quantity** verbs whose lexical entries are given below. They form a very restricted category, since they are used exclusively to focus on particular quantities or measures of those quantities in the last sentence of a pulley problem. This sentence can often take the form of a question, as in "What is the tension in the string?"

Calculate, *find* and *what-is* can all be used to indicate that a particular quantity should be **sought** by the problem-solver. One of the ways the quantity predicates differ from the predicates in the other categories is that they take only quantities or measures as their arguments, and not solid entities. These verbs are all defined in terms of a **seek** predicate, which in turn decomposes into **sought**.

> *calculate* ←
> > seek(Object1,Time)
>
> *find* ←
> > seek(Object1,Time)
>
> *is*(moment) ←
> > equals(Object1,Object2,moment)
>
> *what-is* ←
> > seek(Object1,Time)

The lexical entry for **seek** is

> seek(Object1,Time) ←
> sought(Object1,Time)

Prepositions

One more set of entries has to be added, the lexical entries for prepositions. One of the same semantic relationships that can be expressed by verbs, **contact**, can also be expressed by a WITH preposition, as in ". . . a string with weights 4 and x lb."[5] **Support** can be expressed indirectly by "the mass m just over the edge (of the table)," which indicates that the mass is **not-resting** on the table, but has a location very close to the edge. This location is only possible if the mass is **supported** by something else. Both of these uses of prepositions are represented in the lexical entries below.

---

[5] This is really an example of the LOCATIVE use of WITH, as in "The book with the papers . . ." But since it is always used in this very specific way in the pulley domain, expressing it directly as a **contact** relationship is a short-cut for going through **location** relationship to **support** relationship, and finally to **contact**.

just-over ←
not-rest(Object1,Object2,initial)

with ←
contact(Object1,Object2,duration)

Prepositions are not always used to express basic semantic relationships. They can also be a syntactic cue for indicating semantic roles associated with the semantic relationship indicated by the verb, as in the use of AT to indicate a location point. PERPENDICULAR TO, on the other hand, can indicate an orientation for a semantic role. These prepositional uses occur in the following types of phrases.

"A weightless string . . . is placed on a smooth horizontal table perpendicular to an edge . . ."
". . . a fine string with weights 3 lb and 6 lb at its ends . . ."

Boundaries on the decomposition
For the purposes of the semantic processing, the following set of predicates are not decomposed any further.

locpt(Locpt1,Object1,Time)
sameplace(Locpt1,Locpt2,Time)
force(Down,Object,Time)
acceleration(Object,Acceleration,Time)
velocity(Object,Velocity,Time)
direction(Object,Path,Time)
equals(Object1,Object2,Time)

These are all predicates that occurred in the basic lexical entries described in the preceding sections. They do need to be decomposed further for the problem-solver, but this more detailed level is not mentioned explicitly at the sentence level. The general principle is that the decompositions only need to go far enough to pick up any arguments to the verb that can be mentioned syntactically. A different application that required more detail might introduce new verbs that would result in a further decomposition of some of these predicates.

The predicates were selected with the problem-solver in mind. The problem-solver uses the **support** and **contact** predicates to recognize a pulley system, making well-known facts about pulley systems available for deductions. It also uses same-place predicates as indications of likely locations for forces to be acting. **Support** as defined for the semantic processing is not transitive, since it is associated with direct contacts between the entities being supported. The problem-solver, however, can infer an indirect **support** for entities that have no other means of **support** and are in **contact** with entities being supported. It makes sophisticated use of the time periods for drawing inferences about entities in motion, and the locations of entities along paths at given points in time. None of the information in this more detailed level is mentioned explicitly in any of the sentences of the domain, so it is considered to be solely relevant to the problem-solving.

3.4   Case predicates

The preceding section introduced the simpler verbs whose decompositions are based on concrete semantic predicates. This section will now discuss the more complex verbs, whose decomposition includes a case predicate associated with a particular semantic role. The previous verb decompositions have all included semantic roles as arguments to the predicates, e.g., OBJECT1, OBJECT2, LOCPT1, LOCPT2, etc., but case predicates are distinct in that they do not correspond to a basic concrete semantic relationship, but, rather, to the necessary relationships that must arise out of the presence of a particular semantic role. This is getting into the area of the relationships between the semantic roles. If an AGENT is included, what is its relationship to the other semantic roles? What effect does it have on the decomposition of the verb? This is especially relevant where optional semantic roles, roles that may or may not appear in the surface structure, are concerned.

It is possible for the inclusion of an optional semantic role, such as AGENT or INSTRUMENT, to have an effect on the verb decomposition that is not present when the optional role is not included, and that effect could be to some degree independent of the verb. If the effect of the inclusion of the role can be demonstrated to be independent of the verbs, then this is an example of a case benefit as defined by Charniak (see chapter 2). The following two case predicates, **cause-motion** and **effect**, define exactly that difference in the decomposition of the verb that occurs when the semantic role involved is included, and for at least the **effect** predicate, the difference is demonstrated to be independent of the verb.

3.4.1   Cause-motion AGENTS

There was only one actual instance of an AGENT in the pulley problems, so there can be no claims for generality based on one example. There are, however, indications that the lexical entry involving an AGENT will also apply to more complex uses of **motion** verbs [Palmer and McCoy, in prep.]. The verb that expresses the presence of an AGENT is *pull*, as in "The man pulls himself up the rope."

The use of *pull* in this phrase suggests that some AGENT **caused motion** in an object along a path during a time period by *pulling*. The lexical entry below gives this decomposition. The embedding of the **move** predicate as an argument to **cause-motion** indicates that the AGENT causes a motion "event" which can itself have a decomposition. This follows the standard embedding of events as arguments to **cause** predicates that occurs in many different uses of decomposition, including Conceptual Dependency Nets, the LNR system, generative grammar, etc. (See chapter 2.)

There is a sense in which this is now outside of first-order predicate logic, since a predicate is used as an argument to a predicate. But the **move** predicate does not act as predicate while it is an argument to **cause-motion**. It is only decomposed after **cause-motion** has been rewritten as a conjunction of **apply-force** and **move**. In terms of usage, this **move** predicate can be thought of as a function symbol while it is an argument to **cause-motion**; a function symbol that triggers a decomposition into the actual **move** predicate. The same is true for the embedding of predicates as arguments for **effect**.

> *pull* ←
>   cause-motion(Agent,
>   move(Object1,Path,Time)),
>   direction(Dir,Path,Time)

An AGENT can only be present in a **cause-motion** event if some **force** has been **applied** by the AGENT in order for the **movement** of the object to occur. This is expressed in the lexical entry given below. There is a sense in which the decomposition of **cause-motion** is dependent on the verb belonging to the category of **motion** verbs, so this does not demonstrate a complete independence of the verb. AGENT lexical entries that can be shown to apply to categories of verbs such as **motion** verbs are quite interesting in their own right.

>   cause-motion(Agent,
>   move(Object1,Path,Time)) ←
>   apply-force(Agent,Object1,Time),
>   move(Object1,Path,Time)

The AGENT is an optional semantic role, meaning that it does not have to be mentioned in the sentence. The sentence might have been "The end of the rope is pulled three feet," where no AGENT is mentioned explicitly. In such a case, the AGENT role can be marked absent, and a different decomposition of agent can be applied. The following lexical entry is specifically designed to be applied when AGENTs are absent. Since nothing is known about the AGENT, there is no point in including **apply-force** in the decomposition. A **motion** event without an AGENT is simply a **motion** event.

>   cause-motion(absent,
>   move(Object1,Path,Time)) ←
>   move(Object1,Path,Time)

3.4.2   Effect INTERMEDIARIES

The **effect** predicate defines the influence the presence of an INSTRUMENT has on a particular class of verbs. For this domain, the INSTRUMENT is termed an INTERMEDIARY to indicate that it defines a special subclass of the general usage of INSTRUMENT. INTERMEDIARIES provide additional evidence of legitimate case benefits, since the lexical entry associated with **effect**, to which the INTERMEDIARY is an argument, is independent of whether the verb involved is a **support** or a **contact** verb. This lexical entry allows *the presence of an INTERMEDIARY to impose transitivity upon the semantic relation associated with the verb*. If the verb suggests a semantic relation such as a **contact** between OBJECT1 and OBJECT2, **effecting** this **contact** with an INTERMEDIARY produces an indirect contact between the entities. There are actually two **contacts**: a **contact** between OBJECT1 and INTERMEDIARY, and a **contact** between INTERMEDIARY and OBJECT2. This is expressed by the following lexical entry.

```
effect(Inter,
   contact(Object1,Object2,Time)) ←
      contact(Object1,Inter,Time),
      contact(Inter,Object2,Time)
```

Contact intermediaries

The simplest example of the use of an INTERMEDIARY in the pulley domain is the phrase

"A particle is connected to another particle by a string . . ."

Connect can be classified as a verb that always uses an INTERMEDIARY to express a **contact** relationship. This is expressed in the lexical entries given below.

```
connect ←
   effect(Inter,
      contact(Object1,Object2,duration))

effect(Inter,
   contact(Object1,Object2,Time)) ←
      contact(Object1,Inter,Time),
      contact(Inter,Object2,Time)
```

Up until now semantic roles have all had the semantic feature, or type, "solid" associated with them. INTERMEDIARIES are solid entities as well, but for this domain they must also be flexible line-segments in order to do the connecting. In other domains, possible candidates for a similar semantic role might be glue or screws.

Support INTERMEDIARIES

In this domain, **location** is inferred from **support**. The simple **support** verbs, such as *sustain* and *support*, do not express events involving intermediaries. The more complex verbs, such as *hang* and *suspend*, do. These verbs are primarily **location** verbs. Therefore, the **effect** entry for **support** is specified in terms of **location**. This entry as well as the entries for *hang* and *suspend* are given below. For *hang* and *suspend*, the semantic requirements on the INTERMEDIARY are even more restricted than for *connect*. A hanging relationship first requires a fixed point (Loc) that an entity (Object1) can be hung from. Then, in order for the fixed point to support the entity, some part of the entity must be above the point. This part can minimally have the dimension of a point itself. The rest of the entity being hung is actually below the fixed point that is doing the supporting. In order for the entity being hung to be both below and above the fixed point, it must either have a flexible INTERMEDIARY, as in a string or the loop on a coat, or be curved, as in a horse shoe. All of the entities in the pulley domain are hung by strings, cords or ropes, so the semantic requirement is that the INTERMEDIARY must be a flexible line-segment, i.e., a string.

In a phrase like "The chandelier is hung from a hook on the ceiling by a chain," the chain acts as the INTERMEDIARY, the chandelier is the entity being hung, and the hook represents the fixed point. Part of one loop on the chain will be above the hook, allowing the hook to support the chain, and therefore support the chandelier.

> *hang* ←
> effect(Inter,
> location(Object1,Loc,initial))
>
> *suspend* ←
> effect(Inter,
> location(Object1,Loc,initial))
>
> effect(Inter,
> location(Object1,Loc,Time)) ←
> location(Inter,Loc,Time),
> location(Object1,Inter,duration)

Just as AGENTS can be absent, INTERMEDIARIES can be unmarked. This suggests that a syntactic constituent that does not normally indicate an INTERMEDIARY has as its referent an entity that could normally be an INTERMEDIARY but is playing a dual role (see section 2.3.2). An example of this is "A string hangs from a pulley," where the string could be the INTERMEDIARY, but is also acting as the Object1. For this example, the normal lexical entry for **effect** is not applied, and the following entry is applied instead. Just as motion EVENTS without AGENTS are simply motion EVENTS, location EVENTS without INTERME-

DIARIES are simply location EVENTS. Several examples involving support INTER-
MEDIARIES are given in section 4.3.

> effect(unmarked,
>   location(Object1,Loc,Time)) ←
>   location(Object1,Loc,Time)

Hang adverbials

Hang is the only verb in the pulley domain to appear with two different
adverbs; *freely* and *vertically*. As might be expected, the choice of adverb
affects the use of the verb so strongly that separate lexical entries are given for
each one. They are listed below along with the decompositions of any new
predicates they use. The main difference between the use of ***hang*** and the use of
the ***hang*** adverbials is that the adverbials do not indicate an INTERMEDIARY.

Hang-freely, as in "a mass hanging freely," states that the mass is ***not-resting***
on anything in such a way that movement would be impeded. This in turn
suggests that the mass is being supported from above, possibly by a string.
Not-rest decomposes into a **location** predicate which can decompose into
support from above.

Hang-vertically, as in "with the free portions of the string hanging vertically," suggests a vertical orientation for a line-segment. This can also decompose into the line-segment being supported from above, thus preserving the
orientation.

> ***hang-freely*** ←
>   not-rest(Object1,solid,Time)

> ***hang-vertically*** ←
>   orientation(Object1,vertical,initial)

> ***not-rest*** ←
>   location(Object1,Loc,Time)

> ***orientation*** ←
>   location(Object1,Loc,Time)

3.5   Accommodating alternative syntactic realizations

Lexical entries alone are not sufficient for a method of semantic analysis. A
uniform method of associating syntactic constituents with these lexical entries
is also needed. Since the predicate-arguments are synonymous with semantic
roles, this method should be able to borrow heavily from case theory.
However, as demonstrated in chapter 2, there are certain inadequacies with
case theory, and the question remains: "Is this new method any more ade-

quate?" From a representation point of view it is obviously more adequate, since the representations are not restricted to flat predicate-argument structures, but are richer, more expressive, multiple embedded predicates. Multiple embedded predicates can easily express more than one event, since they can include events as arguments to predicates, and they can also allow the same filler to fill more than one semantic role. Case theory also had problems in associating syntactic constituents with semantic roles. The main difficulty lay in capturing verb idiosyncrasies without losing generalities. The multiple case-frame approach captures the idiosyncrasies at the cost of redundancy. This section demonstrates how the mapping constraints presented here can also capture idiosyncrasies but without the same amount of redundancy. This is possible because the decomposition representation is richer than a flat predicate-argument structure, and allows cross-verb generalizations to be made, while the inclusion of the predicate environment in the mapping constraints can be used to capture verb idiosyncrasies in the form of semantic role interdependencies. The mapping constraints are equivalent to templates in terms of their ability to preserve semantic role interdependencies. In fact, the end of this section demonstrates how the lexical entries together with the mapping constraints can be seen as grammar rules for producing a superset of the set of templates required by the domain. The section following this one presents the additional semantic and pragmatic constraints that are required to test the consistency of the proposed mappings.

3.5.1   Mapping constraints

At first glance, the mapping constraints appear to be identical to the types of generalizations used by case grammarians, such as "the AGENT is the subject if present, else the INSTRUMENT is the subject if present, else the PATIENT is the subject, etc." For this domain, the OBJECT1 semantic role is similar to the PATIENT semantic role, and there are two LOCATIVE semantic roles, LOC and LOCPT1. For example, in the phrase, "A particle is attached to a string at one end," the subject of the clause is particle1. The subject is a likely syntactic constituent for the indication of the OBJECT1 of the **contact** predicate into which **attach** decomposes. The object of the pp(to,Y) is a likely candidate for OBJECT2, the other entity of the **contact** predicate. The syntactic cues below are in the form "semantic role" is X if "syntactic cue" of X. This notation actually indicates that the two variable names represented by X in subj(X) and OBJECT1 are unified so that they will receive the same instantiation. The unification between the variable names constitutes a mapping between a syntactic constituent and a semantic role. This mapping will also be expressed using the short-hand form "syntactic cue" = = "semantic role." The examples below represent most of the syntactic cues that can be used to produce the example phrases from the preceding section, and as such constitute a set of "case-like" general rules for associating syntactic cues with semantic roles that are independent of the verbs involved.

> Object1 is X if subj(X)
> Object2 is X if pp(to,X)
> Object2 is X if obj(X)
> Loc is X if pp(on,X)
> Loc is X if pp(over,X)
> Locpt is X if pp(at,X)

Since semantic roles are defined as predicate-arguments of the decompositions, shared predicates result in shared semantic roles. Along with OBJECT1S and OBJECT2s, it is common for **contact** and **support** verbs to have LOCPTS on one or more of the entities mentioned in the syntactic expression of the verb. On the other hand, it would be unnatural to mention a LOCPT on an **acceleration** or a **velocity**, and there are no predicates associated with one of these that contains a LOCPT1 or LOCPT2 as a predicate-argument.

The purpose of this section is to present the mapping constraints used with the lexical entries, and to compare the efficacy of inference-driven mapping with templates as a method of performing mappings. The best way to make the comparison with templates is to show how the mapping constraints could be used with the lexical entries to generate all of the alternative syntactic realizations, and then compare these realizations with the templates. This is not how inference-driven mapping actually performs the mappings. Inference-driven mapping uses the generative capability of the lexical entries and the mapping constraints to do analysis by synthesis. Rather than generate all of the syntactic realizations, the generation tree is pruned while it is being built so that only the realization corresponding to the actual syntactic parse is generated. This is explained in more detail in chapter 4. The following sections concentrate on the generative capacity of the lexical entries combined with the mapping constraints as a prelude to explaining how they are used to perform analysis by synthesis, and to simplify the comparison with templates.

Lexical entries as templates

The syntactic cues introduced above can be used in conjunction with a lexical entry to produce all the possible sets of mappings of syntactic constituents onto semantic roles for the verb. For a verb like *attach*, for instance, one possible set of mappings is: $subj(X) == OBJECT1$, and $pp(to,Y) == OBJECT2$. The variables corresponding to the semantic roles in the *attach* lexical entry are bound to variables corresponding to syntactic constituents suggested by the mapping constraints, as illustrated below. Function symbols such as $subj(X)$, $obj(Y)$, and $pp(to,Z)$ can be thought of as indicating that any instantiation must be of the same syntactic type. This can be demonstrated by using a **contact** predicate as an example.

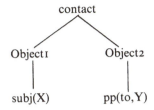

Fig. 3.4. "An entity **contacts** another entity"

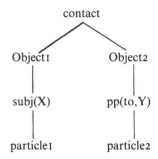

Fig. 3.5. "Particle 1 **contacts** particle2"

contact(Object1,Object2,duration)

The set of bindings between the semantic role variable names and the syntactic variable names represents a possible set of mappings from semantic roles to syntactic constituents, such as subj(X) = = OBJECT1 and pp(to,T) = = OBJECT2. This set of mappings can also be represented as in figure 3.4.

The tree in figure 3.5 can be seen as a semantic representation of a fixed contact relationship between two particles.

The verb **attach** can appropriately be used in a syntactic realization of this semantic representation, such as "a particle is attached to another particle." This is illustrated by the tree in figure 3.6. Since the tree includes the verb and the mappings to syntactic constituents it can easily be translated into a syntactic realization. Such trees will be referred to as *syntactic realizations*.

Another way of representing this syntactic realization is by the set of predicates corresponding to the first two nodes on the tree. The semantic roles of the predicates are instantiated by the syntactic constituents indicated by the set of mappings, as illustrated below. The referents of the syntactic constituents, particle1 and particle2, do not need to be included to indicate the syntactic realization.

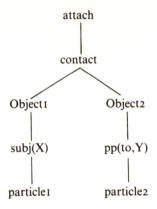

Fig. 3.6. "A particle is attached to another particle"

> **attach**
> contact(subj(X),pp(to,Y))

This representation could be expanded to include the decomposition of **contact** into **locpt** and **sameplace**. The syntactic constituent instantiations would be continued throughout, as in the example in section 3.5.3.

> **attach**
> contact(subj(X),pp(to,Y))
> locpt(NULL,subj(X))
> locpt(NULL,pp(to,Y))
> sameplace(NULL,NULL)

This syntactic realization could also be represented by the following template, which would also match the example sentence:

> ⟨Object1⟩ attach to ⟨Object2⟩

However, before templates and trees can be compared, the use of the predicate environment for preserving interdependencies must be explained. The following section explains how the predicate environment can be used to filter out the application of mapping constraints that would violate context-sensitive restrictions such as semantic role interdependencies.

3.5.2   *Associating syntactic cues with predicate environments*

The mapping constraints just presented are essentially equivalent to the disjunctions described in section 2.1.1 since they allow more than one syntactic cue to be associated with each semantic role. Therefore they would not be able to adequately account for interdependencies, just as the disjunctions could not.

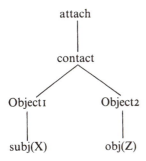

Fig. 3.7.   *"An entity is attached an entity"

For instance, the existing mapping constraints applied to the same lexical entry could also result in the set of mappings: subj(X) = = OBJECT1, obj(Z) = = OBJECT2. This set of mappings is illustrated by the syntactic realization shown in figure 3.7.

Unfortunately, these mappings correspond to an ungrammatical sentence. (It is missing a "to.")

* "An entity is attached an entity."

The procedural interpretation of the lexical entries described in chapter 4 provides an added richness of representation that greatly aids in the handling of interdependencies. This richer representation includes information about the predicate a semantic role is an argument of, as well as whether or not the other arguments of that predicate have already been instantiated and what those instantiations are, and is called the predicate environment. *Verb inter-dependencies are handled by associating the syntactic cues with the predicate environment in which the semantic role occurs.* For example, in the **attach** lexical entry, OBJECT1 has **contact** as a predicate and OBJECT2 and Time as the other arguments. The predicate environment of OBJECT1 is simply "**contact** (Object1,Object2,Time)." Predicate environments can be fine-tuned to particular mapping constraints. If the mapping constraint for this semantic role can always be applied, no matter what the other arguments are or how they have been instantiated, then the other argument positions can simply be indicated by variables. The predicate environment for OBJECT1 becomes "**contact**(Object1,_,_)." The preceding mapping constraints are associated with appropriate predicate environments in the list below. The constraints now take the form "syntactic cue = = semantic role / predicate environment." Note that the constraints now state that OBJECT2 can only be assigned a pp(to,Y) if the predicate head is **contact**, and an obj(Z) if the predicate head is **support**. With a further restriction mentioned in section 3.5.2 this also prevents the generation of a set of mappings that would match "*An entity sustains to another entity."

subj(X) = = Object1 / contact(Object1,.,.)
pp(to,Y) = = Object2 / contact(.,Object2,.)
subj(X) = = Object1 / support(Object1,.,.)
obj(Z) = = Object2 / support(.,Object2,.)
subj(X) = = Object1 / location(Object1,.,.)
pp(on,X) = = Loc / location(.,Loc,.)
pp(over,X) = = Loc / location(.,Loc,.)
subj(X) = = Object1 / move(Object1,.,.)

Notice that OBJECT1 can be indicated by a subj(X) for **contact, support,** and **move.** This generality can be captured by creating a superordinate type, **concrete-rel,** for these semantic predicates. The predicates **contact, support, location,** and **move** are considered to be subtypes of the type **concrete-rel,** and will all match **concrete-rel.** This is not exactly the same as "Relation (Object1,.,.)," since Relation as a variable would match other predicates as well. The expression "subj(X) = = Object1 / concrete-rel(Object1,.,.)" can be substituted for every instance of a subj(X) syntactic cue. The new set of syntactic cues is represented below.

Standard mapping constraints:

subj(X) = = Object1 / concrete-rel(Object1,.,.)
pp(to,Y) = = Object2 / contact(.,Object2,.)
obj(Z) = = Object2 / support(.,Object2,.)
pp(on,X) = = Loc / location(.,Loc,.)
pp(over,X) = = Loc / location(.,Loc,.)

These cues represent a set of general, "case-like" associations between syntactic constituents and semantic roles that account for most of the mappings found in analyzing the sentences in the pulley domain. There are, however, certain associations between syntactic cues and semantic roles, such as the ones involving semantic role interdependencies and verb idiosyncrasies, which are more complex. These are the associations that caused trouble for the case-frames, i.e., templates. The next two sections demonstrate how they can be handled by the use of the predicate environment.

Preserving verb idiosyncrasies

The predicate environment can also be used to preserve verb idiosyncrasies. This results in an increase in the number of mapping constraints required, since the constraints corresponding to the idiosyncrasies are by definition different from the general constraints. However, there is not the same redundancy that is found with the template approach. With the template approach, the necessity of making verb idiosyncrasies explicit resulted in having to make every possible syntactic realization of a verb explicit. This is not true in inference-driven mapping, since the more specialized mapping constraints can co-exist happily with the general ones, and none of the cross-verb generalizations need to be lost.

For example, in the pulley domain **connect** has a larger choice of syntactic cues than **attach** because of the intermediary. Intermediary syntactic cues are given below with associated predicate environments.

subj(X) = = Inter / effect(Inter,_)
pp(by,Y) = = Inter / effect(Inter,_)

This first set of cues represent general cues for INTERMEDIARY, that apply to several different verbs. The second set given below represent mapping constraints that capture a certain idiosyncrasy of **connect**; that it is acceptable to conjoin OBJECT1 and OBJECT2 in a plural noun phrase, rather than indicating each one by a separate syntactic constituent, as in "Two particles are connected by a string." Other INTERMEDIARY verbs such as **hang** do not share this idiosyncrasy, neither does the other **contact** verb, **attach**. **Attach** and **hang** can be handled by the standard mapping constraints described in the previous section, along with the two additional general INTERMEDIARY constraints. The same cues can be used to produce alternative mappings for **sustain** and **pass**, as illustrated by the following examples:

"An entity sustains another entity."
"An entity passes over another entity."
"An entity passes under another entity."

The predicate environment associated with the idiosyncratic constraints must clearly indicate **connect**. The combination of a **contact** predicate embedded in an **effect** predicate is unique to **connect** in this domain. Two new syntactic cues are introduced for these mapping constraints, a plsubj(X) – meaning a member of a plural noun group that is the subject of the clause, and a plobj(Z) – meaning a member of a plural noun group that is the object of the clause.

Inter cues for **connect:**

plsubj(X) = = Object1 /
    effect(Inter,
        contact(Object1,_,_))

plobj(Z) = = Object1 /
    effect(Inter,
        contact(Object1,_,_))

plsubj(X) = = Object2 /
    effect(Inter,
            contact(_,Object2,_))

plobj(Z) = = Object2 /
    effect(Inter,
            contact(_,Object2,_))

These syntactic cues combined with the previous ones would produce alternative sets of mappings for **connect** that would correspond to the following sentences.

> "A string connects an entity to another entity."
> "An entity is connected to another entity by a string."
> "Two entities are connected by a string."
> "A string connects two objects."

The usefulness of associating syntactic cues with predicate environments can also be illustrated by returning to the example from the beginning of this section. It is the association of pp(to,Y) with **contact** that prevents the set of mappings corresponding to "*An entity sustains to another entity" from being produced.

Preserving interdependencies

The previous examples have all dealt with verb idiosyncrasies. The predicate environment is also appropriate for capturing the type of semantic role interdependency mentioned in section 2.1.1. The example from that section concerned the inadmissibility of a sentence such as "50 lb is supported," which attempts to place a 〈force〉 in the subj(X) position without any reference to something that is supporting the force. The problem is to distinguish between this sentence and sentences like, "The right end of the scaffold is supported," and "50 lb is supported by a man standing on a scaffold," which are considered to be acceptable. The predicate environment can be used to make this distinction by allowing tests to be made on the arguments in the environment. The mapping constraints given below are sufficient to make this distinction.

subj(X) = = Object2
    /   support(Object1,Object2,initial)
      AND isatype(solid,Object2)

subj(X) = = Object2
    /   support(Object1,Object2,initial)
      AND isatype(solid,Object2)
      AND already-instantiated(Object1)

A variation on these tests could be used to capture some of the prepositional dependencies mentioned in section 1.2.3. The goal would be to prevent the production of sets of mappings corresponding to the starred sentences below.

> The door was opened by a key.
> *John opened the door by a key.
> John opened the door with a key.
> The door opens with a key.
> John broke the window with a bat.
> The window was broken with a bat.
> *The window broke with a bat.

These interdependencies concern the restrictions that are placed on potential fillers for semantic roles by already filled semantic roles, and could not be handled by disjunctions. Templates handle them by giving a pattern for every alternative syntactic realization. Although a pp(by,Y) can indicate an INSTRU-MENT, it cannot do so when the AGENT is indicated by the subj(X). Neither can an INSTRUMENT always be indicated by a pp(with,Y) when the PATIENT is indicated by the subject. These interdependencies can be captured by the following mapping constraints.

> pp(by,Y) = = Inter
>   /   cause(Agent,effect(Instrument,Predicate))
>   AND not(already-instantiated(Agent))
>
> pp(with,Y) = = Inter
>   /   cause(Agent,effect(Instrument,
>   break(Object)))
>   AND already-instantiated(Agent)
>
> pp(with,Y) = = Inter
>   /   (contact verbs excluding break)

3.5.3 *Comparing lexical entries to templates*

Section 3.5.1 demonstrated how syntactic realizations can be associated with a lexical entry through the application of mapping constraints. One representation of the realization is the tree that associates the syntactic constituent variable with the semantic role variables (see figure 3.7).

The preceding sections have demonstrated that lexical entries are similar to templates in their ability to preserve verb idiosyncrasies and semantic role interdependencies. Yet they are more general in the sense that several alternative syntactic realizations of one verb can be generated automatically from the lexical entry for the verb and a general set of mapping constraints for the domain. They also allow cross-verb generalizations to be made, since one mapping constraint can apply to several different verbs. The template approach has to provide a separate template for every verb the constraint applies to. As demonstrated below, the lexical entries can be extended to be even more like templates by including prepositional phrases. In this way, the entries and the mapping constraints can be used to produce a set of syntactic realizations that includes all of the templates required by the domain. In fact, with the exception of the INTERMEDIARY lexical entries, the entries and the mapping constraints can be seen as grammar rules that generate alternative sets of mappings. These sets of mappings correspond to alternative syntactic realizations that form a superset of the set of templates for the domain.

Generation with lexical entries

The alternative syntactic realizations examined so far have dealt only with the entries associated with the verbs. To give a more complete account of the possible syntactic realizations of each verb, and how they could be generated using lexical entries, the entries for the decomposition predicates along with their associated mapping constraints need to be included as well. There must also be a categorization of constituents into *top-level constituents* such as subj(X), obj(Y), pp(by,Z) and pp(to,R) which can indicate major syntactic constituents such as subject, object or indirect object that can only be assigned at this primary level, and *lower-level constituents*. Later assignments made to the arguments of the concrete predicate decompositions will be concerned with the lower-level syntactic constituents, which include adjuncts such as pp(at,Q). Including these further decompositions allows the production of a more complete syntactic realization from the following underlying semantic representation.

contact(particle1,string1)
locpt(particle1,particle1)
locpt(rtend1,string1)
sameplace(particle1,rtend1)

To produce a syntactic realization of these predicates, first a set of mappings must be found from the semantic roles to the syntactic constituents. Then a specific syntactic realization can be produced from the set of mappings. This would require an additional component with rules about appropriate verb forms, placing the subject at the beginning of the sentence, ordering prepositional phrases and relative clauses, and so on. Novak used templates to express this type of ordering information implicitly, although Woods did not (see chapter 2). For analysis purposes it does not matter, but for generation purposes it is clear that templates can contain information in addition to the set of mappings which is essential for accurate generation. However, there are other types of information which are also essential for generation which

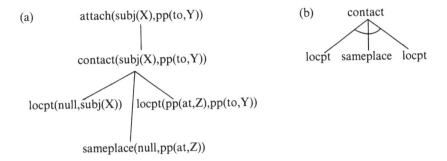

Fig. 3.8. "⟨Object1⟩ is attached to ⟨Object2⟩ at ⟨Locpt1⟩"

cannot be captured so easily in a template. This is discussed more in the next section.

In the semantic representation, the semantic roles are all filled by referents to particular entities. In the syntactic realization, these entities must each be indicated by a particular syntactic constituent. The following set of mappings corresponds to the alternative syntactic realization given below. Mapping a semantic role to null indicates that the semantic role, being an optional semantic role, is not mentioned explicitly in the syntactic realization.

subj(X) = = Object1 = = particle1
pp(to,Y) = = Object2 = = string1
null = = Locpt1 = = particle1
pp(at,Z) = = Locpt2 = = rtend1

The syntactic realization expressed by these mappings matches the sentence, "A particle is attached to a string at its right end." The following template is one way of expressing this set of mappings:

⟨Object1⟩ is attached to ⟨Object2⟩ at ⟨Locpt1⟩

Another way of representing this collection of predicates is as a decomposition tree which illustrates the path through the lexical entries by which the tree is generated (figure 3.8). The Time arguments have been left off for greater simplicity. This could, of course, also be an AND proof tree, representing the application of the Prolog clauses. The three branches from contact would then be "ANDED" together as in part (b).

This type of tree could also be used to display the complete set of mappings, including the semantic roles. In section 3.5.1, a predicate with its semantic roles

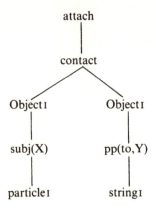

Fig. 3.9.   "A particle is attached to a string . . ."

and the corresponding syntactic constituents was also represented as a tree (figure 3.9.).

In order to combine the predicate-argument trees with the decomposition trees, it is important to keep the argument descendants of **contact** separate from the predicate descendants. This can be done with a three-dimensional tree, where the predicate descendants are along one axis, and the argument descendants are along another. Given a simple predicate tree without any arguments, and tilting it forward, the predicate-arguments can then be connected to the tree with dotted lines, indicating that they descend directly below. The syntactic constituent arguments are given immediately beneath the semantic role arguments (figure 3.10).

The tree in figure 3.10 has a lot of redundancy since many of the arguments are shared by the predicates. A slightly more complex tree results from consolidating the shared predicate-arguments (figure 3.11). The terminal symbols of the tree, i.e., the terms in upper-case, now indicate the set of mappings corresponding to this syntactic realization. By adding a terminal node off of the root of the tree to indicate the verb, *attach*, it can be seen that a particular set of mappings as applied to a decomposition tree gives effectively the same information as the set of mappings given by a template.

In fact, mapping syntactic constituents onto semantic roles as a verb is being composed can be seen as one method for generating a set of mappings corresponding to a particular syntactic realization. In this respect, *the lexical entries with the mapping constraints constitute a set of grammar rules for generating alternative sets of mappings.*

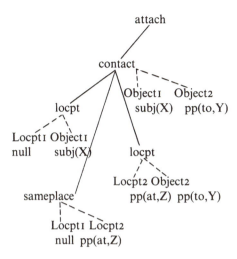

Fig. 3.10. "An entity is attached to an entity at a point"

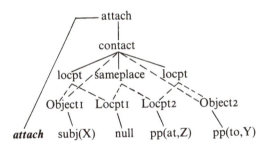

Fig. 3.11. Adding the verb as a terminal node

Limitations with respect to generation

Clearly the lexical entries and mapping constraints can be used to generate sets of mappings that are equivalent to the sets of mappings indicated by templates. However, the current set of mapping constraints and lexical entries would actually generate too many sets of mappings for the domain. Many of them, although not strictly ungrammatical, would still be inappropriate. For example, the syntactic cues alone do not contain any information to prevent the production of the following syntactic realization from the original underlying semantic representation. Notice that the second contact relationship is now being expressed.

An alternative syntactic realization

"A string connects two particles at its right end and at its left end,"

connect
effect(sub(X),contact(plobj(Z),plobj(Q)))
    contact(plobj(Z),subj(X)),
    contact(subj(X),plobj(Q))

    locpt(null,plobj(Z)),
    locpt(pp(at,R),subj(X)),
    sameplace(null,pp(at,R))

    locpt(pp(at,S),subj(X)),
    locpt(null,plobj(Q)),
    sameplace(pp(at,S),null)

This syntactic realization corresponds to the following set of mappings:

subj(X) = = Inter = = string1
plobj(Z) = = Object1 = = particle1
plobj(Z) = = Object2 = = particle2
pp(at,X) = = Locpt1 = = rtend1
pp(at,X) = = Locpt2 = = ltend1

which could also be represented by this template:

⟨Inter⟩ connects ⟨Object1,Object2⟩ at ⟨Locpt1⟩ and at ⟨Locpt2⟩

The sentence corresponding to this syntactic realization might not be strictly ungrammatical, but is somewhat awkward to say the least. However, there is already an assumption that each top-level constituent can only be used once. Allowing this same assumption to hold true for prepositional phrases would prevent the generation of successive "at" prepositional phrases. This assumption alone is insufficient to restrict the production of lexical entries to only those that correspond to well-formed sentences. The sentence corresponding to the previous syntactic realization is grammatical, and is not awkward, but is not as informative as this one. Neither one is the most appropriate expression of the information in the semantic representation.

To consider seriously using a method like this for generating all the possible syntactic expressions of a verb, much more exploration of constituent assignment etiquette is necessary. Strategies for choosing which set of semantic roles should be expressed in a particular sentence are essential. Such strategies would have to use information about discourse coherence and limitations on how much information can be politely contained in a single syntactic clause. The predicate environment is an inappropriate vehicle for expressing this type of information. The rules of assignment etiquette should be general to the domain, and should be expressed at a "meta-level," where they could be used to guide a generation interpreter. There would also have to be rules that could choose the most appropriate syntactic realization of a semantic representation from the set of alternatives that would be generated. In summary, lexical entries are likely candidates for sentence generation, but require several additional strategies for acceptable syntactic expression of semantic roles. Incidentally, the template method would also be inadequate for making these types of choices, and would require additional strategies as well.

3.6   Filling semantic roles

Section 3.5 concentrated on producing a set of mappings between syntactic constituents and semantic roles that could correspond to a particular syntactic realization. This section explains how this important component of semantic analysis can be integrated with other components to ensure the instantiation of the semantic roles with the most appropriate noun phrase referents. The ultimate goal of producing a set of mappings is to instantiate the semantic roles with referents of the syntactic constituents. The referent of each syntactic constituent must be tested for certain semantic properties associated with the semantic role, and a check must be made that the suggested set of mappings includes all of the obligatory semantic roles. *Semantic constraints*, as defined below, are used for testing semantic properties of noun phrase referents, and *pragmatic constraints*, defined in section 3.6.2, test that the obligatory semantic roles have been filled, and decide whether or not unfilled optional semantic roles should be filled by deduction.

3.6.1   Semantic constraints

Section 3.2 introduced the entity hierarchy, and the **isatype, haspart** and **hasprop** rules that can be used to traverse this hierarchy. These are the tools used by the semantic constraints to test semantic features of noun phrase referents. In general, OBJECT1s and OBJECT2s are expected to be solid entities, so it is only necessary for a semantic constraint to test "isatype(solid,Object1)" of the role in question. However, just as the syntactic cues for a particular semantic role can change according to the predicate to which that role is an argument, so can the desired semantic feature. To allow for this, generalizations about semantic features for the semantic roles can be associated with the predicate environment in the same way that syntactic cues are. Since semantic features must be at least partially determined by the type of predicates produced, this may seem more intuitive than the association of syntactic cues with the predicate level.

The following examples use a notation that is similar to the notation used for syntactic cues, with the predicate environment following the "/." An important difference is that the semantic constraint is not unifying one variable name with another; it is predicating something over a variable and a constant, so the " = = " notation is no longer used. Instead, the semantic role can be found as an argument to a predicate, which is usually either **isatype**, **hasprop**, or **haspart**. The constraints in the following example take the form: predicate(constant,semantic-role) / predicate environment. The first two examples state that OBJECT1s and OBJECT2s are expected to be **solid** entities in a physical **concrete-rel**. The second two examples state that in an arithmetic relation such as **equals**, OBJECT1s and OBJECT2s are expected to be **quantities**. The last example states that an INTERMEDIARY that is an argument to an **effect** predicate is expected to be a line segment.

isatype(solid,Object1) / concrete-rel(Object1,_,_)
isatype(solid,Object2) / concrete-rel(_,Object2,_)
isatype(quantity,Object1) / equals(Object1,_,_)
isatype(quantity,Object2) / equals(_,Object2,_)
isatype(line-seg,Inter) / effect(Inter,_)

There is one semantic constraint, the **locpt** constraint, that uses a combination of these simple hierarchy rules. Location points of entities have to be "points," which corresponds to a simple feature check, but they also have to be points on a particular entity, which can only be tested by looking at the instantiation of the other argument of the **locpt** predicate – another example of the usefulness of the predicate environment. This can be written as:

haspt(Y,L) / locpt(L,Y,Per)

where L is the possible location point, and Y is the entity of which it is supposed to be a location point. The predicate **haspt** simply tests that L is a point, and that it is a part of Y, using the **isatype** and **haspart** predicates. The definition of **haspt** is:

haspt(Y,L) ←
    isatype(point,L),
    haspart(Y,L).

If a semantic constraint for any of the proposed mappings in a given set were to fail, then that set is assumed to be inaccurate, and another set must be found. For the pulley domain, there are no alternative possible semantic features for a semantic role as there are alternative possible syntactic cues. Testing the semantic features is therefore more straightforward than selecting appropriate syntactic cues.

3.6.2 Pragmatic constraints

Even if all the semantic features for a proposed set of mappings test out correctly, that does not mean that there will then be a noun phrase referent for every semantic role. Section 3.5 used an example of a location point that was not given an explicit syntactic realization, and was simply mapped to null. This is all right for optional roles, but not for obligatory ones.

Chapter 1 defined two different kinds of semantic roles, optional and obligatory. Obligatory roles have to appear in a syntactic realization of the verb. Optional roles may appear in a syntactic realization, but do not have to. Inference-driven mapping has to recognize that if a proposed set of mappings has not included an obligatory role, then that set must be rejected in favor of an alternative set. It also has to decide whether an optional role that has not been mapped to a syntactic constituent should be filled by deduction. This decision is made partly by subdividing optional roles into two classes; optional roles that are *essential* and optional roles that are not. The *essential* roles must be filled even if there is no syntactic constituent. The location INTERMEDIARY in "a pulley is suspended from another pulley" is an example of an essential role. Essential roles are often filled by defaults. The default for a location INTERMEDIARY is "string57," indicating an arbitrary flexible line-segment. An essential role that does not have a default must be filled by deduction. Pragmatics handles all of these tasks: (1) causing failure when an obligatory role has not been filled, (2) filling essential roles by defaults or by deductions, (3) allowing optional roles that are not essential to remain unfilled.

Pragmatic constraints take much more changeable forms than syntactic and semantic constraints. The semantic role and the predicate environment are still always included. However, the simple check that was sufficient for a semantic constraint is now occasionally expanded to a set of predicates. On the other hand, a simple pragmatic constraint for supplying a default value is very similar to a mapping constraint. The following constraint supplies gravity as a default value for the AGENT of a **cause-motion** event. Notice since "gravity" is a constant, this constraint can only apply if the semantic role has not already been instantiated.

$$\text{gravity} = = \text{agent} \ / \ \text{cause-motion(agent,move(\_,\_,\_))}$$

Location points are essential for an appropriate representation of a **contact** or a **support** relationship. If they are not indicated by a pp(at,X), they must still be filled. All pragmatics has to do is, given the entity that is in need of a location point, find a part of that entity that is the shape of a point and that is not at the **sameplace** as any other location point. This is accomplished by a **findpt** predicate, which is defined below. If the entity is itself a point, as in a particle or a pulley, then it is always its own location point, a kind of default value. This is captured by the first **findpt** clause. The second clause uses **haspart** to pick a part corresponding to that type of entity, and then uses **freepoint** to test whether or not the part has the shape of a point and is not already at the **sameplace** as something else.

>findpt(Obj1,Obj1) ←
>   isatype(point,Obj1)
>
>findpt(Obj1,Part1) ←
>   haspart(Obj1,Part1),
>   freepoint(Part1)

3.6.3 *Similarities between semantics and pragmatics*

The pragmatic constraint for LOCPT1 is very similar to the semantic constraint for the same semantic role. The major difference is that usually when the semantic constraint is applied the semantic roles are already filled, whereas the goal of applying the pragmatic constraint is to fill an unfilled role. Chapter 4 gives an application of the same semantic constraint where it does in fact fill an unfilled role, the OBJECT1, and in doing so performs more like a pragmatic constraint than a semantic one. This unexpected similarity between semantics and pragmatics gives rise to interesting questions about the traditional dividing lines between semantics and pragmatics that should be explored further.

3.6.4 *Summary*

This chapter has presented the formalization of the pulley domain, including the entity hierarchy, the lexical entries of the verbs and case predicates, and the syntactic, semantic and pragmatic constraints on the filling of the semantic roles which are the predicate-arguments to the lexical entries. The next chapter explains how the lexical entries are interpreted procedurally to drive the semantic analysis of the domain. It is during this interpretation that the constraints are applied to find a set of mappings between the semantic roles of the entries involved and the syntactic constituents of the sentence.

4 Inference-driven mapping

This chapter presents the semantic processor that performs the semantic role assignments at the same time as it is decomposing the verb representation. Chapter 3 has described how semantic roles are defined as arguments to the semantic predicates that appear in the lexical entries. These arguments are instantiated as the lexical entries are *interpreted*. A possible instantiation of a predicate-argument is the referent of a syntactic constituent of the appropriate syntactic and semantic type. The syntactic constituent instantiations corres- pond to the desired mappings of syntactic constituents onto semantic roles. Other instantiations can be made using pragmatic information to deduce appropriate fillers from previous knowledge about other syntactic constituents or from general world knowledge.

These tasks are performed by interpreting the lexical entries procedurally similarly to the way that Prolog interprets Horn clauses procedurally [Kowalski, 1979]. The lexical entries are in fact Horn clauses, and the predicate-arguments that correspond to the semantic roles are terms that consist of function symbols with one argument. The procedural interpretation drives the application of the lexical entries, and allows the function symbols to be "evaluated" as a means of instantiating the arguments. The predicate environments associated with the mapping constraints correspond to states that may or may not occur during the procedural interpretation of the entries. Thus the same argument can be constrained differently depending on the state the verb interpretation is in. The state can vary according to instantiations of arguments or by the predicates included in the predicate decomposition. This allows the same lexical entry for a verb to match several different syntactic realizations of the verb without losing necessary context dependencies. It also allows an entry to decompose differently given different instantiations of predicate-arguments. The trace of the interpretation of the lexical entries corresponds to the set of predicates that make up the expanded representation of the verb. The interpreter for inference-driven mapping is completely domain independent which makes it easily transportable to other limited domains which can be similarly formalized.

As demonstrated in the last chapter, the lexical entries can actually be thought of as grammar rules, in that a particular verb entry and the predicate entries that can be associated with it can be combined with the general

mapping constraints to produce all the possible sets of mappings corresponding to syntactic expressions of that verb. The processor effectively performs
analysis by synthesis by using the generative power of the entries to produce a
set of mappings for the syntactic parse. This could obviously be done by
generating the sets of mappings that correspond to all the possible realizations
of a single verb and then selecting the one that matches the parse, in much the
same way that templates are used. The interpreter gains a great deal of
efficiency over this approach by comparing each possible mapping with the
constituent list of the clause and immediately discarding those mappings that
involve constituents not on the constituent list. Only one complete set of
mappings is ever generated, the one that matches the constituent list. These
sets are achieved almost deterministically by using the order of the arguments
of the semantic predicates to control the order in which possible mappings are
considered. The ordering of the mapping constraints and the arguments
follows the natural ordering of syntactic constituents as defined by the precedence relations mentioned in chapter 1. On the rare occasion when the
mappings are not straightforward, the system backtracks to find a new set, as
described in section 4.3.3. The process of matching a syntactic parse to a lexical
entry is almost as efficient as template matching, and includes the performance
of several other semantic tasks as well, such as the pragmatic instantiation of
unfilled roles and verb expansion.

In summary, inference-driven mapping performs analysis by synthesis efficiently and directly using lexical entries for the verbs. One verb entry produces
alternative semantic representations given different sets of syntactic constituents. This allows the processor to cope with the verb idiosyncrasies and
semantic role interdependencies handled by templates. The representations are
in the form of multiple embedded semantic predicates that provide a flexible
and detailed "deep" semantic representation.

4.1   Analysis by synthesis

In inference-driven mapping the traditional syntactic cues associated with
semantic roles perform an essential part of the efficient selection of the
mappings from syntactic constituents to semantic roles. Even more significant
advantages to this approach stem from combining the selection of mappings
with the decomposition of the verb. Inference-driven mapping first selects the
set of mappings for the semantic roles of the verb decomposition. It then looks
for mappings for the semantic roles of the decomposition of the decomposition, and so on, as illustrated by the flow-chart in figure 4.1.

Since a sentence rarely contains an explicit syntactic expression of every
possible semantic role associated with a verb, many of these roles will not find
mappings to syntactic constituents. Inference-driven mapping attempts to
deduce possible fillers for these unfilled semantic roles as soon as it is clear that

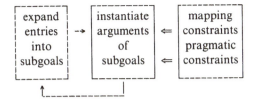

Fig. 4.1.   Basic structure of inference-driven mapping

an appropriate syntactic constituent is not available. Combining these tasks illuminates the close ties between the semantic constraints on the possible mappings and the pragmatic constraints on deducing fillers.

4.1.1   Overview

As mentioned above, one method of analysis by synthesis would be to generate all of the possible syntactic constituent instantiations associated with a particular lexical entry as described in section 3.5. Then each possible syntactic realization could be matched against the syntactic parse of the sentence, just as templates are currently matched against syntactic parses. This section discusses the gains in efficiency occasioned by pruning the generation tree so that only the matching syntactic realization is produced, and this is how inference-driven mapping is implemented.

In comparing the generation of all possible syntactic realizations to the traditional template method, there are two different criteria to be compared: processing requirements and space requirements. The generation approach would result in an increase in computational requirements due to the repeated generation of all the syntactic realizations from lexical entries with a decrease in space requirements due to the smaller representational requirements for those lexical entries and the mapping constraints. The major advantage of the generation approach over the template approach comes from the more general level of representation. This simplifies extending the domain. The multiple embedded predicates of the lexical entries also represent a level of representation that is "deeper" than the canonical level most current systems derive from the schemas. The question is whether or not these advantages are outweighed by the additional computational overhead.

This question can be sidestepped by getting rid of most of the computational overhead. A significant increase in computational efficiency is made by only generating one syntactic realization that is guaranteed to match the sentence. This is accomplished by comparing each mapping constraint that is a candidate for a set of possible mappings with the actual syntactic constituents found by the parse, and discarding any that are not on the constituent list. Only those constraints that correspond to syntactic constituents are left to be considered. After having selected a possible mapping for a semantic role, the referent of the constituent is examined for the appropriate semantic properties of that semantic role. If it does not have these semantic properties, then this mapping is rejected and another mapping for that semantic role is selected. This is the only time more than one possible mapping for a semantic role is considered, and is the only reason the process is not completely deterministic.

Further increases in efficiency are made by comparing the mapping constraints to the constituents in a well-defined order. This order is naturally established by the syntactic parse, where the subject is always first, followed by the objects, etc. It is also seen in the precedence relations between subject, object and BY prepositional phrase mentioned in section 1.2.3. In chapter 1 these precedence relations are defined by the semantic roles, AGENT, INSTRUMENT and PATIENT. In the pulley domain these same precedence relations hold for AGENT, INTERMEDIARY, OBJECT 1 and OBJECT2. This ordering is preserved in the embedded nature of the lexical entries, since the AGENT must be an argument to the outermost predicate, the INTERMEDIARY must be an argument to the next outermost predicate and the OBJECT1 is always an argument to the innermost predicate. This allows left-to-right "evaluation" of the function symbols of the predicate-arguments of the lexical entries to ensure that the appropriate ordering is followed. Using the syntactic parse of the sentence being analyzed to prune the possible mapping constraints for each semantic role as it occurs in the lexical entry allows the selection of mappings to be made almost deterministically.

4.1.2   *Procedural interpretation of lexical entries*

This section describes the interpreter for inference-driven mapping. The primary task of the interpreter, given a syntactic parse, is to prove the well-formedness of a particular verb usage. This includes selecting a lexical entry suggested by the verb, finding mappings from the syntactic constituents of the verb usage to the semantic roles of the lexical entries, filling any unfilled semantic roles, and testing consistency with previous information. The semantic roles of the verb correspond to the arguments of the semantic predicates that make up the lexical entries. The arguments of the general predicates are actually functions that get "evaluated" during the procedural interpretation, thus instantiating the semantic roles [Goguen and Mesequer, 1988]. An instantiation may be indicated by a syntactic constituent or may be deduced from pragmatic information. The functions do not always succeed in finding instantiations, in which case the argument corresponding to the role remains uninstantiated.

The lexical entries already presented make up a major portion of the code for inference-driven mapping as implemented in Prolog. The interpreter explained in this section sits on top of the Prolog interpreter and interprets the lexical entries procedurally similarly to the way Prolog interprets Horn clauses procedurally. The lexical entries were written backwards since this is the way they are used by the interpreter. Backward implications, P ← Q, R, can be read as, "If P needs to be proved, try and prove Q and then try to prove R." Since the clauses are "proven" by a resolution theorem-prover, "starting the program" is accomplished by negating P. The resolution theorem-prover churns away, performing resolutions in an attempt to produce the null clause, and automatically backtracking to try every possible choice [Kowalski, 1979].

For instance, when asked to prove that the usage of *attach* in a particular sentence is semantically well-formed, the interpreter picks up the lexical entry whose left-hand side matches "*attach*." Before looking for a rule that corresponds to the right-hand side of the *attach* rule, the interpreter "evaluates"[1] the function symbols of the predicate-arguments to return values that represent the mappings from syntactic constituents to semantic roles. The mapping constraints described in chapter 3 are used to suggest possible syntactic constituents as fillers for the semantic roles. If there are no appropriate syntactic constituents, the "functions" can use pragmatic constraints to deduce possible fillers. Examples of the function "evaluation," including the application of pragmatic constraints, are given later.

Implementation

The first task of the interpreter is to retrieve the syntactic parse associated with the clause. The syntactic parses are stored in **parse** predicates which have three arguments. The first argument is a token identifying the particular clause. The second argument corresponds to the verb of the clause, and the third argument contains a list of the syntactic constituents occurring in the clause. Executing **parse**(clause1,Verb,Constituents) is equivalent to a data base lookup that causes Verb and Constituents to be instantiated. If the clause associated with clause1 is "A particle is attached to a string at its end . . ." the entry for **parse** is:

> parse(clause1,*attach*,
> [subj(particle1),pp(to,string1),pp(at,right1)])

In order to finish executing successfully, there must not be any constituents left in the list. If there are, it is assumed that the interpreter has failed to find the appropriate set of mappings, and it automatically backtracks to try and find an alternative set. If the constituent list is empty, then the assumption is that the set of mappings is appropriate, and that this particular verb usage is indeed well-formed. The instantiated decomposition of the verb that has just

---

[1]Login, a recent implementation of a typed logic programming language, might prove to be an interesting vehicle for implementing this approach [Ait Kaci and Nasr, 1986]. In Prolog abstract data types and function evaluation have to be simulated for inference-driven mapping.

been achieved constitutes the semantic representation of the sentence and is added to the knowledge base.

The interpreter for inference-driven mapping is modeled after the Prolog interpreter for Prolog given in the Prolog DEC-10 manual, with a few additions. The environment, the proof history and the constituent list, are carried along as an argument, and plural noun groups are distributed according to the possibilities outlined in chapter 1. The most important innovation is highlighted by the following Prolog clause, which is a part of the complete interpreter given in appendix B. Assuming that P is the goal to be "executed," the normal Prolog interpreter matches P to the left-hand side of some clause, and then "executes" the right-hand side of that clause, i.e., Q for the clause P ← Q. In inference-driven mapping, before the search for a clause whose left-hand side matches P is made, an attempt is made to instantiate any uninstantiated variables in P. This step is indicated by the predicate "bind(P,_,_)," in the following example. Then the "define([P,Q])" predicate searches for a rule whose left-hand side matches the newly instantiated P, and whose right-hand side matches Q. The last step, "execute(Q,_,_)" indicates that Q is now set up as the goal to be executed, and the process begins again.

```
execute(P,_,_) ←
    bind(P,_,_),
    define([P,Q]),
    execute(Q,_,_)
```

The instantiation of the variables that occurs during the satisfaction of "bind" is explained in the next section.

4.1.3   *Filling semantic roles*

This section explains "bind," which applies the mapping constraints as well as the semantic and pragmatic constraints defined in chapter 3 to return "values" for the semantic roles, and in doing so simulates function evaluation. The goal of the evaluation is to return an appropriate referent of a noun phrase for the semantic role represented by the predicate-argument. If no suitable mappings are available from the constituent list, pragmatic information is used to deduce a possible referent, as explained in section 4.3.

In this implementation, the referents of the noun phrases have already been determined, so the task is really selecting the noun phrase, and then returning the referent associated with it. In a later implementation, an actual reference resolution component is called at this point which produces a potential referent and uses the semantic constraint on the role to test its suitability [Palmer *et al.*, 1986].

Applying the constraints

To avoid unnecessary complication, up until now the predicate

contact(Object1,Object2,Time)

has simply been instantiated as

contact(particle1,particle2,duration)

However, it is useful to preserve the information that PARTICLE1 and PARTI-CLE2 are playing the roles of OBJECT1 and OBJECT2. The device of a "typed function" can be used in the following way. The function symbol "Object1" can be thought of as a *typed* function, placing *constraints* on the type of argument that can be returned as its value [Goguen and Mesequer, 1988]. The "evaluation" of the function is performed by the "bind" predicate. The main purpose the function symbols serve is to preserve the name of the semantic role involved. When

contact(Object1,Object2,Time)

has been instantiated to

contact(particle1,particle2,duration)

the variable names have been lost, and the semantic role is indicated in a purely positional fashion. Adding the function symbols preserves the semantic role information, and encapsulates the mappings between the semantic roles and the referents. The instantiated predicate is now

contact(object1(particle1),object2(particle2),time(duration))

The flowchart in figure 4.2 describes the manner in which the semantic roles are filled. The "binder" uses the syntactic constraints associated with a particular semantic role to suggest syntactic constituents as potential candidates for instantiation. The list of syntactic constituents from the parse is examined to see if it contains any of the suggestions. If it does, a semantic constraint is used to test the suggested syntactic constituent for appropriate semantic features. If this test is successful, the pragmatic constraints are applied just in case this latest instantiation has supplied a new piece of information that could be useful to pragmatics. If there are no successful syntactic constituents, the pragmatic constraints are still applied, this time in an attempt to supply an appropriate filler for the semantic role.

The following clauses correspond to the process just described and define the algorithm to be followed for the filling of semantic roles:

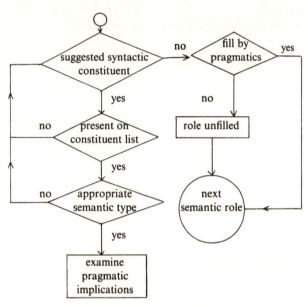

Fig. 4.2.   Filling a semantic role

Binding procedure.

choose(Arg,Rel,_,_) ←
        parsed(Arg,Rel,_,_),
        check(Arg,Rel,_,_),
        select(Arg,Rel,_,_).

choose(Arg,Rel_,_) ←
        select(Arg,Rel,_,_)

The first argument of **choose**, Arg, is the argument to be instantiated. The second argument, Rel, corresponds to the current predicate environment of Arg. **Parsed** applies the syntactic constraints, **check** applies the semantic constraints to the result of **parse**, and **select** applies the pragmatic constraints. The pragmatic constraints are generally thought of as providing fillers for unfilled semantic roles, but it is useful to apply the pragmatic constraints upon choosing a referent to a syntactic constituent as a filler. Sometimes the instantiation that has just been made will provide a crucial piece of information that allows pragmatics to make an important deduction. Calling **select** cannot in any way undo the filling of the semantic role, but it could possibly deduce something new that could not have been deduced before.

If either **parsed** or **check** fails, then no appropriate syntactic constituent is available for the semantic role in question. The second possibility for instantiating a semantic role is the application of pragmatic constraints, as indicated by the right-hand side of the second **choose** clause. This indicates another call to **select**, with the hope that **select** will find a likely binding such as an available default value. It is possible that **select** will not be able to fill the role, in which case it simply leaves it as an uninstantiated variable.

The next section describes how **parsed** and **check** apply the syntactic and semantic constraints defined in chapter 3.

Performing mappings

The actual code for the syntactic and semantic constraints is very similar to the notation that was used to express them in chapter 3, and this code simplifies the task of applying them. For example, the Prolog predicate given below corresponds to the following mapping rule:

Object1 = = subj(X) / concrete-rel(Object1,_,_)

The code for the syntactic constraints takes the form of predicates such as syntax(ARG1,ARG2,ARG3). ARG1 corresponds to a semantic role that has been expressed as a predicate-argument in a lexical entry. ARG2 corresponds to the type of syntactic constituent that might be expected to indicate this semantic role. ARG3 corresponds to the predicate environment that ARG1 should have for this generalization to hold.

```
syntax(object1(Obj),
    subj(Obj),
    concrete-rel(object1(Obj),_,_))
```

The "object1" function symbol indicates a typed function; in other words, the value of the function must be of type "object1." The semantic role is an object1(Obj), which is typically an argument to a **support** or **contact** relationship. The syntactic cue for an object1(Obj) could be the **subject** of the clause, i.e. **subj**(Obj). The suggested syntactic constituents associated with mapping constraints are represented in the program as a function symbol with one argument. The function symbol indicates the "type" of syntactic constituent, and the argument is generally a variable to be instantiated with a referent for the syntactic constituent. The predicate environment for this semantic role is **concrete-rel**(object1(Obj),_,_). **Concrete-rel** can be read as any physical relation such as **contact**, **support** or **move**; object1(Obj) is the first argument of the predicate; and the other two arguments are irrelevant.

To apply this syntactic constraint, it is only necessary for **parsed** to pick up a syntactic constraint for the semantic role in question, and delete the suggested syntactic constituent for the constituent list. The following code does just that:

```
parsed(Arg,Rel,_,_) ←
    syntax(Arg,Constraint,Rel),
    delete(Constraint,Const,Nconst)
```

When **parsed** is called, Rel, the current predicate environment, must match with ARG3 of a **syntax** constraint, the predicate environment of the constraint, for that syntactic constraint to apply. Prolog unification can be used to test the matching of the predicate environments automatically by giving the arguments the same variable name.[2] The second argument of **syntax** is the syntactic constituent that might indicate a possible referent. If the match succeeds, and that particular syntactic constituent is a member of Const, the constituent List,[3] it will be deleted from Const, producing Nconst, a new list of syntactic constituents that no longer contains it. In the original **syntax** rule, the semantic role and the syntactic constituent share the same variable, i.e., Obj. This variable is now bound to the referent of the syntactic constituent, thus binding the semantic role, Arg, to that referent as well. If **parsed** succeeds, it returns with Arg instantiated with a potential referent. A successful semantic analysis should result in every constituent being removed from the constituent list, indicating that all of the constituents have been mapped to semantic roles.

The coding of the semantic constraints is also very similar to the notation that has already been used. The code for the following semantic constraint is given below.

> isatype(solid,Object1) / concrete-rel(Object1,_,_)

The semantic constraints are also of the form: **semantics**(ARG1,ARG2,ARG3). ARG1 corresponds to a semantic role that has been expressed as a predicate argument in a lexical entry. ARG2 corresponds to the semantic test that should be performed on instantiations of this semantic role. Arg3 corresponds to the predicate environment that ARG1 should have for this generalization to hold. The semantic role in the example is indicated by "OBJECT1(Obj)." The semantic test to be performed on this semantic role is the "isatype(solid,Obj)," ensuring that the instantiation of the semantic role is a solid entity. This test is only to be performed if the predicate environment of this semantic role is "concrete-rel(object1(Obj),_,_))."

> semantics(object1(Obj),
>   isatype(solid,Obj),
>   concrete-rel(object1(Obj),_,_))

The code for **check**, given below, performs very similarly to **parsed**, but rather than delete a constituent from a list, **check** asks Prolog to prove that a **semantic** constraint holds for this instantiation. If **check** fails, **parsed** tries again with a new **syntax** constraint. If there are no more appropriate **syntax** constraints, **parsed** fails as well, and the variable is left uninstantiated unless pragmatic information can instantiate it.

---

[2] Preserving the generality in the syntax constraints involves using **concrete-rel** as a supertype of **support**, **contact** and **move**. Prolog unification does not coerce data types, so the pulley domain implementation uses a **match** algorithm given in appendix B to compare the predicate environments.

[3] The constituent List and current predicates are carried around as "global variables."

```
check(Arg,Rel,_,_) ←
    semantics(Arg,Constraint,Rel),
    Constraint
```

Pragmatic constraints are applied by **select**, and they handle three tasks: (1) causing failure when an obligatory role has not been filled, (2) filling essential roles by defaults or by deductions, (3) allowing optional roles that are not essential to remain unfilled. They take a slightly different form from syntactic and semantic constraints; "pragmatics(ARG1,ARG2,_,_) ← BODY." ARG1 is the semantic role as usual, while this time ARG2 is the predicate environment. The other argument places indicate the environment variables, since pragmatics occasionally needs access to the proof history. The BODY can be of arbitrary complexity, since some semantic roles require complicated deductions in order to be filled. Pragmatic constraints that are used to indicate default values are the simplest, and have null BODIES.

The following code corresponds to this pragmatics constraint from chapter 3:

$$\text{gravity} = = \text{Agent} / \text{cause-motion(Agent,move(\_,\_,\_))}$$

This constraint supplies gravity as a default value for the AGENT of a cause-motion event. Notice that this rule can only apply if the semantic role has not already been given a filler.

```
pragmatics(agent(gravity),
    cause-motion(agent(gravity),move(_,_,_)),_,_)
```


4.2 The processor in action

The goal of inference-driven mapping is to "prove" that a particular verb usage is well-formed. This is accomplished by "proving" each component of the verb decomposition. At the end of this process, the instantiated predicates that correspond to the "proven" components contain all of the information normally included in a semantic representation of the verb. In the template method the detailed representation is inferred from the presence of the verb. In inference-driven mapping the "deep" semantic representation is the same as the verb decomposition, and is tested for plausibility and well-formedness while selecting the appropriate lexical entry for the verb. There is no need to apply further inference rules to derive the semantic representation, and the instantiated decomposition is simply added to the knowledge base. Inference-driven mapping shares a key assumption with most other semantic processors; that the clause being examined does in fact reflect an appropriate verb usage and that the analysis will succeed.

While proving well-formedness, the predicate-arguments become instantiated by syntactic constituents and by pragmatic deductions. These instantiations effect how the predicates will be decomposed, since some lexical entries only apply to certain predicate-argument instantiations. Particular instantiations also restrict future instantiations by constraining the application of mapping constraints through the use of the predicate environment. Each new instantiation can be seen as producing a new state of the procedural interpretation. Given a particular state, the number of new states that can be achieved next is very limited, making the processing for any single verb entry almost deterministic.

The application of the lexical entries is illustrated by the following examples.

4.2.1   A simple example

This section presents a detailed example of the processor in action. This example is very similar to the example in chapter 1, but is presented in more detail here, with actual traces of the program's performance. The traces have been edited so that they contain only the rule applications that pertain to the discussion. The sentence to be analyzed is "A particle is attached to a string at its end." The input to the processor is given below, where particle1, string1 and right1 are **referents** for "the particle," "the string" and "the end of the string."

*Verb: **attach***

Constituent list:

[subj(particle1),pp(to,string1),pp(at,right1)]

The processor is given execute(***attach***) as the goal, and applies the only lexical entry that matches, given below. This entry has the effect of decomposing ***attach*** into **contact**.

Decomposition:

attach ←
        contact(object1(O1),object2(O2),time(duration))

Finding mappings

Before decomposing **contact**, the task of filling the semantic roles OBJECT1(O1) and OBJECT2(O2) must be performed. The first suggested syntactic constituent that is found by **parsed** is subj(Obj), which is instantiated by "subj(particle1)" in the application of the following syntactic constraint.

        syntax(object1(Obj),
          subj(Obj),
          concrete-rel(object1(Obj),_,_))

The predicate environment of the first semantic role, OBJECT1(O1), is "contact(object1(O1),object2(O2),time(duration))." This is passed as the second argument to **parsed**, and is matched to the predicate environment of the constraint, "concrete-rel(object1(Obj),_,_)." In applying the constraint, **parsed** deletes subj(particle1) from the constituent list. The final result is the instantiation of OBJECT(O1) to particle1, the referent of the subject. This is illustrated by the following mapping, which represents the first mapping in the set of mappings being generated for the sentence. Alternative syntactic mappings for this particular role are no longer considered, unless backtracking occurs. In this case, backtracking does not occur, since **check** recognizes particle1 as a solid object, which fulfills the semantic constraint required here. Pragmatics has nothing to add.[4]

object1(O1) = = subj(O1) = = particle1

The next role to be filled is OBJECT2(O2), with a predicate environment of

"contact(object1(particle1),object2(O2),time(duration))"

The first syntactic constraint whose predicate environment matches is given below, and suggests pp(to,X) as a syntactic constituent mapping.

syntax(object2(Obj),
    pp(to,Obj),
    contact(_,object2(Obj),_))

In applying this constraint, **parsed** deletes **pp** (to,string1) from the constituent list. This results in string1 being bound to Obj, and then to O2 as illustrated by the following mapping, the second mapping to be added to the set. The only semantic requirement of this OBJECT2(Obj) is that it also be a solid object, which a string is, so **check** is also satisfied. Once again, pragmatics has nothing to add.

object2(O2) = = pp(to,O2) = = string1

The third argument to **contact** is "time(duration)" which in this domain does not act as a semantic role. In any event, it already has a binding, duration, which is abbreviated to "d" in the program traces. The process of binding the semantic roles that has just been discussed is illustrated by the partial trace in figure 4.3. The clause following "call:" corresponds to a goal that is being "proven" by the program. Success results in the program "exiting with" the clause, including any new instantiations that may have occurred during the "proof." A "proof" usually requires the establishment of certain subgoals, which are also indicated by an embedded "call:" and whose satisfaction is

---

[4] The use of the = = here does not correspond to a strict interpretation of unification, since "string" would not unify directly with the pp function symbol. However, its real purpose is to indicate the mapping of string1 onto the OBJECT2 semantic role, and it is sufficient for this. The reader should assume that string1 instantiates Obj.

```
call: bind(
    contact(object1(O1),object2(O2),time(d)),_,_)

    ⋮

    call: parsed(object1(O1),
        contact(object1(O1),object2(O2),time(d)))
    exit with: parsed(object1(particle1),
        contact(object1(particle1),object2(O2),time(d)))
    call: check(object1(particle1),
        contact(object1(particle1),object2(O2),time(d)))
    exit with: check(object1(particle1),
        contact(object1(particle1),object2(O2),time(d)))
    call: select(object1(particle1),
        contact(object1(particle1),object2(O2),time(d)))
    exit with: select(object1(particle1),
        contact(object1(particle1),object2(O2),time(d)))

    ⋮

    call: parsed(object2(O2),
        contact(object1(particle1),object2(O2),time(d)))
    exit with: parsed(object2(string1),
        contact(object1(particle1),object2(string1),time(d)))

    ⋮

exit with: bind(
        contact(object1(particle1),object2(string1),time(d)),_,_)
```

Figure 4.3: "Instantiating OBJECT1(O1) and OBJECT2(O2)"

signaled by a matching "exit with." This example begins with a "call" to bind(**contact**(object1(O1),object2(O2),time(d)),_,_). It then skips to the first call to **parsed** which has been passed "OBJECT1(O1)" as the semantic role to be filled. This call successfully exits, and the suggested mapping as indicated by "OBJECT1(particle1)" is passed to **check** to perform the required semantic checking. This is also successful, so "OBJECT1(particle1)" is finally passed to **select** which in this case does not even perform any tests. Having finished with the first semantic role, **parsed** is soon called again with the second semantic role, "OBJECT2(O2)" and the process begins again. After applying a syntactic constraint as described above, **parsed** exits with the semantic role instantiated to "OBJECT2(string1)." The following calls to **check** and **select** are omitted, since they are essentially the same as the previous ones. Eventually, the call to bind exits successfully, with the previously unfilled semantic roles having now been instantiated.

Decomposing contact

It is now possible to decompose **contact**(object1(particle1),object2(string1), time(d)) by applying the lexical entry whose left-hand side matches. This will, of course, be the original **contact** lexical entry from section 3.3.1, given below, with function symbols added to each argument, and a time period added as well.

> contact(object1(O1),object2(O2),time(_)) ←
>   locpt(locpt(L1),object1(O1),time(_)),
>   locpt(locpt(L1),object2(O2),time(_)),
>   sameplace(locpt(L1),locpt(L2),time(_)),

When **contact**(object1(particle1),object2(string1),time(d)) is matched to the left-hand side of this lexical entry, the variables in OBJECT1(O1), OBJECT2(O2) and time(_) become instantiated with particle1, string1 and d respectively. The general lexical entry for decomposition of **contact** becomes in this case the following, partially instantiated decomposition.

Decomposition:

> contact(object1(particle1),object2(string1),time(d)) ←
>   locpt(locpt(L1),object1(particle1),time(d)),
>   locpt(locpt(L2),object2(string1),time(d)),
>   sameplace(locpt(L1),locpt(L2),time(d))

An example of backtracking

Having matched this rule, the processor tries to bind the unbound arguments of each predicate on the right-hand side of the rule, one at a time, from left to right. The only unfilled semantic roles are LOCPT(L1) and LOCPT(L2). The first occurrence of LOCPT(L1) is as the first argument to LOCPT with OBJECT1(particle1) as the second argument, giving LOCPT(L1) a predicate environment of LOCPT(locpt(L1),object1(particle1),time(d)). There is only one syntactic constraint that will match this predicate environment:

> syntax(locpt(L1),
>   pp(at,L1),
>   locpt(locpt(L1),Y,_))

In applying this constraint, **parsed** deletes the only pp(at,X) from the constituent list, pp(at,right1), and tries to bind right1 to LOCPT(L1), resulting in the following mapping.

locpt(L1) = = pp(at,L1) = = right1

This mapping is tested for semantic well-formedness by **check**, as usual, but this time the test fails. The semantic constraint that applies here and which is given below is the same one that was first introduced at the end of chapter 3 as being the most complex semantic constraint.

semantics(locpt(L),
    haspt(Y,L),
    locpt(locpt(L),Y,_))

When the predicate environment of this constraint, **locpt**(locpt(L),Y,_), matches the predicate environment of the semantic role,

locpt(locpt(right1),object1(particle1),time(d))

all of the variables become instantiated. So the test that is performed in this application of the constraint is **haspt**(particle1,right1). The call to **haspt** tests that a location point for an entity is a part of that entity and has the shape of a point. Since right1 is an end, which can be a part of a string, but not of a particle, it cannot be a location point on particle1.

Since **haspt**(particle1,right1) fails, **check** fails, which forces **parsed** to backtrack, i.e., to throw away the mapping of locpt(L1) = = right1 and try to find another one. In throwing away this mapping, the syntactic constituent that suggested it, pp(at,right1), is replaced on the constituent list, so that it can participate in a mapping for another semantic role at a future date. It is then the task of **parsed** to go through all of the syntactic constraints to see if any have predicate environments that will match. Unfortunately, there is none, and **parsed** fails.

Applying pragmatic constraints
There being no other syntactic constraints whose predicate environments match that of locpt(L1), the first pass at filling the semantic role, locpt, has failed. There is an alternative method, however, which is to call **select** to see if the application of pragmatic constraints can find a filler. The application of the following pragmatic constraint selects "particle1" as a filler for this semantic role by calling **findpt**.

pragmatics(locpt(L),
    locpt(locpt(L),Y,_)) ←
    findpt(L,Y)

As mentioned in section 4.3, **findpt** applies appropriate semantic tests to deduce a suitable location point for an object. In this case, any entity that is the shape of a point is its own location point, so particle1 is its own location point, and **select** binds L1 to particle1.

call: bind(
    locpt(locpt(L1),object2(particle1),time(d)).,.)

    ⋮

    call: parsed(locpt(L1),
        locpt(locpt(L1),object2(particle1),time(d)))
    exit with: parsed(locpt(right1),
        locpt(locpt(right1),object2(particle1),time(d)))
    call: check(locpt(right1),
        locpt(locpt(right1),object2(particle1),time(d)))
    fail: check(locpt(right1),
        locpt(locpt(right1),object2(particle1),time(d)))
    backtrack: parsed(locpt(L1),
        locpt(locpt(L1),object2(particle1),time(d)))
    fail: parsed(locpt(L1),
        locpt(locpt(L1),object2(particle1),time(d)))
    call: select(locpt(L1),
        locpt(locpt(L1),object2(particle1),time(d)))
    exit with: select(locpt(particle1),
        locpt(locpt(particle1),object2(particle1),time(d)))

    ⋮

exit with: bind(
    locpt(locpt(particle1),object2(particle1),time(d)))

Figure 4.4: "Instantiating LOCPT(L1)"

The preceding discussion which results in binding L1 to particle1 is illustrated by the partial trace in figure 4.4. The trace begins with a call to bind **locpt**(locpt(L1),object2(particle1),time(d))), and then skips to the first call to **parsed** which has been passed LOCPT(L1) as the unfilled semantic role. The mapping suggested by **parsed** is indicated by "LOCPT(right1)," but this mapping fails the semantic check, causing **parsed** to backtrack. There are no more possible syntactic mappings, so **parsed** fails as well, and **select** is called. This time the attempt to fill the role is successful, and **select** returns with "LOCPT(particle1)."

There is only one semantic role left to be filled, LOCPT(L2). Once more **parsed** suggests right1 as the binding, and this time **check** does not reject it, since right1 is the right end of string1. The final mapping to be added to the set is:

lopcpt(L2) = = pp(at,L2) = = right1

The last predicate, **sameplace**, inherits these bindings.

Decompositions as semantic representations

In one sense, the goal of the process just described has been achieving an appropriate set of mappings between the syntactic constituents and the semantic roles. The entire set of mappings produced here includes:

object1(O1) = = subj(particle1)
object2(O2) = = pp(to,string1)
locpt(L2) = = pp(at,right1)

However, in testing the semantic consistency of these mappings, and in decomposing the predicates in order to bring in all of the relevant semantic roles, the decomposition has become instantiated with the appropriate referents to syntactic constituents, and certain unfilled semantic roles have been filled by pragmatic deduction. The final instantiated decomposition represents what computational linguists usually mean by a "deep" semantic representation. The history of the goals and subgoals that have been achieved in producing this decomposition have been collected during the course of the "proof" of the semantic well-formedness of the mappings. It is only necessary to now "assert" this history, in other words, to add these instantiated predicates to the knowledge base as the desired "deep" semantic representation of the sentence. The instantiated predicates that represent "A particle is attached to a string at its end" are given below.

Semantic representation:

attach ←

contact(object1(particle1),object2(string1),time(d))
locpt(locpt(particle1),object1(particle1),time(d))
locpt(locpt(right1),object2(string1),time(d))
sameplace(locpt(particle1),locpt(right1),time(d))

4.2.2   *INTERMEDIARY EXAMPLES*

The simplest example of the use of an intermediary in the pulley domain is the phrase

"A particle is connected to another particle by a string . . ."

The input to the semantic processor for this sentence is given below, where particle1, particle2 and string1 are referents for the syntactic constituents.

Verb: **connect**

Constituent list:

subj(particle1)
pp(to,particle2)
pp(by,string1)

The first task is to decompose **connect** into its semantic predicates. This is done by applying the lexical entry for **connect** given below.

Decomposition:

connect ←
    effect(inter(I),
        contact(object1(O1),object2(O2),time(d)))

Filling the intermediary role
Before decomposing **effect** and **contact** in turn, an attempt must be made to find mappings for the semantic roles INTERMEDIARY(I,OBJECT(O1), and OBJECT2(O2). The first syntactic constraint applied by **parsed** is given below, and this suggests a mapping of a subj(X) to the INTERMEDIARY, as in "A string connects two particles . . ."

    syntax(inter(I),
      subj(I),
      effect(inter(I),_))

There is a subj(X) on the constituent list, subj(particle1), that **parsed** can delete, and this results in the following suggested mapping:

Initial inter mapping:

inter(I) = = subj(I) = = particle1

This mapping is passed to **check** to be tested for semantic well-formedness. Since all of the intermediaries in this domain are used to "hang strings over pulleys" or "connect particles together," etc., the semantic constraint is that **isatype**(lineseg,I) be true of inter(I), as illustrated below.

    semantics(inter(I),
      isatype(lineseg,I),
      effect(inter(I),_))

When **check** attempts to prove "isatype(lineseg,particle1)," it fails, since particle1 is a point, and not a line-segment. This causes **parsed** to backtrack, just as it did in the **attach** example, except that this time it is more fortunate.

There is another syntactic constraint whose predicate environment matches, and this constraint suggests a pp(by,X) as a possible mapping.

> syntax(inter(I),
>   pp(by,I),
>   effect(inter(I),_))

There is a pp(by,X) on the constituent list, pp(by,string1), and **parsed** deletes it. (The subj(particle1) was replaced on the constituent list because of the backtracking.) The new mapping is:

> *Final inter mapping:*

> inter(I) = = pp(by,I) = = string1

This time when **check** applies "isatype(lineseg,string1)," the test is successful. Now **parsed** can go on to fill the other two semantic roles, OBJECT1(O1) and OBJECT2(O2) which follows essentially the same process as the filling of the same roles in the *attach* example. The final set of mappings achieved for this stage of the decomposition is:

> inter(I) = = pp(by,I) = = string1
> object1(O1) = = subj(O1) = = particle1
> object2(O2) = = pp(to,O2) = = particle2

> *Decomposing effect*

All of the constituents on the constituent list have been mapped to semantic roles, but the decomposition is not finished, since there is a lexical entry for **effect**, given below.

> effect(inter(I),
>   contact(object1(O1),object2(O2),time(_))) ←
>   contact(object1(O1),object2(I),time(_)),
>   contact(object1(I),object2(O2),time(_))

The left-hand side of this entry matches the instantiated **effect** predicate,

> effect(inter(string1),
>   contact(object1(particle1),object2(particle2),time(d)))

resulting in the following instantiations for the right-hand side:

> contact(object1(particle1),object2(string1),time(d))
> contact(object1(string1),object2(particle2),time(d))

There are no more semantic roles to be filled at this stage, but notice what the decomposition has achieved. In the *attach* example, the end result is a simple contact relationship between the string and the particle. In this example, since the particles are connected "by" the string, the explicit mention of the string results in two contact relationships; one between the first particle and the string, and another between the string and the second particle. The string is quite literally an INTERMEDIARY for the contact between the two particles. The particles do not actually touch each other at all. However, since they are connected by the string, movement of one particle will result in movement of the other particle and vice versa. Section 4.3 describes a similar use of an INTERMEDIARY, but for a **location** verb rather than a **contact** verb. The striking similarity between the use of an INTERMEDIARY for **location** verbs and **contact** verbs allows a decomposition of the semantic role that is independent of the verbs involved.

Semantic representation
It only remains to decompose the two **contact** relationships. This is very similar to the **contact** decomposition described in the ***attach*** example, so is not repeated in detail here. There are no more syntactic constituents in the list, so pragmatics has to fill the LOCPT semantic roles. Each particle is chosen as its own location point, and the right end and left end of the string are chosen as the two location points for the string. The final instantiated decomposition for "A particle is connected to another particle by a string . . ." is as follows:

> ***connect***
> effect(inter(string1),
>   contact(object1(particle1),object2(particle2),time(d)))
>
> contact(object1(particle1),object2(string1),time(d))
>
> locpt(locpt(particle1),object1(particle1),time(d))
> locpt(locpt(right1),object2(string1),time(d))
> sameplace(locpt(particle1),locpt(right1),time(d))
>
> contact(object1(string1),object2(particle2),time(d))
>
> locpt(locpt(left1),object1(string1),time(d))
> locpt(locpt(particle2),object2(particle2),time(d))
> sameplace(locpt(left1),locpt(particle2),time(d))

4.3 Analyzing sentences in context

One of the ways of constraining the decompositions at this stage is looking at the semantic roles that could be mentioned in the surface structure. If for a certain verb it is possible to indicate a location point explicitly in the surface structure, then the decomposition has to go far enough to include a predicate with the location point semantic role as a predicate-argument. This allows a mapping to be found between the semantic role and the syntactic constituent. However, if the location point is not mentioned explicitly, the role remains unfilled. It is up to pragmatics to attempt to deduce an appropriate filler for the role. The preceding examples have briefly illustrated this, by showing that pragmatics recognizes that an entity with the shape of a point is its own location point, etc. These examples have been about sentences in isolation, and the pragmatic deductions have used information that is locally available, as well as information that is known generally about these types of entities. To analyze sentences in context it is sometimes necessary to rely on information that has already been asserted about the other entities involved, i.e., *contextual* information. All of these types of information, local, general and contextual, can be referred to by the term *pragmatic* information. When the pragmatic deductions use contextual information to fill semantic roles with referents from previous clauses, they provide an important bridge between the "given" and "new" information in the clause being analyzed, as discussed in section 1.2.4.

One of the most difficult aspects of this task is deciding when to stop trying to fill a semantic role, and leave it uninstantiated. Inference-driven mapping uses the algorithm described in section 4.3.1 to make this decision. The algorithm relies on distinguishing between optional, obligatory and essential semantic roles, and treating each type accordingly. Obligatory roles must always be filled by syntactic constituents, essential roles must always be filled, but not necessarily by syntactic constituents, and optional roles can be left uninstantiated. Examples are given of the use of pragmatic deductions for filling essential semantic roles in section 4.3.2, which then shows how this technique can be used to derive a contextual semantic representation.

4.3.1   Algorithm for filling unfilled roles

If a semantic role has not been filled, the processor first has to decide if it is obligatory. As mentioned previously, an obligatory role is one that must be mentioned explicitly in the surface structure of the sentence. An obligatory role that is not filled by a syntactic constituent reflects an incorrect analysis of the clause, and an alternative attempt at analysis must be made. In other words, unfilled obligatory roles cause a failure, and the processor backtracks to find a new set of mappings. The obligatory roles in this domain are OBJECT1s. If the role is optional rather than obligatory, then it might need to be filled (if it is an essential role), but it might not, and this can be domain-dependent. For this domain, INTERMEDIARIES, AGENTS, LOCPTS, LOCS, and FORCES are all considered essential roles. OBJECT2s are the only optional roles, and as such can be left unfilled. This approach is indicated by the flowchart in figure 4.5.

This method is applied to unfilled semantic roles as soon as it is clear that a referent for a syntactic constituent cannot be found. Essential roles such as LOCPTS are usually filled by pragmatics immediately after **parsed** and

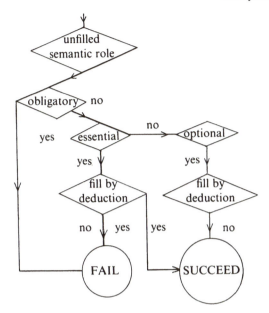

Fig. 4.5. Algorithm for semantics

check have failed to fill them with a syntactic constituent. This kind of application of pragmatic information was illustrated in the previous example. Occasionally there is not enough information at this stage either to successfully fill an essential role, or to cause failure for an obligatory role. For instance, it is only when every semantic role that can be filled has been filled that it is possible for the constituent list to be empty, and to know that an obligatory role cannot possibly be filled. The application of pragmatic constraints is tried again after filling (or not filling) each of the remaining semantic roles in a decomposition, and eventually succeeds or fails. This is somewhat redundant, although reliable, and it is possible that with further research a more precise method of applying pragmatic constraints can be found.

4.3.2   *Filling essential roles*

Section 1.2.4 suggested three different methods of filling essential roles: (1) default values, (2) discourse, and (3) hypothesizing a new referent. Since default values are really just shortcuts to hypothesizing new referents, these methods can be condensed into two methods:

1. selecting a known referent;
2. introducing a new referent.

Selecting a known referent can actually be quite complicated, as with unmarked INTERMEDIARIES. In this case, pragmatics must recognize that the referent that should be playing the INTERMEDIARY role is playing a dual role, and that the normal interpretation of the inclusion of an INTERMEDIARY semantic role does not apply. This section gives examples from the pulley domain of filling semantic roles with known referents as well as creating new referents, with most of the examples based on INTERMEDIARIES and special attention paid to the effect of an unmarked INTERMEDIARY.

Examples using LOCPTS are described first, since they are more straightforward, and can only be filled by known referents. However, there is an interesting twist to the use of LOCPT that has not yet been mentioned. The constraints that were developed for LOCPTS can also be used to fill the OBJECT2 semantic role. This role is considered to be optional, so it does not matter if it is not filled. The example given here shows how the semantic and pragmatic constraints for LOCPTS proved to be more flexible than was originally intended by the author, and can fill an unfilled role as a side-effect.

Filling location points with known referents

In applying the lexical entries for a **contact** relation, location points on each entity are looked for so that it can be asserted that they are in the **sameplace**. These location points are often mentioned explicitly in the sentence, as in "A particle is connected to the end of a string," or "A particle is attached at one end of a string." If they are not mentioned they can be deduced. Since deducing a location point on an entity involves selecting an appropriate part of the entity, this is considered to fall into the category of choosing a known referent. Since the entity has been mentioned explicitly, it is assumed that any parts of the entity that have not also been mentioned explicitly have at least been mentioned implicitly. Therefore all of the parts can be considered to be known referents.

Examples of deducing LOCPTS have already been given in the previous section. The following **pragmatic** constraint is used to deduce an end point for a fixed contact. **Findpt** picks the first available end point on the entity that is not already at the **sameplace** as something else.

$$\text{pragmatics}(\text{locpt}(\text{L}1)$$
$$\text{locpt}(\text{L}1,\text{Object},\_)) \leftarrow$$
$$\text{findpt}(\text{L}1,\text{Object})$$

In all of the previous examples (see section 4.2.1) the entity is known but the location point is not. **Findpt** is used in those examples to deduce location points for the entities, such as "particle1" as a LOCPT for "particle1," and "right1" and "left1" as LOCPTS for "string1."

Filling an optional role

In the original design of the system, it was assumed that OBJECT1s and OBJECT2s would generally be known, and it was most likely that LOCPTs would have to be deduced. There is one example from the pulley domain that violates these assumptions. This involves the processing of a phrase like ". . . weight attached at its other end," where the LOCPT is mentioned explicitly in the syntactic parse, but the OBJECT2 is not.[5] The input associated with this clause is given below, where "weight1" is a referent for "weight" and "left1" is a referent for "its other end."

Verb: **attach**

Constituent list:
subj(weight1)
pp(at,left1)

In previous examples, the semantic constraint for LOCPTs, given below, has been used to make sure that a referent of a syntactic constituent is an appropriate filler for a LOCPT semantic role.

semantics(locpt(L1),
　　haspt(Object,L1),
　　locpt(L1,Object,_))

This constraint applies **haspt** to check that the suggested location point has the shape of a point and is a part of the entity involved. In the example in section 4.2.1 the application of **haspt** caused "right1" to be rejected as a LOCPT of "particle1" because particles cannot have right ends. In this example, **haspt** is being applied to test a LOCPT mapping suggested by **parsed**,

locpt(L1) = = pp(at,L1) = = left1

The following mapping has already been found, but notice that there is no mapping for OBJECT2:

object1(O1) = = subj(O1) = = weight1

This results in a predicate environment for LOCPT(left1) that is

locpt(locpt(left1),object2(O2),_)

The application of **haspt** therefore involves testing whether "left1" is an appropriate location point for an unknown entity, i.e., **haspt**(O2,left1). In this case, **haspt** actually returns with the unknown entity instantiated, since the necessary semantic feature of a location point is that it be a point on the entity. It is already part of the knowledge base that left1 is a part of string1, and of

---

[5] The OBJECT2 is mentioned in a sense, in that the "it" refers to the string, but it is difficult to see how to map a possessive pronoun onto a semantic role in the system being discussed.

call: bind(
    locpt(locpt(L2),object2(O2),time(d))...,.)

⋮

    call: parsed(locpt(L2),
        locpt(locpt(L2),object2(O2),.))
    exit with: parsed(locpt(left1),
        locpt(locpt(left1),object2(O2),.))
    call: check(locpt(left1),
        locpt(locpt(left1),object2(O2),.))
    exit with: check(locpt(left1),
→   locpt(locpt(left1),object2(*string1*),.))

⋮

exit with: bind(
    locpt(locpt(left1),object2(string1),time(d))...,.)

Figure 4.6: Deducing OBJECT2s from LOCPTS

course, being the end of a string, left1 has the shape of a point. Executing **haspt**(O2,left1) results in O2 being bound to string1. Figure 4.6 shows a trace of the decomposition for "a weight attached at its end," where OBJECT2(O2) of **contact** remains a variable until bind(**locpt**(locpt(L),OBJECT2(O2),time(d))) is reached. When **check** is called, O2 is still a variable, but when **check** exits it has been instantiated. This stage of the trace has been indicated by a double arrow, →.

There is no fundamental difference between the semantic checking that **haspt** performs and the use of **findpt** to deduce a location point as described in the preceding section. The same tests for the "partness" and the "pointness" of the location point are made. **Findpt** then goes on to ensure that the potential location point is not already known to be in the **sameplace** as another object. This is not done explicitly by **haspt**, since the assumption is that **haspt** is dealing with new information from the sentence, and that this information is correct. But immediately after **haspt** provides a referent for a location point, a **sameplace** predicate is examined with respect to this location point and another location point. Exactly the same semantic predicates are relevant to the semantic checking and to the pragmatic deduction. Trying to combine semantic checking and pragmatic deductions more closely is an interesting area for future research.

Unmarked intermediaries

This section describes the use of the unmarked concept for filling INTERME-DIARY roles. Since unmarked INTERMEDIARIES in a sense play dual roles, this is an example of filling a role by a known referent, rather than creating a new one. The next section describes an example where a new referent, a string57, has to be created to fill the INTERMEDIARY role.

All of these examples have to do with filling INTERMEDIARY roles for *hang* and *suspend*. In this domain *hang* and *suspend* are considered to be synony-mous, and have exactly the same decompositions. The predicate "time(initial)" has been shortened to "time(i)" for simplicity.

> *hang* ←
>   effect(inter(I,
>   location(object1(O1),loc(L),time(i))))

> *suspend* ←
>   effect(inter(I,
>   location(object1(O1),loc(L),time(i))))

In section 2.3.2, unmarked INSTRUMENTS are first introduced. Levin noted that, although the INSTRUMENT role is usually indicated by a pp(by,X), a pp(with,Y) or a subj(Z), occasionally an entity that seems to be acting similarly to an INSTRUMENT is indicated by an unexpected syntactic constituent. For example, a marked INSTRUMENT is the rock in

> S1: John cut his foot with a rock.

On the other hand, in

> S2: John cut his foot on a rock.

the rock is still acting very similarly, but is indicated by an unexpected syntactic constituent, a pp(on,X). Levin suggested that in S2, "on the rock" introduces an unmarked INSTRUMENT, and that some of the meaning associ-ated with INSTRUMENTS is preserved by the unmarked INSTRUMENT, but some of the meaning is lost. In S1 there is a certain element of control being exercised by John over the rock that is missing from S2. This control relation could be introduced by the presence of the marked INSTRUMENT, and would therefore be absent when the INSTRUMENT is unmarked.

"At one end of a string a weight is suspended . . ." is an example of an unmarked INTERMEDIARY in the pulley domain. An unmarked INTERMEDIARY in this domain is considered to be an entity that is usually expected to act as an INTERMEDIARY, such as a string, but has been indicated in the surface structure by a syntactic constituent that does not normally indicate INTERMEDIARIES. The string in this phrase is the object of a pp(of,Y) which is the object of a pp(at,X). It is not even seen by the verb, since the pp(of,Y) has been processed in determining the referent for the pp(at,X), the "end." At best the "end" can be considered a location point. The processor is given the following input, and *suspend* as the goal.

> *Verb:* **suspend**

> Constituent list:
> subj(wt1),
> pp(at,right1)

By adding a new syntactic constraint to the constraints used in our previous examples,

> syntax(loc(above(L)),
>   pp(at,L),
>   location(_,loc(L),time(_)))

the following mappings are made to the decomposition of the *suspend* lexical entry. There is no available syntactic constituent for inter(I), and at its first attempt, pragmatics fails to supply one.

> object1(O1) = = subj(O1) = = wt1
> loc(L) = = pp(at,L) = = right1

The last semantic role that is filled is LOC, and it is passed to **select** as an argument along with its predicate environment before the mapping is considered complete. As mentioned before, this call to **select** cannot in any way undo the mapping, but is included to allow pragmatics a last attempt to fill any other unfilled semantic roles. The predicate environment at this stage is the following partially instantiated predicate:

> effect(inter(I),
>   location(object1(wt1),loc(right1),time(i)))

At this stage, pragmatics recognizes that right1 is a part of a string, so an INTERMEDIARY has been referred to, if somewhat indirectly, and there is no need to deduce one. This is considered to be an instance of an unmarked INTERMEDIARY, so pragmatics instantiates INTERMEDIARY(I) with "unmarked," indicating that the INTERMEDIARY is considered to have been mentioned, but is playing another semantic role as its primary role.[6] This instantiation changes the way **effect** is decomposed.

---

[6] Exactly which other role the INTERMEDIARY is playing does not have any effect on any of these examples. In other implementations it might be useful, and could be captured by changing unmarked to unmarked-right1 or something similar.

There are two alternative decompositions for **effect**. The standard decomposition, given below, decomposes **effect**(I,Pred) into two copies of the Pred relationship, with the I acting as an argument to each one.

effect(inter(I),
  location(object1(O1),loc(O2),time(_))) ←
    location(object1(I),loc(O2),time(_)),
    location(object1(O1),loc(I),time(d)))

This is considered to be the verb-independent decomposition of the case predicate **effect** and applies equally to **contact** and **location** verbs when a marked INTERMEDIARY has been recognized. However, just as Levin suggested that the unmarked INSTRUMENT no longer conveyed the notion of control between John and the rock, an unmarked INTERMEDIARY no longer produces two copies of the basic semantic predicate involved. The following lexical entry is applied instead:

effect(inter(unmarked,Predicate) ← Predicate

The unmarked **effect** entry essentially discards the **effect** predicate, and treats the **location** predicate independently. The **location** predicate in turn decomposes into the **support** and **contact** predicates that **location** normally decomposes into, and which are given below. This does not mean that the INTERMEDIARY is not playing an essential role. It is the presence of the INTERMEDIARY in an unmarked position that allows the verb to be decomposed in this way. An INTERMEDIARY that is completely missing, as in the example in the next section, results in a very different decomposition.

suspend
effect(inter(unmarked),
  location(object1(wt1),loc(right1),time(i)))

location(object1(wt1),loc(above(right1)),time(d))

support(object(right1),object2(wt1),time(d))

force(up(F1),object1(right1))
force(down(F1),object2(wt1))
contact(object1(right1),object2(wt1),time(d))

locpt(locpt(right1),object2(right1),time(d))
locpt(locpt(wt1),object1(wt1),time(d))
sameplace(locpt(wt1),locpt(right1),time(d))

Hypothesizing a new referent

The following phrase describes another example of a ***hanging*** event in which the INTERMEDIARY, usually a string, plays an essential role, but the INTERMEDIARY is never indicated by an expected syntactic constituent.

"a pulley is suspended from another pulley"

In this phrase, the INTERMEDIARY is not mentioned at all, and cannot be derived from context. In order to fill this role, a new referent must be hypothesized.

Section 3.4.2 introduced the rule for ***hang*** and gave an example of how INTERMEDIARIES are used to **effect location** relations that decompose into **support** relations. The lexical entries for ***hang*** and *suspend* are repeated here.

> *hang* ←
>   effect(inter(I,
>   location(object1(O1),loc(L),time(i))))

> *suspend* ←
>   effect(inter(I,
>   location(object1(O1),loc(L),time(i))))

In "a pulley is suspended from another pulley," the missing role is the INTERMEDIARY, and there is not even an indirect reference to an entity that could fill that role. The input for the processor is given below:

Verb: **suspend**

Constituent list:
subj(pulley1)
pp(**from**,pulley2)

By adding another new syntactic constraint to the constraints used in our preceding examples,

> syntax(loc(**above**(L)),
>   pp(**from**,L),
>   location(_,loc(L),time(_)))

the following set of mappings for the decomposition of *suspend* can be produced:

> object1(O1) = = subj(O1) = = pulley1
> loc(L) = = pp(from,L) = = pulley2

When **parsed** initially fails to find a syntactic constituent for INTERMEDIARY(I), pragmatics is also unable to find a filler. However, after filling the other semantic roles, OBJECT1 and OBJECT2, when pragmatics is called for the last time it finally has enough information to deduce a filler. This is another example of the advantage of being able to postpone a decision about filling an essential role until all of the other roles are filled.

In this case, since neither pulley1 nor pulley2 could **effect** the ***hanging*** relationship, it is clear that the INTERMEDIARY role has not been mentioned at all. Neither is anything already known about the pulleys, such as their being in contact with strings that might supply a referent from context. A flexible entity must be added to the set of semantics roles, and it must be done by hypothesizing the existence of an entity not mentioned previously. Default values are just short cuts to hypothesizing new entries, and a default value is appropriate here. The following pragmatic constraint instantiates I with string57, the standard default value for an INTERMEDIARY.

> pragmatics(loc(above(L)),
>   effect(inter(string57),location(object1(O1),loc(above(L)),_)), . . .) ←
>   isatype(point,L),
>   not(isatype(string,O1))

Note that this constraint can only apply when the INTERMEDIARY in the predicate environment is uninstantiated. The BODY of the constraint checks that the OBJECT1 is not already a string, a possible "unmarked" INTERMEDIARY, and that the LOC of the OBJECT1 is a solid entity with the shape of a point. The constraint is examining the semantic features of the other semantic roles to make sure that this is a situation where the INTERMEDIARY should be filled by hypothesis.

Having satisfactorily filled the INTERMEDIARY role, the standard **effect** decomposition can be applied, and two location predicates, one between pulley1 and string57 and the other between string57 and pulley2, are then decomposed in turn. The final set of semantic predicates that represents the decomposition of "A pulley is suspended from another pulley . . ." is given below.

suspend

> effect(inter(string57),
>   location(object1(pulley1),loc(pulley2),time(i)))
>
> location(object1(pulley1),loc(above(string57)),time(i))
>
> support(object1(string57),object2(pulley1),time(i))
>
> force(up(F1),object1(string57))
> force(down(F1),object2(pulley1))
> contact(object1(string57),object2(pulley1),time(i))

locpt(locpt(right57),object1(string57),time(i))
locpt(locpt(pulley1),object2(pulley1),time(i))
sameplace(locpt(right57),locpt(pulley1),time(i))

location(object1(string57),loc(above(pulley2)),time(d))

support(object1(pulley2),object2(string57),time(d))

force(up(F1),object1(pulley2))
force(down(F1),object2(string57))
contact(object1(pulley2),object2(string57),time(d))

locpt(locpt(pulley2),object1(pulley2),time(d))
locpt(locpt(midpt57),object2(string57),time(d))
sameplace(locpt(pulley2),locpt(midpt57),time(d))

Using new referents as known referents

The usefulness of filling essential roles is illustrated by examining the rest of the sentence beginning with "A pulley is suspended from another pulley . . ." The phrase continues with

". . . and is offset by a particle of mass 8 pounds."

In order to produce an appropriate representation for the second phrase, two of the semantic roles have to be filled by pragmatics. These roles are in fact filled by referents from the first phrase, counting as still another example of filling roles with known referents. It is interesting to note that one of the "known referents" in this example, string57, was in fact created as a "new referent" in the analysis of the first phrase.

The first clause is analyzed as described above, with string57 being introduced as a new referent that fills the INTERMEDIARY role. The predicates that represent the final decomposition are added to the knowledge base. The analysis of the second clause, "the pulley is offset by a particle," is discussed here, assuming the constituent list and referents below as input.

Verb: **offset**

Constituent list:
subj(pulley1),
pp(by,particle1)

The verb entry for *offset* is presented below, along with an additional lexical entry for the predicate it decomposes into, **balance**. *Offset* in this domain is taken as suggesting a balance relationship between two entities, while **balance** decomposes into a "double suspension"; the equivalent of two hanging relationships, each one *balancing* the other. The definition of balance is clearly geared to a pulley domain where entities to be balanced are expected to be supported by hanging.

> *offset* ←
>   balance(object1(O1),object2(O2),time(i))
>
> balance(object1(O1),object2(O2),time(i)) ←
>   effect(inter(I),
>   location(object1(O1),loc(L),time(i)))
>   effect(inter(I),
>   location(object1(O2),loc(L),time(i)))

An additional syntactic constraint

> syntax(object2(O2),
>   pp(by,O2),
>   balance(object1(O1),object2(O2),_))

allows the arguments of **balance** to be instantiated with pulley1 and particle1, resulting in the following set of mappings:

> object1(O1) = = subj(O1) = = pulley1
> object2(O2) = = pp(by,O2) = = particle1

The lexical entry for **balance** is now applied to the following instantiated predicate to decompose it further.

> balance(object1(pulley1),object2(particle1),time(i))

The first predicate in this new decomposition is given below, and it contains two unfilled semantic roles, the INTERMEDIARY and the LOC.

> effect(inter(I),
>   location(object1(pulley1),loc(L),time(i)))

There are no more syntactic constituents so these semantic roles must be filled by pragmatics. This is appropriate, since this predicate represents the first half of the double suspension relationship, and is the suspension relationship that is to be "balanced." It should have already been described elsewhere, and pragmatics recognizes that the uninstantiated semantic roles should be filled by context. The OBJECT1, pulley1, is the entity being suspended, and the knowledge base does in fact already contain information about that suspension relationship. The analysis of "A pulley suspends another pulley" supplied an INTERMEDIARY and a LOC as illustrated by the following predicate taken from page 141. Pragmatics fills the semantic roles for the first half of the suspension relationship with the same referents, binding INTERMEDIARY to string57 and LOC to pulley2.

effect(inter(string57),
　　location(object1(pulley1),loc(pulley2),time(i))))

The second **effect** predicate shares some of these semantic roles, so these
arguments are instantiated in the same way. The fully instantiated **balance**
entry is given below.

effect(inter(string57),
　　location(object1(pulley1),loc(pulley2),time(i))))
effect(inter(string57),
　　location(object1(particle1),loc(pulley2),time(i))))

This entry is further decomposed into the relevant **support** and **contact**
relationships. The predicates representing the final decomposition of "... and
is offset by a particle ..." are as follows:

offset

balance(object1(pulley1),object2(particle1),time(i))

⟨effect(inter(string57),
　　location(object1(pulley1),loc(pulley2), time(d)))
– duplicate of previous predicate, so not decomposed⟩
effect(inter(string57),
　　location(object1(particle1),loc(pulley2),time(d)))

location(object1(particle1),loc(above(string57)),time(i))
⟨location(object1(string57),loc(above(pulley2)),time(i))
– duplicate of previous predicate, so not decomposed⟩
support(object1(string57),object2(particle1),time(d))

force(up(F1),object1(string57))
force(down(F1),object2(particle1))
contact(object1(string57),object2(particle1),time(d))

locpt(locpt(left57),object1(string57),time(d))
locpt(locpt(particle1),object2(particle1),time(d))
sameplace(locpt(left57),locpt(particle1),time(d))

Since the first **effect** predicate duplicates a predicate already in the knowledge base, it is not decomposed, or added to the knowledge base. The final
representation is quite similar to the representation of the first clause, except
that particle1 is put at the left end of string57 instead of being at the right end,
as illustrated by figure 4.7.

The complete set of **location** and **support** predicates listed at the end of the

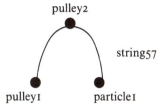

pulley1   particle1

Fig. 4.7.   "... and is offset by a particle of mass 8 pounds"

last section and just above give a semantic representation of a pulley system, where pulley1 and particle1 are hung by string57 from pulley2, one at each end of string57 (figure 4.7). This is clearly the intended meaning of "A pulley is suspended from another pulley and is offset by a particle of mass 8 pounds," but the analysis requires a complicated interaction between syntax, semantics and pragmatics. In particular, this example demonstrates that for a particle to offset a pulley suspended from another pulley, a string must be involved. In order to continue with the semantic processing of the sentence, it is necessary for pragmatics to first fill the INTERMEDIARY role of *suspend* with a new referent.

4.3.3   *Obligatory roles causing failure*

This section describes how an unfilled **obligatory** role can cause the processor to discard a set of incorrect mappings, backtrack and produce a set of new mappings. The phrase involved is "A string hangs over a pulley." This is still another example of an unmarked INTERMEDIARY, but it is not recognized as such on the first pass. Given an input of

> *Verb:* **hang**
>
> Constituent list:
> subj(string1)
> pp(over,pulley1)

the first set of mappings achieved is:

> *First set of mappings:*
>
> inter(I) = = subj(I) = = string1
> loc(L) = = pp(over,L) = = pulley1

It is only after the last mapping has been found, and **select** has been called, that it is recognized that the constituent list is now empty, and the **obligatory** OBJECT1 semantic role is still uninstantiated. This causes a failure, and backtracking occurs. The original set of mappings is discarded, and an attempt is made to find a new set. There are no other syntactic constituents to indicate an INTERMEDIARY, so that role is left unfilled. The following set of mappings is suggested.

Second set of mappings:

object1(O1) = = subj(O1) = = string1
loc(L) = = pp(over,L) = = pulley1

Now when **select** is called to examine the last mapping for the LOC, it is parsed

effect(inter(I),
    location(object1(string1),loc(pulley1),time(i)))

as a predicate environment. This time pragmatics notices an unfilled INTERME-DIARY role, while a string is filling another role. This set of circumstances indicates an unmarked INTERMEDIARY, just as it did in the previous example, and INTERMEDIARY is instantiated with "unmarked." This allows the special **effect** entry for unmarked INTERMEDIARIES to be applied (see section 4.3.2).

4.3.4   *Summary*

Several examples have been given here of filling unfilled semantic roles by the application of pragmatic constraints. Sometimes these roles are filled by known referents that have occurred in previous semantic representations, and sometimes they are filled by new referents that are created for no other reason than to fill a particular semantic role that cannot be filled in any other way. The pragmatic constraints that fill the roles make use of general knowledge about the type of role to be filled, knowledge about the other semantic roles that have been filled, and knowledge about previous representations to deduce appropriate fillers. The examples have illustrated how useful these pragmatic-ally deduced fillers are to the continued operation of the semantic processor. A filler for a semantic role may be a new referent in one decomposition, such as string57, and then may be referred to as a known referent later on in order to fill a semantic role in another decomposition.

However, it is not always possible to fill an unfilled semantic role through pragmatic deduction. By classifying semantic roles into obligatory, essential and optional roles, the processor can determine when the inability to fill a role is unimportant, and when it should cause a failure. For example, the unfilled OBJECT1 in the last section correctly caused the current set of mappings to be discarded and a new set of mappings to be found. Since OBJECT1s are oblig-atory roles, pragmatics never even makes an attempt to fill the OBJECT1. Unfilled optional roles can be marked as *absent* or *unspecified*. This kind of classification could easily be applied to other domains with the same effect. It seems to be the case that the roles that pragmatics does fill, the essential roles, are defined by being fundamental to the semantic decomposition in the sense that other decompositions and other roles depend on them. Whether or not this is a sufficient way of ascertaining essential roles, or whether there is another way that is more linguistically oriented, is yet to be determined and offers an interesting area for future research.

Pragmatic deductions are just one means of filling semantic roles, and the examples in section 4.2.1 concentrated on the use of syntactic and semantic constraints to fill semantic roles. The general method of inference-driven mapping is to decompose a verb into its basic semantic predicates, and then try to fill the semantic roles associated with those predicates. The syntactic constraints are tried first in an attempt to find a mapping from the syntactic parse of the sentence to a semantic role, and it is only after the syntactic constraints have been attempted that the pragmatic constraints are applied. The pragmatic constraints may fill a role that syntax has just failed to fill, or they may use information about a referent syntax has just filled a semantic role with to find a filler for a role previously left unfilled. It is clear, however, that whatever information syntax may be able to supply about a semantic role is very important to the application of the pragmatic constraints, and that information must always be sought first. The examples given here, especially the ones relating to unmarked INTERMEDIARIES, illustrate the complex inter-action of syntactic, semantic and pragmatic information that is necessary for producing an appropriate semantic representation. The decomposition of the verb can change depending on the fillers of the semantic roles that have been supplied by syntax and by pragmatics.

The processor that produces the semantic representations does so by inter-preting the lexical entries procedurally, which decomposes the verbs into semantic predicates, and evaluating the function symbols corresponding to the semantic roles during this interpretation. The evaluation of the function symbols results in the application of the syntactic, semantic and pragmatic constraints that usually return an instantiation for the semantic role. The interpretation then goes on to decompose the semantic predicates themselves, resulting in the introduction of new semantic roles which are also instantiated. The history of the interpretation corresponds to the "deep" semantic represen-tation, and is added to the knowledge base when the predicate cannot be decomposed any further.

5   Results of inference-driven semantic analysis

This chapter summarizes the results that have been presented in the preceding chapters, in particular the process by which inference-driven mapping goes directly from the syntactic parse of a sentence to a "deep" semantic representation that corresponds to a traditional linguistic decomposition. The summary illustrates two of the most important benefits offered by inference-driven mapping over the template approach, namely, (1) the clear distinction between the verb definition and the final semantic representation achieved, and (2) an integrated approach to semantic analysis. The first benefit is of special relevance to linguistic theories about semantic representations, in that it provides a testing ground for such theories. The second benefit is of more relevance to computational models of natural language processors, in terms of interfacing semantic processing with syntactic parsing. The last section suggests directions of future research for pursuing these objectives.

5.1   Integrated semantic analysis

As discussed in chapter 2, traditional approaches to semantic processing need several levels of description to produce a "deep" semantic representation from a syntactic parse. The most popular of these approaches, termed the template approach, can be seen as using at least two intermediate levels of description, (1) the template level which is used for assigning mappings from syntactic constituents and semantic roles, and (2) the canonical level where the semantic roles are grouped together to simplify derivation of a "deep" semantic representation. These separate levels of description impose several stages of processing on the implementations, since only certain pieces of information are available at any one stage. Each of the semantic analysis tasks defined in chapter 1 and repeated below has to be performed separately, using a separate level of description and a separate stage of processing, resulting in unnecessary redundancies and inefficiencies.

Inference-driven mapping bypasses both of the intermediate levels by mapping the syntactic constituents directly onto the predicate-arguments, i.e., semantic roles, of the "deep" semantic representation. This is an approach that can be used for limited domains where the sublanguage has been formalized into a set of basic semantic predicates with corresponding decompositions, and the verbs of the domain have been defined in terms of these basic predicates. The goal of inference-driven mapping is the expansion of the verb into its decomposition, and the assignment of the syntactic constituents to the semantic roles of the verb during this expansion. All the semantic roles will not be filled by syntactic constituents, and these unfilled roles can be filled by pragmatic deduction during the process of the expansion. This allows the semantic analysis tasks to be solved simultaneously, with resulting gains in efficiency and clarity. This section reviews these tasks and the method by which inference-driven mapping solves them using an example from the pulley domain:

1. establishing referents for the noun phrases;
2. finding appropriate mappings from the syntactic constituents of the parse onto the underlying semantic representation of the verb;
3. using pragmatic information to assign fillers to semantic roles that do not have an explicit syntactic realization;
4. expanding the representation of the verb into a more detailed representation that fulfills the requirements of the processing task;
5. constraining allowable inferences so that this semantic representation does not become explosive;
6. appropriately integrating the final representation of the clause with the representations of prior clauses.

5.1.1 Basic structure

The input to inference-driven mapping includes the syntactic parse of the sentence to be analyzed as well as fully determined referents for the syntactic constituents (task 1). The input assumes that a sophisticated noun phrase component has already been at work, which has determined referents for the noun phrases and processed some of the prepositional phrases. This level of representation is based on the author's interpretation of the original goals of the Mecho project. The remaining tasks, tasks 2 through 6, are handled by the following process. The basic semantic predicates that compose a verb definition are given in the lexical entry of the verb which is a Horn clause, with the verb as the consequent. Expanding the verb representation (task 4) is performed by decomposing the verb into its semantic predicates through the procedural interpretation of the lexical entry. Traditional semantic roles are defined as **types** of arguments of the semantic predicates that appear in the lexical entries. The predicate-arguments can be instantiated during the procedural interpretation of the lexical entries by either syntactic constituents of the appropriate type or by a referent deduced from pragmatic information, also of the appropriate type. Then the basic semantic predicates are themselves decomposed, and any new semantic roles that are introduced are also instantiated if possible. This process continues until the semantic predicates cannot be decomposed any further. The expansion of a verb is restricted to only those predicates whose arguments can act as semantic roles to the verb; an implicit constraint on the decomposition that achieves task 5, the constraining of allowable inferences.

The expansion process is illustrated by figure 1.2 (see page 22).

Task 2, the task of finding mappings from syntactic constituents to semantic roles, is considered to be a member of the set of problems involved in finding instantiations for the arguments to the semantic predicates. The mappings are derived by providing a set of syntactic and semantic constraints on the instantiation of each **type** of predicate-argument, depending on the particular **predicate environment** it is in.

If there is no syntactic constituent for a particular semantic role it may be filled by deductions based on pragmatic information (task 3). The use of pragmatic deductions depends on whether the semantic role is considered to be optional, obligatory, or essential. Optional roles are merely marked "absent," essential roles are filled by deduction, and an unfilled obligatory role causes a failure resulting in the derivation of a new set of mappings. The ability to instantiate arguments by syntactic constituents or by pragmatic deduction is essential for the correct integration of the sentence representation within the current model of the scene being described (task 6) since the appropriate filler is often a known referent from a previous sentence. The following sections describe this process in more detail.

Lexical entries

In inference-driven mapping, producing a semantic representation for a sentence is accomplished by decomposing the verb involved, and establishing the semantic well-formedness of that decomposition with regard to the major syntactic constituents. By mapping the syntactic constituents onto the predicate-arguments of the decomposition, and expanding the decomposition further, the semantic consistency of the mappings is tested. All of the verbs are defined in terms of a small set of semantic predicates, and they all share the decompositions of these predicates. The mapping constraints are associated with this small set of predicates and their decompositions, and they are also shared by many verbs. For example, R1, the lexical entry for *hang*, can be read as, "A location for an entity (O1) can be another entity (L) and can be effected by means of an INTERMEDIARY (I)." This can be expressed using the verb *hang*. In order to "prove" that *hang* has been used appropriately, effect(inter(I),Predicate) can be set up as a subgoal. The "time" arguments have been left off in the following entries for simplicity.

R1:

hang ←
    effect(inter(I),
        location(object1(O1),loc(L)))

Several lexical entries are applied during the decomposition of **hang**. The **effect** entry, R2, is applied first.

R2:

effect(inter(I),
    location(object1(O1),loc(L)) ←
        location(object1(O1),loc(I))
        location(object1(I),loc(L))).

The **effect** predicate decomposes into two **location** predicates, indicating that the location of the entity being *hung* is the INTERMEDIARY, and the location of the INTERMEDIARY is the second entity, the location entity. The **location** predicate is then decomposed into **support**, which is decomposed further into **contact**, and so on.

The semantic representation for sentence S1 is produced from R1 by gathering up all of the subgoals that have been established during the process of demonstrating the consistency of the decomposition. It is only by finding the appropriate set of mappings from the syntactic constituents to the predicate-arguments that the appropriateness of the decomposition for a particular sentence can be confirmed.

S1:

"A particle is hung from a pulley by a string."

Performing mappings
The input to inference-driven mapping includes a surface syntactic parse of the sentence as well as referents for the noun phrases of the sentence. The input for S1 is given below, with "string1" as a referent for the string, "particle1" as a referent for the particle, and "pulley1" as a referent for the pulley.

Verb: **hang**

Constituent list:
subj(particle1)
pp(from,pulley1)
pp(by,string1)

Chapter 3 introduced the mapping constraints that are applied during the expansion of the decompositions to instantiate the predicate-arguments with syntactic constituents. As mentioned previously, three factors complicate the mapping of syntactic constituents onto semantic roles:

1. the large number of choices available for syntactic realization of any particular semantic role;
2. the ability of syntactic constituents to indicate several different types of roles given appropriate contexts;
3. semantic role interdependencies, i.e., the appropriateness of a mapping for a particular semantic role is often dependent on the mappings given to the other semantic roles.

Inference-driven mapping introduces the notion of the predicate environment to account for semantic role interdependencies without losing case-like cross-verb generalizations. Some mapping constraints, such as "subj(X) = = AGENT," are quite general and can apply in many situations. Other constraints, such as "pp(with,Z) = = INSTRUMENT," are much less general, and can only apply under a set of specific circumstances. For some verbs, in order for the pp(with,Z) constraint to apply, the AGENT must be mentioned explicitly in the syntactic realization, as in "John broke the vase with a hammer." Checking for the mention of the AGENT can disallow inappropriate applications of this constraint, such as "*The vase broke with a hammer." The predicate environment is used to check for explicit mention of the AGENT, or any other context-sensitive information that affects the application of a mapping constraint, thus preserving semantic role interdependencies, while still allowing many mapping constraints to have very general predicate environments that will match most verb decompositions.

In the R1 lexical entry, a general mapping rule, M1, finds the instantiation of the first semantic role, the INTERMEDIARY,

$$\text{M1: inter(I)} = = \text{pp(by,I)} \mid Y$$

Application of this constraint results in the following mapping being included as the first member of the set of mappings being postulated for this sentence.

$$\text{inter(I)} = = \text{pp(by,I)} = = \text{string1}$$

Another general constraint, M2, instantiates the second semantic role, OBJECT1(O1). OBJECT1s are similar to PATIENTS, and like PATIENTS can usually be indicated by the subject.

$$\text{M2: object1(X)} = = \text{subj(X)} \mid Y$$

Given S1, application of this constraint results in OBJECT1(O1) being instantiated with "PARTICLE1."

To instantiate the LOCATION, a third mapping constraint, M3, is applied. M3 states that LOCATIONS can be indicated by pp(from,Z)s, but only when the LOCATION is a predicate-argument embedded in an **effect** predicate. This occasions the use of the predicate environment which restricts the application of this constraint to a particular set of circumstances that can be defined in terms of the predicate name and the surrounding arguments of the semantic role.

M3: loc(L) = = pp(from,L) | effect(_,location(_,loc(L)))

The three semantic roles in the decomposition of *hang* have all been filled by syntactic constituents, adding the following two mappings to the mapping for the INTERMEDIARY to complete the set of mappings for this sentence:

object1(O1) = = subj(O1) = = particle1
loc(L) = = pp(from,L) = = pulley1

These mappings correspond to the fully instantiated predicate given below.

effect(inter(string1),
    location(object1(particle1),loc(pulley1)))

This predicate is decomposed in turn by applying R2 from the preceding section. There are now two **location** predicates to be decomposed, with the following instantiations, but there are no more syntactic constituents on the constituent list. The following section describes the rest of the lexical entries that are involved in the decomposition, and then the next section describes how pragmatic information is used to fill any uninstantiated semantic roles that are introduced during the final stages of the decomposition.

location(object1(particle1),loc(string1))
location(object1(string1),loc(pulley1))

Explicit relationships between semantic roles
In traditional approaches to semantic analysis, the emphasis has been on defining the semantic roles associated with a particular verb. For example, in "John broke the vase with a hammer," John is the AGENT, the vase is the PATIENT and the hammer is the INSTRUMENT. It has become clear that to derive "deeper" semantic representations, an attempt must be made to make explicit the relationships *between* the semantic roles themselves. Does John touch the hammer, does he want the vase to be broken, does the hammer touch the vase, and so on? An important question related to the validity of case theory rests on whether or not these semantic role relationships can generalize to more than one verb.

In the *hang* decomposition, there has already been one example of an explicit relationship *between* the semantic roles associated with the verb, namely the **effect** lexical entry. This lexical entry spells out precisely the way that the inclusion of the INTERMEDIARY semantic role influences the verb decomposition. As illustrated by the examples in section 4.3, if the INTERMEDIARY role is included, then there are two location relationships, one between the INTERMEDIARY and the entity being given a location, and the other between the INTERMEDIARY and the location itself. If the INTERMEDIARY role is not marked explicitly, that is, if it is included but only as an unmarked INTERMEDIARY, then there is only one location relationship involved. The explicit inclusion of the INTERMEDIARY role has the same influence on *connect* as well, causing two **contact** relationships to be established rather than just one. This illustrates that the influence of the INTERMEDIARY on a verb decomposition is not restricted to a particular verb, but is general to the class of verbs that include that type of INTERMEDIARY in their decomposition.

There are other semantic role interrelationships that can be made more explicit, such as what it means for one semantic role to be given a LOCATION. In the pulley domain, if an entity is given another entity as a LOCATION, it is assumed that there must be a **support** relationship between them (because of the existence of gravity). The **location** predicates in the example are decomposed into **support** predicates, by the application of R3.

R3:

location(object1(O1),loc(L)) ←
    support(object1(L),object2(O1))

Applying R3 derives the following two **support** predicates from the instantiated **location** predicates. Notice that these predicates indicate that pulley1 is supporting string1, and string1 is supporting particle1, exactly the expected interpretation of a *hanging* relationship.

support(object1(pulley1),object2(string1))
support(object1(string1),object2(particle1))

For an entity to **support** another entity, there must be some sort of direct **contact** between them, so **support** decomposes into **contact** with the application of R4.

R4:

support(object1(O1),object2(O2)) ←
    contact(object1(O1),object2(O2))

Applying R4 to the instantiated **support** predicates results in the following two instantiated **contact** predicates.

contact(object1(pulley1),object2(string1))
contact(object1(string1),object2(pulley1))

Finally, **contact** decomposes into two **locpt** predicates and a **sameplace** predicate through the application of R5, given below. Up until now none of the new predicates have introduced any new semantic roles, but applying R5 introduces the LOCPT semantic roles. There are no more syntactic constituents on the constituent list to fill these new roles, although it is possible for a LOCPT to be indicated explicitly at the surface level, as in the following sentence, "A particle is hung from a pulley at the left end of a string." R5 can be read as "If a location point on an entity, LOCPT(L1), and a location point on another entity, LOCPT(L2), are at the **sameplace**, then the entities are in contact with each other." Location points are classified as essential roles, so that if they are not filled by syntactic constituents they have to be deduced. The filling of the LOCPTS by pragmatic deduction is described in the following section.

R5:

contact(object1(O1),object2(O2)) ←
    locpt(locpt(L1),object1(O1)),
    locpt(locpt(L2),object2(O2)),
    sameplace(locpt(L1),locpt(L2)).

Filling unfilled semantic roles

Chapter 4 described how pragmatic information is used to fill unfilled semantic roles. In "the pulley is suspended from a pulley," it is clear from pragmatic information about suspension that a STRING, or some type of flexible line-segment, is doing the "suspending," but it is never mentioned explicitly. This sentential unit is followed by "and offset by a particle," meaning that the pulley is being counter-balanced by a particle, as in the following figure. The appropriate representation for *offset* is achieved by pragmatics supplying "string57" as a default value in the preceding representation of *suspend*. The methodology that allows an unfilled semantic role to be instantiated with string57 is summarized below.

"pulley is suspended from a pulley"
"and offset by a particle"

In order to accomplish this, traditionally semantic roles are divided into two classes, syntactically **obligatory** roles that have to be mentioned explicitly in the surface structure of a sentence, and syntactically **optional** roles that do not. Inference-driven mapping divides optional roles into two subcategories; **essential** roles that are *semantically* **obligatory**, and **optional** roles that are both syntactically and semantically **optional**. Labelling roles as essential is similar to the marking of roles as "elliptical" in the Lunar project [Nash Webber, 1975]. The classification of semantic roles as **optional**, **essential** or **obligatory** is used to constrain the application of pragmatic inference rules as follows:

1. unfilled **optional** roles are simply marked as "absent;"
2. unfilled **essential** roles are filled by deduction;
3. unfilled **obligatory** roles cause failure resulting in the derivation of a new set of mappings.

Fillers for **essential** roles basically fall into two categories.

1. new referents: these include default values and fillers hypothesized from general world knowledge;
2. known referents: these can be supplied by discourse information or deduced from general world knowledge.

In this domain, INTERMEDIARIES (similar to INSTRUMENTS) are considered to be essential roles, so when an INTERMEDIARY is not mentioned explicitly, as in "a pulley is suspended from another pulley," if no appropriate known referents can be found, pragmatics is allowed to create string57 as a default value, i.e., a *new referent*. The lexical entries associated with *offset*, in trying to represent a "counter-balancing" event, need to know what the "pulley" has been supported by in order to copy the support relationships. Since the "supporter" of the pulley, string57, was filled in the analysis of "a pulley is suspended from another pulley," local context can now recognize string57 as a *known referent* that is the supporter of the "particle."

Going back to sentence S1, there are four new semantic roles that are introduced as the following **location** relationships are decomposed into their respective **support** and **contact** relationships according to R3, R4 and R5. The roles in question are the four location points on the objects that are necessary to establish the **contact** relationship.

contact(object1(pulley1),object2(string1))
contact(object1(string1),object2(particle1))

Pragmatics recognizes that pulley1 and particle1 are solid entities with the shape of a point, so they are their own location points. The string requires two location points to be found, one for the **contact** with pulley1, and one for the **contact** with particle1. For the **contact** with the particle, which is considered to be a fixed **contact**, any unattached endpoint of string1 will do, say the right end, right1. The **contact** with the pulley is slightly more complicated, since given the nature of pulley systems in this domain it is necessarily a movable contact. For the location point on the string to change, it cannot be an endpoint, but must be some sort of midpoint. This is also supplied by pragmatics, and the resulting **sameplace** predicates are given below.

sameplace(locpt(particle1),locpt(right1))
sameplace(locpt(midpt1),locpt(pulley1))

This section and one of the preceding ones have explained how semantic roles can be filled by syntactic constituents or by pragmatic deduction, tasks 2 and 3. These two tasks are simply two different methods of finding instantiations for the predicate arguments, and can be performed as part of the application of the lexical entries. The ability to instantiate arguments by syntactic constituents or by pragmatic deduction is essential for the correct integration of the sentence representation within the current model of the scene being described, as explained below.

Controlling expansion

There could still be a problem with uncontrollable verb expansion, although it would now be seen as too great a proliferation of subgoals for decomposition. As explained in section 3.3.1, possible subgoals are limited to predicates involving semantic roles that can be realized as syntactic arguments of the verb which helps solve the problem of uncontrolled inferences, task 5. Other information may come into play when pragmatics is used to fill semantic roles, but this process is driven by the role-filling task, so it is still effectively constrained. Also, R5 demonstrates the high degree of generalization that can be achieved, since entries such as R5 are applicable to most of the verbs in the domain. **Support** and **location** relationships all eventually require **contacts** being made explicit. They can also all have location points for the **contacts** indicated by AT prepositional phrases, another cross-verb generalization.

Integrating semantic representations

To achieve an appropriate representation for a sentence, the piece of the scene being described must be represented accurately, and this representation must be integrated correctly with the current model of the scene derived from previous sentences, task 6. Semantic roles play an important part in the necessary integration since pragmatic information can sometimes use entities that have already been described to fill roles that are not mentioned explicitly in the sentence. This was illustrated by the *offset* example. Another example involves selecting an appropriate location point for the **contact** relationship between string1 and particle1. If the string1 is already in **contact** with something else, such as a fixed point on the ceiling, then one location point on the string would already be assigned. In selecting a location point for the particle, it is necessary to pass over any potential location points that are in the same place as another entity. This ensures that the new semantic representation being built is consistent with the existing model of the scene.

Another important component of successful integration is reference evaluation, task1. Previously described entities can be referred to directly in order to provide new information about them. Correct evaluation of such references is crucial to distinguishing between the information in the sentence that is "given" and the information that is "new." This component of the integration is currently assumed to be performed by another system with the fully determined referents being passed to inference-driven mapping as input. A more sophisticated processor would include control of this task as well.

Summary

In summary, a key component of inference-driven mapping is the division of domain-specific information into entries that spell out relationships between semantic roles, and pragmatic constraints that encode domain information useful for deducing fillers for these roles. As the entries are applied to expand the verb into its subgoals, the pragmatic constraints can be used along with syntactic mapping constraints to instantiate the arguments of the entries. The complete set of instantiated subgoals corresponds to an appropriate semantic representation of the sentence, and is produced directly from the original set of syntactic constituents by collecting each subgoal as it is established. This representation is given below. The process simultaneously performs the five tasks discussed above during the expansion of the verb representation. In performing these tasks, it is not necessary to go through separate levels of representation corresponding to templates and case-frames, since all of the information normally contained at these levels is now contained in the mapping constraints and the lexical entries themselves. The semantic representation that is produced by inference-driven mapping corresponds to the type of decompositional level of representation generally favored by linguists as being more capable of representing complex events and interactions between these events. In fact, the very complexity of the representation allows for the efficacy of the predicate environments, a major factor in the ability of inference-driven mapping to perform the tasks associated with semantic analysis simultaneously, without requiring the separate levels of description and corresponding separate stages of processing used by templates.

5.2   Distinguishing between definitions and representations

A fundamental assumption of inference-driven mapping is that the same lexical entry can correspond to several different syntactic realizations, depending on the application of the mapping constraints. Another fundamental assumption is that the same lexical entry can also produce several quite different semantic representations depending on how the semantic roles have been filled. This is the essence of a procedural interpretation; that the final state of the procedure can differ, depending on the parameters that are passed to it. This section illustrates this capability with several examples based on the same lexical entries used in the example for the preceding section. These examples have all been described in detail in chapter 4, and are briefly recapped here. A comparison of this approach to the template approach is included, with a brief summary of certain advantages. Finally, possible implications for linguistics that are suggested by the clear distinction between the definition of the verb, i.e., the lexical entry, and the semantic representation corresponding to the verb usage are suggested.

5.2.1   *Representing alternative syntactic realizations*

As discussed in chapter 2, the template approach is fundamentally similar to the multiple case frame approach in providing separate patterns for alternative syntactic realizations of the same verb. Separate patterns also have to be provided for other definitions of the same verb, and there is no inherent distinction between an additional pattern that corresponds to a slight syntactic variation and an additional pattern that corresponds to a new definition. In contrast, the procedural interpretation used by inference-driven mapping produces all of the alternative syntactic realizations from the same lexical entry of the verb. Other verb definitions would be represented by other lexical entries, so there is no possible confusion between different syntactic realizations and different verb meanings. In inference-driven mapping the same lexical entry can also produce quite different semantic representations for the alternative syntactic realizations. There is a clear distinction between the definition that is being used to produce the representations and the representations themselves.

One of the original problems from chapter 1 centered on *hang* verbs. "Do the uses of *hang* and *suspend* in the following sentences constitute several different verb predicates or are they all really the same?" One of the disadvantages of case frame representations and templates is that they do not provide any answer to such questions. Every different syntactic realization of a verb requires a new pattern, whether it corresponds to a different verb usage or not.

1. "a pulley is suspended from a pulley"
2. "at one end of a string a weight is suspended"
3. "a string hangs over a pulley"
4. "weights hang freely on the ends of a string"

5.2.2   *The template approach*

Templates are constructed by listing, for a particular domain, all of the possible syntactic expressions of a single verb, and as such are very similar to multiple case frames for the verb. Generally, appropriate semantic features are associated with the syntactic constituents. The objective of the processor involved is to match the syntactic parse of a sentence with one of the templates involving the main verb of the clause. Each template has its own set of inference rules to either derive the required semantic representation directly or to alternatively map the template onto a more general representation of the verb from which the semantic representation is derived by applying another set of lexical entries. A set of templates minus the associated inference rules is given below. The syntactic constituents indicated in these templates are implicit in the word ordering. Each one of the phrases from above would match a different template.

Templates:

⟨physobj⟩ SUSPEND from ⟨physobj⟩
at ⟨location⟩ ⟨physobj⟩ SUSPEND
⟨line-segment⟩ HANG over ⟨physobj⟩
⟨physobj⟩ HANG freely on
      ⟨locpt⟩ of ⟨line-segment⟩

There is no attempt to indicate whether the templates given above are merely different alternative syntactic realizations for the same verb definition, or whether they actually indicate four distinct verb definitions. This is presumably taken care of in the application of the inference rules. Each template can have its own set of inference rules, so any variations in meaning can be handled by drawing different inferences. Or possibly the templates are associated with different canonical forms, which then allow different types of inferences to be drawn. Either way, there is nothing in the templates themselves to distinguish between them.

Extending the toy template system suggested here to also accept "at one end of a string a weight is hung" would require an additional template with its corresponding set of inference rules. No advantage can be taken of the similarity between this phrase and one of the existing phrases. Template systems quickly become explosive when attempts are made to extend them to larger domains.

5.2.3   *The inference-driven mapping approach*

By comparison, the following examples clearly illustrate that for inference-driven mapping, the first three of the phrases are accommodated by the same lexical entry, while the fourth requires a different lexical entry. The three phrases using the same lexical entry all indicate the same definition of the verb, although their semantic representations are quite different. The fourth phrase indicates some similarity in meaning, but the lexical entry is really quite distinct. The ability of several phrases to be analyzed by the same lexical entry has advantages in terms of economy of information storage as well as interesting implications for linguistics.

The main lexical entry that is used is shared by *hang* and *suspend*, and is given below. It is used in conjunction with mapping constraints to handle the first three phrases. These constraints could theoretically be used to generate the template given above, as well as other syntactic expressions of the verbs. The same lexical entry can also be used to accept "at one end of a string a weight is hung," as well as "a weight is hung from a pulley." Adding verbs that are semantically similar to existing verbs is straightforward. It is only necessary to define the verb in terms of the semantic predicates that define the other verbs, and if the verb has unique syntactic realizations, add the necessary mapping constraints.

> **hang** ←
>> effect(inter(I),
>>> location(object1(O1),loc(L)))

> **suspend** ←
>> (the same as **hang**)

Example 1

The processing of three of the four example phrases has been described in detail in section 4.3, and is briefly restated here, as well as the processing of the fourth example. Each of the examples uses some of the mapping constraints listed below.

> *Mapping constraints:*

> object1(O1) = = subj(O1)
> loc(L) = = pp(from,L)
> loc(L) = = pp(over,L)
> loc(Loc) = = pp(at,Loc)

The first phrase is

> "a pulley is suspended from another pulley."

The input is:

> *Verb:* **suspend**

> Constituent list:
> subj(pulley1)
> pp(from,pulley2)

Using the lexical entry for **suspend**, inference-driven mapping finds the following set of mappings from the syntactic constituents to the semantic roles.

> object1(O1) = = subj(O1) = = pulley1
> loc(L) = = pp(from,L) = = pulley2

Pragmatics supplies an instantiation for the INTERMEDIARY, a default value which is "string57," and the **effect** lexical entry, R2, from section 5.1 is applied to decompose the **effect** predicate. The rest of the decomposition is basically the same as the decomposition discussed in section 5.1. The final representation for "a pulley is suspended from another pulley" is given below.

suspend

effect(inter(string57),
    location(object1(pulley1),loc(pulley2),time(i))))

location(object1(pulley1),loc(above(string57)),time(i))

support(object1(string57),object2(pulley1),time(i))

force(up(F1),object1(string57))
force(down(F1),object2(pulley1))
contact(object1(string57),object2(pulley1),time(i))
locpt(locpt(right57),object1(string57),time(i))
locpt(locpt(pulley1),object2(pulley1),time(i))
sameplace(locpt(right57),locpt(pulley1),time(i))

location(object1(string57),loc(above(pulley2)),time(d))

support(object1(pulley2),object2(string57),time(d))

force(up(F1),object1(pulley2))
force(down(F1),object2(string57))
contact(object1(pulley2),object2(string57),time(d))

locpt(locpt(pulley2),object1(pulley2),time(d))
locpt(locpt(midpt57),object2(string57),time(d))
sameplace(locpt(pulley2),locpt(midpt57),time(d))

Example 2
On the other hand, in

"At one end of a string a weight is suspended,"

the same lexical entry produces a very different semantic representation. The input is:

Verb: **suspend**

Constituent list:
subj(wt1)
pp(at,rt1)

The mapping constraints above choose the following mappings from syntactic constituents to semantic roles:

object1(O1) = = subj(O1) = = wt1
loc(L) = = pp(at,L) = = rt1

Again there is no explicit mention of an INTERMEDIARY doing the suspending, but there is an indirect reference to a string. The string is thus considered to be an unmarked INTERMEDIARY, an entity that normally acts as an

INTERMEDIARY but plays a dual role in this sentence. The normal lexical entry for the **effect** predicate is not applied, and the entry that corresponds to unmarked INTERMEDIARIES is applied instead. This entry effectively ignores the presence of the INTERMEDIARY since it is unmarked, and proceeds with the decomposition of the semantic predicate. The lexical entry for unmarked INTERMEDIARIES is given below.

> effect(inter(unmarked),Predicate) ←
> Predicate

The application of this entry results in only one **location** predicate being included in the final representation given below. This is, of course, quite different from the semantic representation of the preceding example, and it is the inclusion of the unmarked INTERMEDIARY that influences the representation, rather than anything to do with the lexical entry for ***hang***.

> ***suspend***
> effect(inter(unmarked),
>   location(object1(wt1),loc(rt1)))
> location(object1(wt1),loc(rt1))
>
> support(object1(rt1),object2(wt1))
>
> contact(object1(rt1),object2(wt1))
>
> locpt(locpt(wt1),object1(wt1))
> locpt(locpt(rt1),object2(rt1))
> sameplace(locpt(wt1),locpt(rt1))

> *Example 3*

The third example also involves an unmarked INTERMEDIARY.

> "a string hangs over a pulley,"

The input is:

> *Verb:* ***hang***
>
> Constituent list:
> subj(string1)
> pp(over,pulley1)

String1 would first be mapped onto the INTERMEDIARY role, as in "A string hangs a particle from a pulley." But the absence of an OBJECT1, which is an **obligatory** semantic role, causes the program to backtrack in order to find a new set of mappings. This time the string plays the role of the OBJECT1, resulting in the following set of mappings:

object1(O1) = = subj(O1) = = string1
loc(L) = = pp(over,L) = = pulley1

Pragmatics recognizes that the normal INTERMEDIARY is playing a dual role, with the primary role being OBJECT1. There is no need to create a referent for an INTERMEDIARY, but neither is a marked INTERMEDIARY included in the set of mappings. The lexical entry for unmarked INTERMEDIARIES is applied again, resulting in the following representation.

hang
effect(inter(unmarked),
   location(object1(string1),loc(pulley1)))
location(object1(string1),loc(pulley1))

support(object1(pulley1),object2(string1))

contact(object1(pulley1),object2(string1))

loctp(locpt(midpt1),object1(string1))
locpt(locpt(pulley1),object2(pulley1))
sameplace(locpt(midpt1),locpt(pulley1))

Example 4
The last example,

"weights hang freely on the ends of a string,"

is fundamentally different, since the inclusion of the adverb invokes a different lexical entry, given below.

hang-freely ←
   not-rest(object1(O1),object2(solid))

not-rest(object1(O1),object2(solid)) ←
   location(object1(O1),loc(L),time(Per))

The input is:

Verb: **hang-freely**

Constituent list:
pl(subj([wt1,wt2]))
pl(pp(on,[right1,left1]))

In spite of the entries being so different, the end result still contains a **location** predicate. The importance of the adverb is that it adds information to what is normally supplied by the unmodified verb.

hang-freely
not-rest(object1(wt1),object2(solid))
location(object1(wt1),loc(right1))

hang-freely
not-rest(object1(wt2),object2(solid))
location(object1(wt2),loc(left1))

Summary

In summary, inference-driven mapping gives an explicit answer as to whether or not different syntactic realizations require different verb definitions. The answer makes a distinction between the lexical entry used to produce the representations and the representations themselves. The procedural interpretation of the entry can differ, depending on the presence or absence of a filler for a semantic role, or even on the type of filler. This can result in very different semantic representations. The lexical entry involved in three of the four examples given above is essentially the same. The final representations, although they all share **location** predicates, are indeed different. The ability to distinguish clearly between definitions and semantic representations may provide a useful tool for exploring certain questions in linguistics, as explained in the next section.

5.2.4   *Causative forms*

Another question specifically involves potentially causative verbs such as *hang*: in changing from the causative to the stative form of *hang* do the definitions change? Or rather, are the verb definitions the same for the transitive and intransitive forms of *hang*?

> John hung a mass from a pulley.
> A mass hangs from a pulley.

One example from the pulley domain, *pull*, illustrates how inference-driven mapping can deal with the traditional decompositional definition of **cause**, with an AGENT and an Event as arguments to a **cause** predicate. In the lexical entry for *pull* given below, the causal predicate is specified as a **cause-motion** predicate that requires an AGENT and a **move** Event.

pull ←
cause-motion(agent(A),
    move(object1(O1),path(P),time(T)))

A more general lexical entry for **cause** that does not require a **move** Event could handle both of the *hang* examples from above, and is given below. This type of entry could handle a more general class of causative verbs that would still not necessarily include all causative verbs, but rather a well-defined subset. This approach has already been illustrated by the use of the **effect** predicate to indicate a class of verbs whose INTERMEDIARIES behave in a similar way. This allows one general lexical entry to be associated with the verb that can produce either a causative interpretation or a stative interpretation. The stative interpretation would occur when the AGENT is marked "absent," and the causative interpretation would follow from an instantiated AGENT. This does not imply that AGENTS have to be **obligatory** or even **essential** semantic roles, simply that their absence should be noted.

> cause(agent(absent),event) ←
>   achieves(unknown,occurs(Event))

> cause(agent(A),Event) ←
>   desire(A,Event),
>   achieves(A,occurs(Event))

The lexical entry for *hang* would now include a **cause** predicate, as illustrated by the example below. The first sentence, "John hung a mass from a pulley," would result in the AGENT being instantiated, and the decomposition into predicates indicating that John desired the *hanging* Event, and John achieved the *hanging* Event, etc. These predicates are just suggestions of a possible representation of **cause**, that could certainly be refined by further research. On the other hand, the second sentence, "A mass hangs from a pulley," would result in the AGENT being marked "absent," and no decomposition into desire would occur. The possibility of using the same lexical entry for interpreting both causative and stative forms of the same verb has interesting implications for linguistics. The assumption up until now is that the lexical entries correspond to the verb definitions for the verbs within the sublanguage of the limited domain. This would suggest that, for a limited domain, causative and stative verbs share the same definition. Whether or not such a definition can be extended to other domains, and would indeed have relevance to causative and stative verbs in general, is an interesting question for future research.

> *hang* ←
>   cause(agent(A),
>   effect(inter(I),
>   location(object1(O1),loc(L),time(initial)))))

5.2.5   *Summary*

This section has illustrated advantages of producing verb representations via the procedural interpretation of lexical entries, i.e., inference-driven mapping. The procedural interpretation can differ according to the presence or absence of fillers for particular semantic roles, which allows alternative syntactic realizations of the same verb or of synonymous verbs to be recognized as being produced by the same verb definition, even though the representations achieved may be quite different. This represents an advantage over multiple case frames and templates, since they have different patterns for every different syntactic realization of a verb, whether the syntactic realization corresponds to a different semantic representation or not. It also has interesting ramifications for certain theoretical questions in linguistics, such as the status of causative and stative forms of the same verb.

5.3   Future research

This method of semantic processing is sufficiently distinct from previous methods that it immediately suggests several possible extensions. Many of these extensions, such as using lexical entries for generation and exploring the formal properties of lexical entries as a grammar, have already been discussed in some detail in chapter 3, so those discussions are not repeated here. The most obvious extension is the integration of this method of semantic processing with existing syntactic parsers. There is enough disparity between the inference-driven mapping and previous assumptions about semantic processing that it is not immediately obvious how such an integration could be achieved. Section 5.3.1 speculates on some of the more obvious constraints on such an integration. Another important consideration for future research discussed in section 5.3.2 is the potential for transporting some of the lexical entries and mapping constraints to other domains. The generality of the domain formalization is interesting not only from a practical standpoint, but also in terms of applicability to linguistic theories about semantic analysis.

5.3.1   Integration of syntax with semantics

One of the most eagerly sought goals in natural language processing is a clean integration of syntax and semantics. The semantic processor described here assumes a syntactic parse has already been produced. Future systems based on this method of semantic processing should investigate the integration of syntax with semantics. Since most previous attempts have been based on verb representations such as case frames or templates, there will be major differences. The two most important differences will revolve round the potential contributions to the guiding of syntactic parsing offered by the mapping rules and the greater flexibility achieved by using the same verb definition for transitive and intransitive verbs.

The most likely candidate for integration would be DCGs [Pereira, 1980] since their logical implementation already represents verbs as predicates with syntactic constituents as potential arguments to those predicates.

The verb predicate exemplified by "loves(john,mary)" is the link between the syntactic parse described in chapter 1 and inference-driven mapping. For most of the verbs used in this domain, there would be a straightforward match between the standard predicate used in syntactic parsing and the left-hand side of the lexical entry.

For example, the DCG verb predicate could correspond directly to the left-hand side of the following lexical entry:

attach(object1(O1),object2(O2)) ←
contact(object1(O1),object2(O2))

For this example, the semantic processor would no longer have access to a constituent list, since the constituents would be supplied as they were parsed by the DCG. All the procedures for the simple transitive verbs would fit into the syntactic parsing neatly, since the syntactic parse of the example corresponds to the syntactic constituents associated with these verbs.

The problems would arise with the more complex lexical entries that involve AGENTS and INSTRUMENTS. The verb predicate on the left-hand side of *hang* only includes **obligatory** semantic roles. If **optional** AGENTS were to feature in the syntactic parse, it is not clear how they should be handled. At present, parsers simply include alternative predicate representations that commit to the presence or absence of **optional** semantic roles. Whether or not a syntactic parser can be designed to take advantage of the greater flexibility allowed by procedural interpretation of the following entry is an interesting research question.

hang(agent(A),inter(I),object1(O1),loc(L)))
←
cause(agent(A),
effect(inter(I),
location(object1(O1),loc(L)))

To sum up, taking advantage of the goal-oriented nature of inference-driven mapping and the clean ties between syntactic cues and semantic roles represented by the mapping constraints, would require a very flexible strategy for syntactic parsing. Close integration with such a parser might result in using the procedural verb interpretation to find the semantic role assignments; taking suggestions for parsing from the syntactic cues associated with the semantic roles; and including a level of description that captured the essence of the verb usage while still preserving the information conveyed by the surface syntactic structure. This level of description would include much of the information mentioned in chapter 3 as being required for accurate generation of sentences. In any event, the most desirable interaction between inference-driven mapping and a syntactic parser would be clearly defined communication between two independent processors running in parallel.

5.3.2 Transportability

All of the mapping constraints and lexical entries described here have been presented as being domain-specific. However, there are certain indications that some of the mapping constraints as well as some of the lexical entries might transport to other domains. The most likely candidates are the ones that deal with the semantic roles that closely correspond to the traditional cases, such as AGENT and INTERMEDIARY. Certainly the syntactic cues for these semantic roles, as evidenced by the mapping constraints, are in accord with Fillmore's original association of syntactic cues with certain cases. For example, INTERMEDIARIES can be indicated by subj(X)s, and pp(by,Y)s. In the pulley domain they were never indicated by a pp(with,Z), but it is easy to construct a sentence for this domain that would use a pp(with,Z) in such a manner.

"John hung the particle from the pulley with a string."

In fact, the absence of INTERMEDIARIES being indicated by pp(with,Z)s would seem in agreement with a restriction on certain types of INSTRUMENTS that has already been mentioned, namely that they can only be indicated by a pp(with,Z) if an AGENT is mentioned explicitly. Since, with respect to strings being hung, AGENTS are never mentioned explicitly in the passive world of pulleys, it is appropriate that the INTERMEDIARIES are never indicated by pp(with,Z)s. In applying this approach to other limited domains, special attention should be paid to similarity of mapping constraints for particular semantic roles.

Special attention should also be paid to transportability of lexical entries that are specifically associated with semantic roles, such as the **effect** and **cause-motion** entry. In trying to develop more transportable lexical entries for such semantic roles, relevant work in linguistics should be consulted. Bresnan's work on *polyadicity*, the number of arguments associated with verb predicates, deals with the issue of how INSTRUMENTALIZATION, for instance, can add an argument to the basic verb predicate [Bresnan, 1982]. This is very similar in spirit to the use of the **effect** predicate in inference-driven mapping. Developing semantic analysis systems for limited domains does not require a thorough linguistic analysis of INSTRUMENTS in general, but general rules for the effect of INSTRUMENTS that prove easily transportable from one domain to another may well derive from such a linguistic analysis. The lexical entry for **effect** presented in chapter 3 seems to be somewhat transportable in its own right, as illustrated by the following example.

Section 5.2.4 has already introduced a possible general entry for a **cause** predicate. By examining the *shoot* example from chapter 2 in more detail, it can be demonstrated that the **effect** predicate has potential for transportability as well. The problem with *shoot* is coming up with a representation that captures the complex interaction of a CONTACT event and a LAUNCH event. The representation suggested in chapter 2 is repeated below.

"John shot the turkey with a bullet from a rifle"

shoot ←
effect(instrument(bullet),
    contact-event(object1(john),object2(turkey),time(P))),

effect(instrument(rifle),
    cause-motion(agent(john),
    move(object1(bullet),object2(Path),time(Per))))

The first **effect** predicate in this representation can be decomposed using the general lexical entry for **effect** that applied to the pulley domain, given here. A **contact-event** is assumed to be a concrete-rel.

effect(instrument(I),
   concrete-rel(object1(O1),object2(O2),time(P))) ←
     concrete-rel(object1(O1),object2(I),time(P)),
     concrete-rel(object1(I),object2(O2),time(P))

The application of this lexical entry to the first effect predicate in the definition of *shoot*,

effect(instrument(bullet)
    contact-event(object1(john),object2(turkey),time(P))),

results in the following two **contact** predicates:

contact-event(object1(john),object2(bullet),time(P)),
contact-event(object1(bullet),object2(turkey),time(P))

The application of a similar entry for **effect** that has been tailored for **cause-motion** events,

effect(instrument(I),
  cause-motion(agent(A),
    move(object1(O1),object2(Path),time(Per))) ←

cause-motion(agent(A),
  move(object1(I),object2(Path1),time(Per1))
cause-motion(agent(I),
  move(object1(O1),object2(Path),time(Per))

to the second **effect** predicate in the *shoot* definition,

effect(instrument(rifle),
  cause-motion(agent(john),
    move(object1(bullet),object2(Path),time(Per)))

results in the following two **cause-motion** predicates:

cause-motion(agent(john),
  move(object1(rifle),object2(Path),time(Per))
cause-motion(agent(rifle),
  move(object1(bullet),object2(Path),time(Per))

This collection has still not fully captured an appropriate semantic representation for "John shot the turkey with a bullet from a rifle," but it is an approximation of such a representation. It has at least demonstrated the generality of the **effect** lexical entry, and the likelihood that it will prove transportable to other domains. An important area for further research is the possibility of such definitions being associated with classes of INSTRUMENTS, such as an INTERMEDIARY class, and also with classes of AGENTS such as AGENTS of motion events.

In general, when applying this approach to other domains, an attempt should be made to produce lexical entries that are as general as possible within the bounds of the domain, and to use lexical entries from other domains whenever appropriate. Eventually it should be possible to produce a core of lexical entries with associated mapping constraints that would act as a starting point for most domains, greatly improving the transportability of the system.

5.4 Conclusion

Chapter 2 specified several criteria for comparing and contrasting implementations that perform semantic analysis. They are repeated below, and this section goes on to briefly discuss the advantages and disadvantages of inference-driven mapping as compared to previous systems with respect to such criteria.

1. The linguistic theories themselves;
2. the adherence or non-adherence to those theories;
3. any variation in the processing of similar theories;
4. how well a theory lends itself to processing;
5. the transparency of the processing techniques;
6. overall advantages and disadvantages of an individual implementation.

The linguistic theory that inference-driven mapping is supposed to adhere to most closely is Jackendoff's theory of semantic analysis based on Gruber's thematic relations [Gruber, 1976; Jackendoff, 1972; Jackendoff, 1983]. This is certainly true from the point of view of the definitions of the verbs. There are several definitions in his latest work [Jackendoff, 1983] that could be translated directly into lexical entries for inference-driven mapping. For example, Jackendoff's analysis of *keep* [Jackendoff, 1983, page 175], as in

"Suzanne kept the books on the shelf."

can be expressed straightforwardly in inference-driven mapping notation, where "things" are similar to "objects," and "places" are similar to "locs," as:

cause-event(thing(suzanne)),
stay-event(thing(books),place(on-shelf))

In terms of a linguistic theory lending itself to processing techniques, this would seem to be ideal. However, it is not that simple, since inference-driven mapping does not even attempt to adhere to Jackendoff in terms of going from the syntactic parse to the semantic representation. Inference-driven mapping uses a system of procedural interpretation of the lexical entries combined with syntactic cues for semantic roles that are applied to the semantic roles at the decompositional level, and this approach is not reflected in Jackendoff or in any other theory of semantic analysis.

All of the existing systems for semantic analysis, such as conceptual dependency nets, preference semantics, LNR, etc. achieve deep semantic representations that are similar to linguistic decompositions. Inference-driven mapping differs from all of these systems in providing a transparent method of mapping the syntactic constituents of the parse directly onto the semantic roles of the decomposition. The previous implementation that inference-driven mapping is closest to in spirit is the LNR system, which also had a procedural interpretation of a "deep" representation. However, the LNR system had also already mapped the syntactic constituents onto semantic roles before this stage of the processing, and did not use the procedural interpretation to drive the mapping process. In practice, inference-driven mapping is also similar to Winograd's SHRDLU, by identifying the semantic decomposition of the verb meanings with the procedural interpretation of the verbs. Inference-driven mapping has an advantage over SHRDLU in allowing for flexible assignment of syntactic constituents to semantic roles, a feature SHRDLU did not include.

Comparisons between inference-driven mapping and templates, i.e., the multiple case frame method, have already been discussed thoroughly in this chapter. They can be summarized into two main advantages that inference-driven mapping has over templates: (1) not having intermediate levels of description allows inference-driven mapping to perform the tasks associated with semantic analysis simultaneously, resulting in a more integrated and efficient system, and (2) the clear distinction between the lexical entries corresponding to the verb definitions and the semantic representations that are produced using the entries provides interesting evidence for instances of similar verb usage and instances of dissimilar verb usage not provided by templates.

The biggest drawback suffered by inference-driven mapping is that it performs the semantic analysis after the parse has been completed, and does not currently interact with a syntactic parser during the production of the parse. As mentioned previously, this is an important area for future research, and it will only be when such a system has been successfully completed that this approach can be said to be a component of a coherent method of semantic analysis. It is possible that interfacing the system with a syntactic parser will cause several fundamental changes, which may result in a system that is closer to existing systems, or possibly even more dissimilar.

A general advantage inference-driven mapping enjoys is the transparency of the processing offered by the procedural interpretation of the lexical entries. The lexical entries are actually the procedures, and it only remains to fill in the semantic roles while they are being executed. This capability is provided by reliance on a highly sophisticated programming language, Prolog, and it is hoped that future research relating to interfacing inference-driven mapping with a syntactic parser will result in equally transparent processing methods.

Appendix A
The pulley problems

1. (Humphrey, p. 84, no. 2)
   Two pulleys of weights 12 lb and 8 lb are connected by a fine string hanging over a smooth fixed pulley. Over the former is hung a fine string with weights 3 lb and 6 lb at its ends, and over the latter a fine string with weights 4 lb and x lb. Find x so that the string over the fixed pulley remains stationary, and find the tension in it.

2. (Part of Humphrey, p. 75, nos. 566)
   A mass of 9 lb resting on a smooth horizontal table is connected by a light string, passing over a smooth pulley at the edge of the table to a mass of 7 lb hanging freely. Find the common acceleration, the tension in the string and the pressure on the pulley.

3. Two particles of mass B and C are connected by a light string passing over a smooth pulley. Find their common acceleration.

4. Particles of mass 3 and 6 lb are connected by a light string passing over a smooth weightless pulley; this pulley is suspended from a smooth weightless pulley and offset by a particle of mass 8 lb. Find the acceleration of each particle.

5. A man of 12 stone and a weight of 10 stone are connected by a light rope passing over a pulley. Find the acceleration of the man. If the man pulls himself up the rope so that his acceleration is one half its former value, what is the upward acceleration of the weight?

6. (Street, p. 99, no. 58)
   A string carrying masses M, m at its two ends is placed over a fixed rough peg, the free portions of the string hanging vertically. Find the acceleration when the system is free to move.

7. (McKenzie, p. 76, no. 28)
   Two weights, of 500 g each, hang freely on the ends of a weightless cord which runs over a frictionless pulley. If they are initially at rest, calculate how long it is after 1 g weight has been added to one of them that this latter has dropped 1 m and find its velocity at this point. What is the tension in the string?

8. (Laney, p. 230, no. 6)
   A weightless string, of length a, with masses m and 3 m attached to its ends is placed on a smooth horizontal table perpendicular to an edge

with the mass m just over the edge. If the height of the table above the inelastic floor is also a, show that the mass 3 m will strike the floor at a distance a from the mass m.

9. (Laney, p. 233, no. 29)
   At one end of a light string passing over a small fixed pulley a weight of 3 lb is suspended and a light pulley is suspended at the other end. Over this pulley another light string passes with weights of 2 lb and 1 lb suspended at its ends. The whole system is let go from a position of rest; find the pressure on the fixed pulley while the system is moving and also the acceleration of the greatest weight.

10. (Laney, p. 23, no. 35)
    A string, one end of which is fixed, has slung on it a mass of 3 lb, and then passes over a smooth pulley and has a mass of 1 lb attached to its other end; show that the larger mass descends with acceleration $g/7$ and that the tension of the string is $1\frac{2}{7}$ lb.

11. (Laney, p. 234, no. 39)
    A string sustains a mass P at one end, then passes over a fixed pulley, then under a movable pulley to which a mass R is attached, and then over a fixed pulley and is attached to a mass Q at its other end. Assuming the masses of the string and pulleys to be negligible and that the parts of the string not in contact with the pulleys are vertical, find the acceleration of R and the tension of the string.

12. (Laney, p. 235, no. 45)
    Over a smooth light pulley is passed a string supporting at one end a weight of mass 4 lb and at the other a pulley of mass 1 lb. A string with masses 2 lb and 3 lb attached at its ends passes over the second pulley; show that the acceleration of the 4 lb mass is $9\,g/49$.

13. (Laney, p. 236, no. 51)
    A small smooth pulley of mass M is lying on a smooth table; a light string passes round the pulley and has masses m and m' attached to its ends, the two portions of the string being perpendicular to the edge of the table and passing over it so that the masses hang vertically. Show that the acceleration of the pulley is $4mm'g/(M(m + m') + 4mm')$.

Appendix B
The interpreter

The main code for the interpreter is given in figure B.2. The interpreter is accessed by the Prolog clause in figure B.1. **Expand** is called with three arguments, a token that refers to the clause to be expanded, a list of assertions from previous expansions (usually[ ]), and a variable that will be instantiated with the assertions produced by the semantic processing of this clause. For example, **expand** is usually first called with ":- expand(clause1,[ ],Assertions)" The goal of **expand** is to retrieve the syntactic parse associated with the clause and pass it to the interpreter, **execute**, as a parameter. The syntactic parses are stored in **parse** predicates which have three arguments. The first argument is a token identifying the particular clause. The second argument corresponds to the verb of the clause, and the third argument contains a list of the syntactic constituents occurring in the clause. In Prolog, executing **parse**(clause1,Verb, Constituents) is equivalent to a database lookup that causes Verb and Constituents to be instantiated. If the clause associated with clause1 is:

"A particle is attached to a string at its end . . ."

the entry for **parse** is:

```
expand(Clause,Asserts,Newasserts) :-
    parse(Clause,Verb,Constituents),
    execute(Verb,envi(Constituents,Asserts),envi([],Newasserts)).
```

Figure B.1: Accessing the interpreter

```
parse(clause1,
        attach(time(initial)),
        [subj(particle1),pp(to,string1),pp(at,right1)])
```

After executing **parse**, the arguments passed to **execute** become:

```
execute(attach(time(initial)),
```

envi([subj(particle1),pp(to,string1),pp(at,right1)],[ ]),
envi([ ],Newasserts))

The third argument ensures that there are not any constituents left in the list after **execute** has finished. If there are, **execute** will have failed to find the appropriate set of mappings, and Prolog will automatically backtrack to try and find an alternative set.

B.1   Execution

The interpreter for the semantic processor is modelled after the Prolog interpreter given in the Prolog DEC-10 manual, with a few additions. Each **execute** clause has three arguments, corresponding to (1) the current inference that is being drawn, whose validity is being tested, (2) the current environment which includes the constituent list and any other inferences that have been drawn, and (3) a possible new environment that could result from any inferences drawn from the first argument. The first clause in figure B.2 returns true if there are no more inferences to be drawn, ending execution. The second clause

```
execute([],Envi,Envi).

execute([P | Q],Envi,NEnvi):-
    !,   execute(P,Envi,PEnvi),
    execute(Q,PEnvi,NEnvi).

execute(P,envi(Const,Asserts),envi(Const,Asserts)) :-
    done(P,Asserts).

Execute(P,envi(Const,Asserts),envi(Nconst,Nasserts)) :-
    bind(P,P,envi(Const,Asserts),envi(Fconst,Basserts)),
    plurals(P,envi(Fconst,Basserts),envi(Plconst,Plasserts)),
    define([P | Q]),
    execute(Q,envi(Plconst,[P | Plasserts]),envi(Nconst,Nasserts)).
```

Figure B.2: The interpreter for the semantic processor

expects the first argument to be a list of inferences, and calls **execute** for the first member of the list, P, and for the rest of the list, Q. The third clause takes the current inference, P, and calls **done** to see if this inference with exactly the same instantiations has been drawn previously. The fourth clause is the one that does all the work. It first calls **bind** to evaluate the function symbols in the current inference, P, and then calls **plurals** to distribute any plural noun groups that need to be distributed to copies of P. It finally calls **define** which attempts to match P to the left-hand side of a member of the set of inference rules. If it succeeds (and it always does), then **execute** is called recursively to validate the new set of current inferences, Q, corresponding to the right-hand side of the rule.

B.2   Distributing plural noun groups

The plural noun groups in this domain always refer to small finite sets of objects, so there was no reason to delay distributing these objects among an appropriate number of copies of the inference involved. The three ways in which a plural noun group can be distributed are illustrated in figure B.3.

1. 'Two particles resting on the table . . .''

2. ". . . particles attached at its ends . . .''

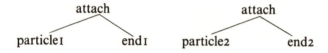

3. "A string carrying masses at its two ends"

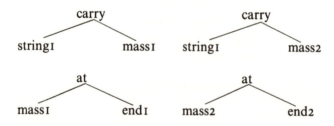

Figure B.3: Alternative distributions of plural noun groups

The Prolog clauses in figure B.4 accomplish this distribution. In the first clause of **plurals, plbind** first produces a copy of P, P2, and then tries to bind any uninstantiated arguments of P to a member of a plural noun group referred to by a syntactic constituent still on the constituent list. If **plbind** succeeds, and if there are still members of the plural noun group to be distributed, then **plcopy**

```
plurals(P,envi(Const,Asserts),envi(Nconst,Nasserts)) :-
    plbind(P,P2,envi(Const,Asserts),envi(Bconst,Basserts)),
    plcopy(P2,envi(Bconst,Basserts),envi(Nconst,Nasserts)).

plurals (P,Envi,Envi).

plbind(P,P2,envi(Const,Asserts),envi(Bconst,Basserts)) :-
    not(P =.. [Pred,time(Per)]),
    not(allbound(P)),
    memberchk(pl(Y),Const),
    copy(P,P2),
    bind(P,P,envi([plurals | Const],Asserts),envi(Bconst,Basserts)),
    !.

plcopy(P2,envi(Bconst,Basserts),envi(Nconst,Nasserts)) :-
    delete(copy,Bconst,Plconst),
    execute(P2,envi(Plconst,Basserts),envi(Nconst,Nasserts)).

plcopy(P2,Envi,Envi).
```

Figure B.4: Distributing plural noun groups

executes the copy of P, which will eventually call **plurals** and repeat the entire process. When the last member of the plural noun group has been distributed, **plcopy** simply succeeds without executing P2.

B.3 Function evaluation

This section explains the process by which the function symbols corresponding to the predicate argument positions are "evaluated." The goal of the evaluation is to return a referent for the semantic role represented by the predicate argument. The syntactic and semantic constraints described in chapter 4 are used to perform appropriate mappings from members of the constituent list to the semantic roles. If no suitable mappings are found pragmatic information is used to deduce a possible referent, as explained in chapter 4.

The term "OBJECT1(O1)" represents a function symbol, "OBJECT1," that has one argument, usually "O1." The function symbols can be thought of as a *typed* function, placing *constraints* on the *type* of argument that can be returned. This section describes the "binder," implemented in Prolog, that simulates the evaluation of the typed function. The binder first looks at syntactic constituents from the syntactic parse to see if any of them satisfy both the syntactic and semantic constraints associated with the function symbols of the argument in question. If no syntactic constituents are appropriate, the binder tries to **select** a referent using the pragmatic constraints described in section 3·6·2. If no obvious selections occur, the argument is left as a variable, and the interpreter looks for a rule whose left-hand side matches the semantic predicate whose arguments have just been instantiated.

The Prolog clauses in figure B.5 first make sure the argument has not already been instantiated. If not, **parsed** is executed to try and find a mapping to a syntactic constituent. The possible mappings are **checked** to be sure they are of the correct semantic type. Then **select** is called to assess any pragmatic implications of the referent of the syntactic constituents that has now been chosen to instantiate the argument representing the semantic role. If no appropriate mapping is found, **select** is also called in an effort to deduce an appropriate filler based on pragmatic constraints.

The first argument of **choose** is obviously the ARGUMENT to be instantiated. The second argument, **Rel**, corresponds to the current predicate environment of ARG. The third and fourth arguments are the same as the third and fourth arguments of **execute**. The third argument carries along the current constituent list, **Const**, and any inferences that have been drawn. The fourth argument can return a new constituent list and set of inferences.

Parsed and **check** have the same four arguments. When **parsed** is called, **Rel**, the current predicate environment, must match with the third argument of a **syntax** constraint, the predicate environment of the constraint itself, for that syntactic constraint to be chosen. A matching algorithm uses Prolog unification to test the matching of the predicate environments. The second argument of **syntax** is the syntactic constituent that might indicate a possible referent. If the match succeeds, and that particular syntactic constituent is a member of Const, it will be deleted from Const, producing Nconst, a new list of syntactic constituents that no longer contains it. In the original **syntax** constraint, the semantic role and the syntactic constituent shared the same variable, i.e., **O1**. This variable is now bound to the referent of the syntactic constituent, thus binding the semantic role, ARG, to that referent as well. So **parsed** succeeds, returning with ARG instantiated with a potential referent.

Check is very similar to **parsed**, but rather than delete a constituent from a list, **check** asks Prolog to prove that a **semantic Constraint** holds for this instantiation. If **check** fails, **parsed** tries again with a new **syntax** constraint. If there are no more appropriate **syntax** constraints, **parsed** fails as well, and the variable is left uninstantiated.

Even if **parsed** and **check** succeed, **select** is called. Sometimes the instantiation that has just been made will provide a crucial piece of information that allows pragmatics to make an important deduction. Calling **select** cannot in any way undo the assignment of the semantic roles that has just been made, but could possibly deduce something new that could not have been deduced before.

The last possibility to fill the argument is for **select** to find a likely binding using only pragmatic information. Chapter 4 explains **select** in more detail.

```
choose(Arg,Rel,Envi,Envi) ← bound(Arg).

choose(Arg,Rel,Oldenvi,Newenvi) ←
    parsed(Arg,Rel,Oldenvi,Newenvi),
    check(Arg,Rel,Newenvi,Newenvi),
    select(Arg,Rel,Newenvi,Newenvi).

choose(Arg,Rel,Envi,Newenvi) ←
    select(Arg,Rel,Envi,Newenvi).

choose(Arg,Rel,Envi,Envi).

parsed(Arg,Rel,envi(Const,Asserts),envi(Nconst,Asserts)) ←
    syntax(Arg,Constraint,Rel),
    delete(Constraint,Const,Nconst).

check(Arg,Rel,Envi,Envi) ←
    semantics(Arg,Constraint,Rel),
    Constraint.
```

Figure B.5: Choosing a syntactic constituent

Appendix C
The syntactic, semantic, and pragmatic rules

Syntax rules

```
syntax(agent(A),
       subj(A),
       cause(agent(A),Y)).

syntax(inter(I),
       subj(I),
       effect(inter(I),Y)).

syntax(inter(I),
       pp(by,I),
       effect(inter(I),Y)).

syntax(object1(Obj),
       subj(Obj),
       relation(object1(Obj),Y,Per)).


syntax(object1(Obj),
       obj(Obj),
       cause(A,move(object1(Obj),Y,Per))).

syntax(object1(Obj),
       pl(subj(Obj)),
       effect(inter(I),contact(object1(Obj),Y,Per))).

syntax(object2(Obj),
       obj(Obj),
       relation(object2(Obj),Y,Per)).

syntax(object2(Obj),
       pl(subj(Obj)),
       effect(inter(I),contact(Y,object2(Obj),Per))).
```

```
syntax(object2(Obj),
       pp(to,Obj),
       relation(Y,object2(Obj),Per)).

 syntax(object2(Obj),
       pp(by,Obj),
       balance(Y,object2(Obj),Per)).

syntax(object2(O2),
       pp(up,O2),
       direction(direction(up),object2(O2),Per)).

syntax(object2(O2),
       pp(from,O2),
       velocity(O1,object2(O2),Per)).

syntax(object2(O2),
       pp(with,O2),
       acceleration(O1,object2(O2),Per)).

syntax(locpt(L),
       pp(at,L),
       locpt(locpt(L),Y,Per)).

syntax(loc(above(L)),
       pp(at,L),
       location(Y,loc(above(L)),Per)).

 syntax(loc(above(L)),
       Const,
       location(Y,loc(above(L)),Per)) :-
           syntax(above(L),Const,
            location(Y,above(L),Per)).

 syntax(above(Obj),
       pp(on,Obj),
       location(Y,above(Obj),Per)).

 syntax(above(Obj),
       pp(over,Obj),
       location(Y,above(Obj),Per)).
```

```
syntax(above(Obj),
       pp(from,Obj),
       location(Y,above(Obj),Per)).

syntax(above(Obj),
       pp(round,Obj),
       location(Y,above(Obj),Per)).

syntax(loc(below(Obj)),
       pp(under,Obj),
       location(Y,loc(below(Obj)),Per)).

syntax(time(Per),
       pp(at,Per),
       seek(X,Y,time(Per))).
```

Semantics rules

```
semantics(agent(A),
          hasprop1(A,animate),
          cause(agent(A),Y)).

semantics(inter(I),
          isa1(lineseg,I),
          effect(inter(I),Y)).

semantics(object1(O1),
          isa1(animate,O1),
          seek(object1(O1),Y,Per)).

semantics(object1(O1),
          isa1(solid,O1),
          relation(object1(O1),Y,Per)).

semantics(object2(O1),
          isa1(solid,O1),
          relation(Y,object2(O2),Per)).

semantics(object2(O2),
          isa1(quantity,O2),
          seek(Y,object2(O2),Per)).
```

```
semantics(object1(O1),
          isa1(quantity,O1),
          equals(object1(O1),Y,Per)).

semantics(object2(O2),
          isa1(quantity,O2),
          equals(Y,object2(O2),Per)).

semantics(object2(O2),
          isa1(quantity,O2),
          velocity(O1,object2(O2),Per)).

semantics(object2(O2),
          isa1(quantity,O2),
          acceleration(O1,object2(O2),Per)).

semantics(object2(O2),
          path(S,E,distance(O2)),
          cause(A,move(Y,object2(O2),Per))).

semantics(object2(O2),
          isa1(lineseg,O2),
          direction(D,object2(O2),Per)).

semantics(loc(below(B)),
          isa1(pulley,B),
          location(Y,loc(below(B)),Per)).

semantics(loc(above(L)),
          isa1(solid,L),
          location(Y,loc(above(L)),Per)).

semantics(locpt(L),
          haspt(Y,L),
          locpt(locpt(L),Y,Per)).

semantics(time(Per),
          isa1(moment,Per),
          seek(X,Y,time(Per))).
```

```
/****** Pragmatic Rules  *********/


/****** Obligatory Roles    **********/

context(object1(unfilled),
        location(object1(unfilled),L,P),
        C,C) :-
    !,fail.

context(loc(unfilled),
        location(X,loc(unfilled),P),
        C,C) :-
    !,fail.


/****** Default Values        ********/

context(agent(gravity),
        cause(agent(gravity),move(O1,O2,P)),
        E,E).


context(object1(you),
        seek(object1(you),O2,Per),
        Context,Context).

context(loc(above(L)),
        effect(inter(string57),
         location(O1,loc(above(L)),Per)),
        E,E) :-
      bound(L),isa1(pulley,L).


context(inter(unmarked),
        effect(inter(unmarked),Predicate),
        C,C).

/****    Deducing fillers from context    ****/
```

```
context(inter(I),
        effect(inter(I),
         location(object1(Obj1),L,P)),
        E,E) :-
   bound(Obj1),
   effect(inter(I),location(object1(Obj1),L,P)).

context(loc(above(L)),
        location(object1(O1),loc(above(L)),Per),
        envi(C,Asserts),envi(C,Asserts)) :-
   var(L),
   bound(O1),
   could_support(L,O1,Asserts).

context(locpt(Var),
        locpt(locpt(Var),Arg,time(duration)),
        envi(Const,Asserts),envi(Const,Asserts)) :-
   split(Arg,Type,Var2),
   nonvar(Var2),var(Var),
   findpt(Var2,Var,Asserts).

context(locpt(Var),
        locpt(locpt(Var),Arg,time(Per)),
        envi(Const,Asserts),envi(Const,Asserts)) :-
   (same(Per,initial);same(Per,moment)),
   split(Arg,Type,Var2),
   nonvar(Var2),var(Var),
   findmidpt(Var2,Var,Asserts).


/****  Optional roles left unfilled    ****/


context(object2(Obj),
        Rel,
        Context,Context),

context(up(Var),
        Rel,
        Context,Context).

context(down(Var),
        Rel,
        Context,Context).
```

Appendix D
Verb, case, and relation definitions

```
define([
 add(time(Per)),
 contact(object1(O1),object2(O2),time(duration))]).

define([
 attach(time(duration)),
 contact(object1(O1),object2(O2),time(duration))]).

define([
 calculate(time(Per)),
 seek(object1(Q1),object2(O2),time(Per))]).

define([
 carry(time(Per)),
 support(object1(O1),object2(O2),time(Per))]).

define([
 connect(time(duration)),
 effect(inter(I),
  contact(object1(Obj1),object2(Obj2),time(duration)))]).
define([
 descend(time(Per)),
 move(object1(O1),object2(Path),time(Per)),
 direction(dir(down),object2(Path),time(Per))]).

define([
 drop(time(Per)),
 move(object1(O1),object2(Path),time(Per)),
 direction(dir(down),object2(Path),time(Per))]).

define([
 free_to_move(time(Per)),
 not_rest(object1(O1),object2(solid),time(Per))]).
```

```
define([
 find(time(Per)),
 seek(object1(O1),object2(Q1),time(Per))]).

define([
 fixed(time(duration)),
 location(object1(O1),loc(above(point)),time(duration))]).

define([
 hang(time(initial)),
 effect(inter(I),location(object1(Obj1),loc(Obj2),time(initial)))]).

define([
 hang_vertically(time(initial)),
 orientation(object1(O2),object2(vertical),time(initial))]).

define([
 hang_freely(time(Per)),
 not_rest(object1(O1),object2(solid),time(Per))]).

define([
 isv(time(Per)),
 equals(object1(O1),object2(O2),time(moment))]).

define([
 is_at_rest(time(initial)),
 velocity(object1(O1),object2(zero),time(initial))]).

define([
 let_go(time(Per)),
 velocity(object1(O1),object2(Q),time(initial))]).

define([
 lie(time(initial)),
 location(object1(O1),loc(L),time(initial))]).

define([
 offset(time(duration)),
 balance(object1(O1),object2(O2),time(initial))]).
```

```
define([
 pass(time(initial)),
 location(object1(O1),loc(L),time(initial))]).

define([
 place(time(initial)),
 location(object1(O1),loc(L),time(initial))]).

define([
 pull(time(Per)),
 cause(agent(A),move(object1(O1),object2(Path),time(Per))),
 direction(direction(Dir),object2(Path),time(Per))]).

define([
 remains_stationary(time(duration)),
 velocity(object1(O1),object2(zero),time(duration))]).

define([
 rest(time(initial)),
 location(object1(O1),loc(L),time(initial))]).

define([
 run(time(initial)),
 location(object1(O1),loc(L),time(initial))]).

define([
 sling(time(initial)),
 location(object1(O1),loc(L),time(initial))]).

define([
 seek(object1(O1),object2(O2),time(Per)),
 sought(object2(O2),time(Per))]).

define([
 strike(time(moment)),
 contact(object1(O1),object2(O2),time(moment))]).


define([
 supportv(time(initial)),
 support(object1(O1),object2(O2),time(initial))]).
```

```
define([
 suspend(time(initial)),
 effect(inter(I),location(object1(O1),loc(L),time(initial)))]).

define([
 sustain(time(initial)),
 support(object1(O1),object2(O2),time(initial))]).

define([
 what_is(time(Per)),
 seek(object1(O1),object2(Q1),time(Per))]).


/* Prepositions */


define([
 at(time(duration)),
 contact(object1(O1),object2(O2),time(duration))]).

define([
 just_over(time(initial)),
 not_rest(object1(O1),object2(O2),time(initial))]).

define([
  perpendicular_to(time(initial)),
  perpendicular(object1(O1),object2(O2),time(initial))]).


 define([
   with(time(duration)),
   contact(object1(O1),object2(O2),time(duration))]).
```

Appendix E
A worked example

---

1. (Humphrey, p. 84, no. 2)
Two pulleys of weights 12 lb and 8 lb are connected by a fine string hanging over a smooth fixed pulley. Over the former is hung a fine string with weights 3 lb and 6 lb at its ends, and over the latter a fine string with weights 4 lb and x lb. Find x so that the string over the fixed pulley remains stationary, and find the tension in it.

Input for problem 1
```
mass(pulley1,m1,duration).
measure(m1,12,lbs).
mass(pulley2,m2,duration).
measure(m2,8,lbs).
mass(string1,zero,duration).
fixed(pulley3,duration).
mass(string2,zero,duration).
mass(wt1,m3,duration).
measure(m3,3,lbs).
mass(wt2,m4,duration).
measure(m4,6,lbs).
mass(string3,zero,duration).
mass(wt3,m5,duration).
measure(wt3,4,lbs).
mass(wt4,m6,duration).
hasprop(string1,tension1).

parse(clause1,connect(time(Per)),
  [pl(subj(pulley1)),pl(subj(pulley2)),
   pp(by,string1)]).

parse(clause2,hang(time(Per)),
  [subj(string1),pp(over,pulley3)]).
```

```
parse(phrase1,with(time(Per)),
   [subj(string2),pl(obj(wt1)),pl(obj(wt2)),
   pl(pp(at,right2)),pl(pp(at,left2))]).

parse(clause3,hang(time(Per)),
   [subj(string2),pp(over,pulley1)]).

parse(clause4,hang(time(Per)),
   [subj(string3),pp(over,pulley2)]).

parse(phrase2,with(time(Per)),
   [subj(string3),pl(obj(wt3)),pl(obj(wt4))]).

parse(clause5,find(time(Per)),
   [obj(m6)]).

parse(clause6,remains_stationary(time(Per)),
   [subj(string1)]).

parse(clause7,find(time(Per)),
   [obj(tension1)]).
```

Output for problem I: (by clause)
''Two pulleys of weights 12 lb and 8 lb are connected by a fine string''

```
parse(clause1,connect(time(Per)),
 [pl(subj(pulley1)),pl(subj(pulley2)),pp(by,string1)]).

sameplace(locpt(left1),locpt(pulley2),time(duration))
locpt(locpt(pulley2),object2(pulley2),time(duration))
locpt(locpt(left1),object1(string1),time(duration))
contact(object1(string1),object2(pulley2),time(duration))
sameplace(locpt(pulley1),locpt(right1),time(duration))
locpt(locpt(right1),object2(string1),time(duration))
locpt(locpt(pulley1),object1(pulley1),time(duration))
contact(object1(pulley1),object2(string1),time(duration))
effect(inter(string1),
  contact(object1(pulley1),object2(pulley2),time(duration)))
connect(time(duration))
```

''string hanging over a smooth fixed pulley.''

```
parse(clause2,hang(time(Per)),
  [subj(string1),pp(over,pulley3)]).
```

```
sameplace(locpt(pulley3),locpt(midpt1),time(initial))
locpt(locpt(midpt1),object2(string1),time(initial))
locpt(locpt(pulley3),object1(pulley3),time(initial))
contact(object1(pulley3),object2(string1),time(initial))
force(down(_6038),object2(string1),time(initial))
force(up(_6038),object1(pulley3),time(initial))
support(object1(pulley3),object2(string1),time(initial))
location(object1(string1),loc(above(pulley3)),time(initial))
effect(inter(unmarked),
  location(object1(string1),loc(above(pulley3)),time(initial)))
hang(time(initial))
```

''Over the former is hung a fine string''

```
parse(clause3,hang(time(Per)),
   [subj(string2),pp(over,pulley1)]).
```

```
sameplace(locpt(pulley1),locpt(midpt2),time(initial))
locpt(locpt(midpt2),object2(string2),time(initial))
locpt(locpt(pulley1),object1(pulley1),time(initial))
contact(object1(pulley1),object2(string2),time(initial))
force(down(_16251),object2(string2),time(initial))
force(up(_16251),object1(pulley1),time(initial))
support(object1(pulley1),object2(string2),time(initial))
location(object1(string2),loc(above(pulley1)),time(initial))
effect(inter(unmarked),
  location(object1(string2),loc(above(pulley1)),time(initial)))
hang(time(initial))
```

''a fine string with weights 3 lb and 6 lb at its ends,''

```
parse(phrase1,with(time(Per)),
   [subj(string2),pl(obj(wt1)),pl(obj(wt2)),pl(pp(at,right2)),
    pl(pp(at,left2))]).
```

```
sameplace(locpt(left2),locpt(wt1),time(duration))
locpt(locpt(wt1),object2(wt1),time(duration))
locpt(locpt(left2),object1(string2),time(duration))
contact(object1(string2),object2(wt1),time(duration))
sameplace(locpt(right2),locpt(wt2),time(duration))
locpt(locpt(wt2),object2(wt2),time(duration))
locpt(locpt(right2),object1(string2),time(duration))
contact(object1(string2),object2(wt2),time(duration))
with(time(duration))
```

``and over the latter a fine string (is hung)''

```
parse(clause4,hang(time(Per)),
  [subj(string3),pp(over,pulley2)]).
```

```
sameplace(locpt(pulley2),locpt(midpt3),time(initial))
locpt(locpt(midpt3),object2(string3),time(initial))
locpt(locpt(pulley2),object1(pulley2),time(initial))
contact(object1(pulley2),object2(string3),time(initial))
force(down(_20935),object2(string3),time(initial))
force(up(_20935),object1(pulley2),time(initial))
support(object1(pulley2),object2(string3),time(initial))
location(object1(string3),loc(above(pulley2)),time(initial))
effect(inter(unmarked),
  location(object1(string3),loc(above(pulley2)),time(initial)))
hang(time(initial))
```

``a fine string with weights 4 lb and x lb.''

```
parse(phrase2,with(time(Per)),
  [subj(string3),pl(obj(wt3)),pl(obj(wt4))]).
```

```
sameplace(locpt(left3),locpt(wt3),time(duration))
locpt(locpt(wt3),object2(wt3),time(duration))
locpt(locpt(left3),object1(string3),time(duration))
contact(object1(string3),object2(wt3),time(duration))
sameplace(locpt(right3),locpt(wt4),time(duration))
locpt(locpt(wt4),object2(wt4),time(duration))
locpt(locpt(right3),object1(string3),time(duration))
contact(object1(string3),object2(wt4),time(duration))
with(time(duration))
```

``Find x''

```
parse(clause5,find(time(Per)),
    [obj(m6)]).


sought(object2(m6),time(_29289))
seek(object1(you),object2(m6),time(_29289))
find(time(_29289))
```

``so that the string over the fixed pulley remains stationary,''

```
parse(clause6,remains_stationary(time(Per)),
    [subj(string1)]).


velocity(object1(string1),object2(zero),time(duration))
remains_stationary(time(duration))
```

``and find the tension in it.''

```
parse(clause7,find(time(Per)),
    [obj(tension1)]).


sought(object2(tension1),time(_30814))
seek(object1(you),object2(tension1),time(_30814))
find(time(_30814))
```

References

Ait-Kaci, Hassan and Nasr, Robert (1986). LOGIN: a logic programming language with built-in inheritance. *Logic Programming Journal*, **3**, 185–215.

Brachman, Ronald and Levesque, Hector (1985). *Readings in Knowledge Representation*. Morgan Kaufmann, Los Altos, CA.

Bresnan, Joan W. (1982). Polyadicity. In Bresnan, Joan W. (ed.), *The Mental Representation of Grammatical Relations*, pp. 149–72. MIT Press, Cambridge, MA.

Bruce, Bertram (1975). Case systems for natural language. *Artificial Intelligence*, **6**(4), 327–60.

Bundy, Alan (1979). Solving mechanics problems using metalevel inference. In Michie, D. (ed.), *Expert Systems in the Micro-electronic Age*. Edinburgh University Press, Edinburgh, UK.

Cardelli, Luca (1984). *Semantics of Multiple Inheritance*. Technical Report, Bell Labs. Internal Publication.

Charniak, Eugene (1975). *A Brief on Case*. Working Paper 22, Castagnola Institute for Semantics and Cognitive Studies.

Charniak, Eugene and Wilks, Yorick (eds.) (1976). *Computational Semantics: an Introduction to Artificial Intelligence and Natural Language Comprehension*. North Holland, Amsterdam.

Clark, Keith (1978). Negation as failure. In Gallaire, H. and Minker, J. (eds.), *Logic and Data Bases*. Plenum Press, New York.

Fillmore, C. (1977). The case for case reopened. In Cole, P. and Sadock, J.M. (eds.), *Syntax and Semantics*, Volume 8: *Grammatical Relations*. Academic Press, NY.

(1980). The case for case. In Bach and Harms (eds.), *Universals in Linguistic Theory*, pp. 1–88. Holt, Rinehart, and Winston, New York.

Fodor, Janet D. (1980). *Semantics: Theories of Meaning in Generative Grammar*. *Language and Thought Series*, Harvard University Press.

Goguen, J.A. and Mesequer, J. (1988). Equality, types, modules and generics for logic programming. CSLI-84-5. Center for the Study of Language and Information, Stanford University.

Gruber, J.S. (1976). *Lexical Structures in Syntax and Semantics*. North Holland, Amsterdam.

Halpern, Joseph Y. (ed.) (1986). *Theoretical Aspects of Reasoning about Knowledge. Proceedings of the 1986 Conference*. Morgan Kaufmann, Los Altos, CA.

Hobbs, Jerry, Croft, William, Davies, Todd, Edwards, Douglas, and Laws, Kenneth (1986). Commonsense metaphysics and lexical semantics. In *Proceedings of the 24th Annual Meeting of the Association for Computational Linguistics, June 1986*. Published by the Association for Computational Linguistics.

197

Jackendoff, R. S. (1970). A system of semantic primitives. In Nash-Webber, Bonnie, L. and Schank, Roger C. (eds.), *Theoretical Issues in Natural Language Processing*, pp. 24–9. Ginn, Cambridge, MA.

(1979). *Semantic Interpretation in Generative Grammar*. MIT Press, Cambridge, MA.

(1983). *Semantics and Cognition*. MIT Press, Cambridge, MA.

Kay, Martin (1973). The MIND system. In Rustin, Randall (ed.), *Natural Language Processing*, pp. 155–88. Algorithmics Press, New York.

Kowalski, Robert (1979). *Logic for Problem-solving*. North Holland, Amsterdam.

Levin, B. (1977). Predicate-Argument Structures in English. MA Thesis Proposal.

(1979). *Instrumental With and the Control Relation in English*. MIT AI Memo 552, MIT, MIT Master's Thesis.

McCawley, James (1968). Lexical insertion in a transformational grammar without deep structure. In Darden, B.J., Bailey, C.N. and Davison, A. (eds.) *Proceedings of the Fourth Regional Meeting of the Chicago Linguistic Society*. Department of Linguistics, University of Chicago, Chicago, IL.

Mellish, Chris. (1981). *Incremental Evaluation*. PhD thesis, University of Edinburgh.

Nash-Webber, Bonnie (1975). The role of semantics in speech understanding. In Bobrow, D. and Collins, A. (eds.), *Representation and Understanding: Studies in Cognitive Science*. Academic Press, New York.

Norman, Donald A. and Rumelhart, David E. (1975). *Explorations in Cognition*. Freeman, San Francisco.

Novak, G.S. (1976). Computer understanding of physics problems stated in natural language. *American Journal of Computational Linguistics*. Microfiche 53.

Palmer, M. and McCoy, K. (in preparation). Motion verbs: a semantic analysis.

Palmer, Martha S., Dahl, Deborah A., Passonneau, Rebecca J. [Schiffman], Hirschman, Lynette, Linebarger, Marcia, and Dowding, John (1986). Recovering implicit information. In *Proceedings of the 24th Annual Meeting of the Association for Computational Linguistics, June 1986*. Published by the Association for Computational Linguistics.

Pereira, Fernando C.N. and Warren, David H.D. (1980). Definite clause grammars for language analysis – a survey of the formalism and a comparison with augmented transition networks. *Artificial Intelligence*, **13**(3), 231–78.

Pereira, Fernando and Shieber, Stuart (1987). *Prolog and Natural-Language Analysis*. University of Chicago Press, Chicago, IL.

Schank, Roger C. (ed.) (1975). *Conceptual Information Processing*. North Holland, Amsterdam.

Simmons, R.F. (1967). Answering English questions by computer. In Borko, Harold (ed.), *Automated Language Processing: The State of the Art*. Wiley and Sons, NY. Also appears in *Communications of the Association for Computing Machinery*, **13**, 1970.

(1973). Semantic networks: their computation and use for understanding English sentences. In Schank and Colby (eds.), *Computer Models of Thought and Language*. W.H. Freeman, San Francisco.

Stockwell, Robert P., Schacter, Paul, and Partee, Barbara (1973). *The Major Syntactic Structures of English*. Holt, Rinehart and Winston, New York.

Weiner, J. and Palmer, M. (1981). The design of a system for designing knowledge representation systems. In *Proceedings of the International Joint Conference on Artificial Intelligence*. Kaufmann, Los Altos, CA.

Wilks, Yorick (1975*a*). An intelligent analyzer and understander of English. *Communications of the Association for Computing Machinery*, **18**, 264–74.

(1975*b*). Preference semantics. In Keenan, Edward L. (ed.), *The Formal Semantics of Natural Language*. Cambridge University Press.

(1976). Processing case. *American Journal of Computational Linguistics*, **4**, Microfiche 56.

(1982). Some thoughts on procedural semantics. In Lehnert, W. and Ringle, M. (eds.), *Strategies for Natural Language Processing*. Lawrence Erlbaum Associates, Hillsdale, NJ.

Winograd, T. (1972). *Understanding Natural Language*. Academic Press, New York.

Woods, William A. (1973). Progress in natural language understanding: an application to lunar geology. In *American Federation of Information Processing Societies, Conference Proceedings*, vol. 42. AFIPS Press, Montvale, NJ.

(1977). *Semantics and Quantification in Natural Language Question Answering*. Report 3687, BBN, Cambridge, MA, November.

(1981). Procedural semantics as a theory of meaning. In Joshi, A., Webber, B.L. and Sag, I. (eds.), *Elements of Discourse Understanding*. Cambridge University Press.